"Between lines of tex
It is an uncomfortable gray a
Barbara Hand Clow, with her inimitable ability, peered into this world
with laser-like vision and has thrust it before us in a way that cannot be
ignored. As an engineer who is 'grounded' in three-dimensional reality,
Catastrophobia *reads between my lines with insight and clarity."*

Christopher Dunn, author of The Giza Power Plant:
Technologies of Ancient Egypt

"In **Catastrophobia** *Barbara Hand Clow,*
with a perceptive voice, invites us to explore the unknown
crevices of the past through her uncommon spiritual eye."

Rand Flem-Ath, author of When the Sky Fell

"I find this book mind-expanding, provocative, and offering
an important contribution to our self-understanding as a species,
especially as we face important decisions in these critical times."

Matthew Fox, author of Original Blessing

"Grandmother Sky (Barbara Hand Clow)
has captured the essence of Mother Earth as a living energy
within the Universal Circle in **Catastrophobia.** *It sometimes takes*
a writer such as Barbara to revisit Old Wisdom for us to
better appreciate our purpose here on Mother Earth.
She has tapped in to the knowledge that helps us as humans
cross over into the future. The book reveals some universal dynamics
that help us understand our connection to the past here on
Turtle Island. We can truly learn from Turtle Medicine or the past
that we have the ability to change and to begin again."

J. T. Garrett, Ed.D. M.P.H.
Member of the Eastern Band of Cherokee Indians

Other books by
Barbara Hand Clow

Eye of the Centaur:
A Visionary Guide into Past Lives

Heart of the Christos:
Starseeding from the Pleiadians

Liquid Light of Sex:
Kundalini, Astrology, and the Key Life Transitions

The Pleiadian Agenda:
A New Cosmology for the Age of Light

Signet of Atlantis: *War in Heaven Bypass*

Chiron: *Rainbow Bridge*
Between the Inner and Outer Planets

CATASTROPHOBIA
The Truth Behind Earth Changes
in the Coming Age of Light

Barbara Hand Clow

Illustrations by Christopher Cudahy Clow

Bear & Company
Rochester, Vermont

Bear & Company
One Park Street
Rochester, Vermont 05767
www.InnerTraditions.com

Library of Congress Cataloging-in-Publication Data

Clow, Barbara Hand.
Catastrophobia : the truth behind earth changes in the coming age of light/
Barbara Hand Clow ; illustrated by Chris Clow.
p. cm.
Includes bibliographical references and index.
ISBN 1-879181-62-2
1. Pleiades—Miscellanea. 2. Spiritual life.
3. Cosmology—Miscellanea. I. Title.
BF1999 .C593 2001
909—dc21

2001001715

Printed and bound in Canada

10 9 8 7 6 5 4 3 2 1

Text design and layout by Cindy Sutherland
This book was typeset in Caslon with Meridien as a display face

Contents

List of Illustrations viii

Acknowledgments xi

Foreword *by J. Bernard Delair* xv

Introduction 1

1. Seizing the Cycles of the Stars 9

The Galactic Winter Solstice
Precession of the Equinoxes
Archeoastronomy
The Platonic Great Year
Individuation by Celestial Archetypal Forces
Cataclysmic Theory
Generational Change and Dematerialization
Turtle Medicine

2. The Great Cataclysm and the Fall 33

Hamlet's Mill *and the Precession of the Equinoxes*
The Terrible Days of Flood, Wind, and Fire
Crustal Shifting Models
The Geological Column
The Prediluvial Landscape
The Holocene Epoch: Earth after the Cataclysm

3. The Bicameral Brain & the Sphinx 53

The Breakdown of the Bicameral Brain
Reawakening the Bicameral Brain
The Orion Correlation and the Riddle of the Sphinx

Contents

Cyclopean Nonincized Stone Monuments
The Mysterious Blank Phase and Nile Ecology
The Giza Plateau as a Cosmic Clock
Numinousness and Stellar Genius
Maat and the Djed Pillar

4. The Story of the Prediluvial World 79

Science Brings Back a Lost World
Plato's Description of Atlantis in the Critias
  and the Timaeus
Prediluvial Cultures
Atlantis as the Primal Root of the Magdalenian Culture
"First Man and the Primordial Bull" Summarized
  from Plato Prehistorian
A Three-Part "Fall of Atlantis" Scenario
The Goddesses Neith and Athena

5. Geomancy & Primordial Memory 103

Geomancy and Sacred Sites
Sacred Sites, the Ether, and Time Discontinuities
Sacred Sites as Energetic Safety Zones
Axial Tilt Theory
The Mystery Plays in the Temples
The Emergence of the Primeval Mound and the Divine Cow
The Battle of Horus and Seth
The Mystery Play of the Succession
The Heb Sed Ceremony
The Standard of Abydos

6. Çatal Hüyük & Noah's Flood 131

The Wanderers after the Cataclysm
Archaic Mediterranean Archeological Sites
Noah's Flood and the Rising Seas
Crustal Shifting in the Cradle of Civilization
Çatal Hüyük and the Precession of the Equinoxes
The Earliest Writing and the Platonic Solids

7. The Fallen Angels & the Stones of Ica 155

Draco and the Great Bear
The Collective Nightmare of the Global Elite
Underground Cities and the Survival Times

Archaic Sacred Texts and Zarathustra
The Watchers, the Nephilim, and the Fallen Angels
Vulture Shamanism and the Birth of Zal
The Mysterious Stone Library of Ica
Ancient Astronomers Study the Sky and Global Maritime Maps
The Great Pyramid Is a Power Plant!

8. The Stargate Conspiracy & the Kosmokrater 185

Support the Heretics!
The Stargate Conspiracy
Edgar Cayce and the Search for the Hall of Records
The Lost Civilization on Mars
The Mars Announcement
The Council of Nine
Symbols as Transmitters of the Divine Mind
Perseus Slays the Medusa
Zoroaster and the Age of Asa
Blood Rituals and the Ahriman

9. Goddess Alchemy & the Heliopolitan Mysteries 213

The Pleiadian Agenda Model and Interactive Time
Bringing the Divine into Everyday Life
The Collective Awakening
Past-Life Regression under Hypnosis
Dancing on Turtle's Back
Chiron as the Wounded Healer
The Liquid Light Principle
The Alternate Reality and Ecstatic Body Postures

Appendix A: *Egyptian Time Line* 241

Appendix B: *Earth Changes During the Holocene Epoch* 243

Appendix C: *Holocene Chronological Highlights* 250

Appendix D: *Reflections on Earth's Tilting Axis* 252

Notes 260

Suggested Reading 281

Bibliography 283

Index 291

List of Illustrations

Chapter 1

Fig. 1.1.	The Precession of the Equinoxes	12
Fig. 1.2.	Pisces and Aquarius on the Ecliptic	13
Fig. 1.3.	The Great Sphinx on the Giza Plateau	15
Fig. 1.4.	Sekhmet	16
Fig. 1.5.	The Platonic Great Year	17
Fig. 1.6.	Observing the Milky Way River of Stars	19
Fig. 1.7.	The Beginning of the Great Ages in 9500 B.C.	20
Fig. 1.8.	The Osireion of Abydos	27
Fig. 1.9.	Watering Osiris who Grows Corn in His Body	28
Fig. 1.10.	Turtle Medicine	29

Chapter 2

Fig. 2.1.	The Great Cataclysm in 9500 B.C.	39
Fig. 2.2.	The Icosahedral Earth	41
Fig. 2.3.	The Geological Column	43
Fig. 2.4.	Tentative Reconstruction of the Prediluvial World	45
Fig. 2.5.	Revised Chronology of the Euro-American Quaternary Subdivisions	46

Chapter 3

Fig. 3.1.	The Electromagnetic Spectrum	56
Fig. 3.2.	The Valley Temple of Giza	60
Fig. 3.3.	Sacsayhuaman Temple in Peru	61
Fig. 3.4.	The Osireion of Abydos	62
Fig. 3.5.	Nile Valley Cross-Section Near Tahta	64
Fig. 3.6.	Round Head Art from Tassili n'Ajjer with inset of Osiris and Nut in the Primeval Waters	67
Fig. 3.7.	Tutankhamen's Throne and the Aker	70
Fig. 3.8.	The Solar System between the Orion Star System and the Galactic Center	72
Fig. 3.9.	Setyi I Erecting the Djed Pillar	75
Fig. 3.10.	The Pyramid as a Power Plant and the Pleiadian Agenda Energy Model	77

Chapter 4

Fig. 4.1.	The Atlantean Seal	83
Fig. 4.2.	The Sacrifice of the Bull in the Temple of Poseidon	85
Fig. 4.3.	Paleolithic Bridled Horses	88
Fig. 4.4.	First Man and the Primordial Bull	89
Fig. 4.5.	Prediluvial Global Maritime City	91
Fig. 4.6.	Neith and Athena	100

Chapter 5

Fig. 5.1.	Callanish Stone Circle	105
Fig.5.2.	The Sedge and the Bee	112

Fig.5.3. Everyday Life by the Nile   117
Fig.5.4. Geb and Nut   118
Fig.5.5. The Heb Sed Ceremony   125
Fig.5.6. The Standard of Abydos   128

Chapter 6

Fig. 6.1. Bulls' Heads of the Tomb of Uadji   134
Fig. 6.2. Nevali Çori Courtyard   135
Fig. 6.3. The Ibn ben Zara Map and the Modern Aegean Map   136
Fig. 6.4. The Sea of Marmara and the Black Sea   139
Fig. 6.5. Knossos Palace on Crete   141
Fig. 6.6. Three Ladies of Knossos Palace   142
Fig. 6.7. Çatal Hüyük Bull Shrine   144
Fig. 6.8. Goddess Giving Birth on the Double Leopard Throne   144
Fig. 6.9. Goddess Giving Birth to a Ram
             above the Three Bull Heads Shrine   145
Fig. 6.10. Wheeled Cross Mural   146
Fig. 6.11. Twelve Hands Above and Seven Below   148
Fig. 6.12. Near Eastern Clay Tokens   152

Chapter 7

Fig. 7.1. Draco and the Great Bear   156
Fig. 7.2. Vulture Shaman   170
Fig. 7.3. Prehistoric Egyptian Vase   170
Fig. 7.4. Three views of Phaeton on an Ica Stone   175
Fig. 7.5. Thermal Equilibrium Map   176
Fig. 7.6. Pangaea   178
Fig. 7.7. Closed Thermic System   180
Fig. 7.8. The Great Pyramid in the Center of Earth's Landmass   183

Chapter 8

Fig. 8.1. The Black Sea Region and the Eastern Mediterranean   202
Fig. 8.2. Perseus Hovering Over the Ecliptic   204
Fig. 8.3. The Narmer Pallette   205
Fig. 8.4. Tauroctony   207
Fig. 8.5. Halafian Geometrical Pottery Designs   209

Chapter 9

Fig. 9.1. The Pleiadian Agenda Energy Model   214
Fig. 9.2. Megalithic Spirals   223
Fig. 9.3. The Bear Spirit Posture   237
Fig. 9.4. The Empowerment Posture   238

Appendix B

Fig. B.1. Lake Algonquin and the Great Lakes   246

This book is dedicated to
Matthew Clow
(November 15, 1968–June 26, 1998)
and his generation.

Acknowledgments

I honor my Celtic/Cherokee grandfather, Gilbert Hand, for his teachings and wisdom, which is bearing fruit fifty years later. Grandfather noticed when I was seven that I was afraid the sky was going to fall. Since he was my medicine guide, he ordered me to sit under a tree in the backyard every day after school to watch the sky. Soon I got bored and I put my horse's saddle on a branch in the apple tree and hitched up a bridle on a branch. I fantasized I was riding my horse Lucky, and I never took my eyes off the sky. When I became thoroughly tired of the vigil, Grandfather ordered me to study *Chicken Little.* Then for the next twelve years, he instructed me in the oral tradition of ancient civilizations and guided me through archeology and the most important sources. His mother gave him the Cherokee secrets, then he passed these teachings to me. Thank you, Grandmother Hand, for the songs and stories of the Celtic People. I hope I have spoken truly about your subtle ways.

Thank you, J. T. Garrett and Michael Walkingstick Garrett, Hunbatz Men, Alberto Ruiz Buenfil, Don Alejandro Oxlac, José and Lloydine Arguelles, White Eagle Tree, Benjamin of Tana Toraga, Heyoka Merrifield, Abdel Hakim, Frank Aon, Sam Kaai, Nicki Scully, Felicitas Goodman, Michael Stearns, Meinrad Craighead, Chris Griscom, Gregory Paxson, and Gerry and Liz Clow, for knowing the medicine and sharing it so graciously with me.

The greatest joy while writing this book has been working with the illustrator and cover artist, Christopher Clow, who is my third son. Thank you, Hampshire College in Amherst, Massachusetts, for encouraging Chris to execute the illustrations for his senior project, which resulted in a fantastic exhibit during May 1999. In this case, the edge of joy is also the edge of sorrow. While Chris and I were collaborating on June 26, 1998, we received the news that my son and Chris's older brother, Matthew Clow, had drowned in Lower Red Rock Lake near Dillon, Montana. I would not have been able to complete *Catastrophobia* alone, and Chris inspired me to keep writing, because he loved the material and wanted to graduate in 1999. Chris, the illustrations and cover are beautiful!

Matthew Clow was a dedicated environmentalist, and he lost his life while doing graduate research to save native trout from Whirling Disease. As a devoted young scientist, Matthew expressed deep skepticism about my intuitive work. We shared a similar intensity: As I have suffered because our human emotional range is so retarded by unresolved trauma, Matthew suffered over the precarious condition of our ecosystem. Six weeks before the end of his short life of twenty-nine years, he read my most recent and speculative book, *The Pleiadian Agenda: A New Cosmology for the Age of Light.* During my last conversation with him, he said this work had enabled him to remember the multidimensional ranges. I remember telling him then that some esoteric thinkers, such as Rudolph Steiner and Christopher Bird, actually believe that life is maintained by spirits who participate in Nature; these beings are Nature. Matthew helped me write this book through Nature. He permeated my reality while I was writing it, and his spiritual participation is a voice in this book. Matthew was happy at Montana State University while studying with his beloved professor, Dr. Kal Kaya, and Kal, I thank you for mentoring him and recognizing his genius. Thank you, Montana State, for working with us on the Matthew Clow Grant that was established in his honor. I hope my work will inspire Matthew's generation to discover the spiritual participation in Nature in the coming age of light. And thank you, Hillary Weinberg Clow, Matthew's wife, for your deep communications and your lively interest in the text as it unfolded.

Thank you, D. S. Allan and J. B. Delair, for *Catalclysm! Compelling Evidence of a Cosmic Catastrophe in 9500 B.C.* which is the foundation of this book. Derek Allan passed away in late 2000, and the world has lost a great science historian, especially regarding his research on recent geological change. J. B. Delair spent countless hours reviewing a manuscript that was usually in very rough condition. This book would not exist without his extraordinary support, and I am deeply honored by his foreword. Thank you, Andrew Collins, Rand Flem-Ath, John Michell, Belinda Goodman, and Chris Dunn, for reviewing the manuscript. Your criticisms and suggestions have greatly improved it, and thank you for your own books, which are building blocks for this one. Many thanks to the anonymous donor for the illustrations, which was a beautiful way to say thank you to Bear & Company. Your generosity enabled Chris to do more than we had originally planned. Thank you, brother Robert Hand, for your geological background that got me interested in the subject when I was young. Your passion about the fate of Earth and its processes has been more of an influence than you realize. Thank you, Cindy Clark, for your wonderful mind that bridges the Paleolithic and Holocene epochs.

Thank you, Gerry Clow, for all your editorial work on the book. You really helped me clarify my thoughts. We are a team, just as we were when we wrote a book together for Little Brown twenty-five years ago. I am still writing because you always help me, and yes, I am very tired of burning the midnight oil. Nicholas Dalton was a secondary reader and a great editor—thank you for staying up until 4:30 A.M. the night of the year 2000 presidential election. The staff at Inner Traditions/Bear & Company was consistently excellent, especially Jon Graham, Jeanie Levitan, Kathleen Achor, Janet Jesso, and Cindy Sutherland. Thank you, Ehud Sperling, for taking Bear & Company under your wing so that I had the time to accomplish so much research. Lastly, this book would not exist without the constant support of our cleaning goddess, Tina Riley, and our gardener and personal Deva, Jane Tanner.

Foreword

The past decade or so has seen a spate of books on the subject of world catastrophes. Of variable quality, these books have ranged from considerations of the believedly traumatic termination of the reign of the dinosaurs at the end of the Cretaceous times about 65 million years ago, to that which evidently brought the so-called Pleistocene Ice Age to an abrupt close approximately 11,500 years ago, when, in the opinion of some, the legendary island of Atlantis was cataclysmically swallowed by the sea.

These studies have focused chiefly on the physical evidence for the onetime reality of those events, on the mechanisms that apparently caused their irruption, and on some of the multifarious long-term aftereffects they unleashed.

Very significantly, the presence in the Pleistocene calamity's dossier of an impressively varied mass of ancient, globally scattered, human "eyewitness" accounts of the event (now preserved as traditions and legends), complementing the associated field evidence, is a factor understandably absent from the file on the far older Cretaceous catastrophe. Such legends and traditions, of course, are themselves very much a *part* of "catastrophism" in its wider sense. The resultant Pleistocene "mosaic" is thus an especially fertile one for in-depth scholastic investigation.

It is, therefore, somewhat curious that comparatively few writers have dealt to any extent with the now deeply etched psychological scars and subsequent social reactions (phobias) generated by early humanity's *en bloc* experience of the disaster 11,500 years ago; that is until now, for this mold has now been shattered by the publication of a remarkable book by Barbara Clow, the aptly titled *Catastrophobia*.

For those already familiar with this author's previous writings, it will be superfluous to emphasize her breadth of scholarship or facility in expressing succinctly otherwise naturally complex data. But for those to whom Clow will be a new author, *Catastrophobia* should prove a most enlightening read, offering coherent explanations of many vexed aspects of mankind's past beliefs and social behavioral patterns, and how that has in turn led to the stultifying conservatism and orthodoxy sadly all too commonly still with us.

Using the latest findings of earth science, of prehistorians, and of what may now be best termed "new wave" archeology, *Catastrophobia* traces the evolution of human psychology during the past 15,000 years or so, and concentrates on how that has been modified by the horrendous benchmark event that, around 11,500 years ago, cut short an older benign terrestrial regime, disrupted much of the adjacent solar system, and ushered in the harsher and more disturbed one of present (Holocene) times.

The marauding cosmic agencies responsible for such dire devastation are now identifiable with reasonable accuracy and are still graphically remembered as the hydras, griffins, dragons, and Medusas, the world encircling serpents and vast "monsters" of popular mythology (the aforementioned traditions and legends); actually symbolized cosmic phenomena. *Catastrophobia* relates this cosmic event to a coincidental change in Earth's axial tilt and the inception of the calendrical precession of the equinoxes—an element of great importance for Holocene Man, and one linked to the newly discovered planet Chiron, which Clow argues may, like zodiacs, have been influential in the development 10,000 years ago of astrology. The destruction of an ancient equable world regime, the so-called Golden Age of precataclysmic days, gave rise among the survivors to the notion that its loss was, along with the coeval Noachian Deluge or Great Flood, a vengeful god's punishment of a sinful antediluvian humanity.

During the ensuing millennia that idea spawned a great and varied raft of penitentiary and propitiatory practices, which were often expressly tied to equinoctial dates in the then new Holocene precessional cycle. Thus guilt, penance, and sacrifice became mainstays of practically all the many religions and cults that arose following the initiation of the Holocene epoch—assumed "guilt" (to explain the "need" for a retributional catastrophe), voluntary "penance" (to atone for the imagined "sin"), and eager "sacrifice" (to hopefully avert a repetition of "divine cleansing")—themselves each long-established facets of "Catastrophobia" itself.

Clow examines these and other psychological human changes in relation to what she terms the Bicameral Mind, its one-time degeneration, and later reawakening. Citing several leading authorities on the subject, she posits that in terms of a general awareness of Nature precatastrophic man possessed a more highly developed sense of it than his Holocene descendants, and that the terrible cataclysm that separated prediluvial from postdiluvial humankind produced a "perceptual narrowing" of that awareness. The original ancient awareness, Clow contends, has only lately begun to reemerge, and then not universally.

Clow emphasizes the important point that almost every ancient civilized society recognized to date not only first appears at a surprisingly advanced technological level, with, furthermore, connections to some thriving, globally active, maritime culture, but that such expertise and sophistication must originally have been acquired before the onset of Holocene times, that is, prior to the Pleistocene catastrophe. Clow wonders if this primal font was the fabled Atlantis of Plato's writings.

In that connection she duly acknowledges the late Charles Hapgood's pioneer work (1966) on the series of enigmatic early maps, yet extant, depicting *bygone* topographical conditions both north and south of the present equator; and, like Hapgood, Clow believes that these maps represent a legacy of this self-same ancient maritime race. She then goes on to consider some of the technological achievements of these mystery mariners, and the original location of Plato's lost continent.

The suggestion recently advanced by the Flem-Aths *When the Sky Fell* that Atlantis occupied part of presently ice-smothered Antarctica—an idea mooted many years ago in an unpublished manuscript by Harold T. Wilkins about a now ice-covered prehistoric Antarctic metropolis called "Rainbow City"—is reviewed in connection with the actual portrayal of a partially ice-free Antarctica on several of the aforementioned ancient maps.

Mirroring the opinions of older writers such as Mainage (1921), Spence (1924), Merekhovsky (1933), and others, Clow concludes that Plato's Atlanteans were culturally associated with the gifted Magdalenian and

Cro-Magnon peoples of so-called Upper Paleolithic times, and, with Settegast (1990) and Rudgley (1999), suggests that the numerous similarities between the primitive scripts of the slightly younger Vinca culture and the Cretan Linear A, early Indus Valley, and the pre-Hellenic alphabetical signs are links in a long chain uniting the fabled primeval Atlantean civilization with the preclassical Indo-Mediterranean examples just listed.

On this basis the age-old belief of the Greeks, Romans, and various medieval chroniclers in a lost but formerly inhabited southern continent conceivably rests on a foundation of fragmented fact, while the many curious cultural similarities between ancient Old and New World civilizations—especially those of South America, significantly the *closest* southern landmass geographically to Antarctica—are very possibly explicable as pieces of the same ancient puzzle and for similar reasons.

Clow's wide-ranging evidence embraces the changing climatic history of the Nile Valley of the past 12,000 years or so, the fluctuating water levels and actual course of the Nile River during that period, and the detail that the Valley Temples of the Sphinx and the Second Pyramid were once situated nearer the Nile than today. Such factors, and the progressive desertification and impoverishment of an originally more densely wooded Nile Valley, from about 4,000 B.C. onward, materially affected early Nilotic culture and its development. This culture, we are told, allegedly derived from the legendary "First Time," or Zep Tepi, when semidivine sages, the Shemsu Hor, reputedly ruled Egypt and instituted all the principal elements comprising ancient Egyptian Dynastic civilization.

Attention is drawn to the Egyptians' claim that their records extended back to 36,525 B.C., and that it was Egyptian priests who, in Greek times, first told Plato's ancestor Solon about the former existence of Atlantis.

In that connection and the possibility that Atlantis's original site was Antarctica, the fact that the massive cut masonry of the Osireion, a temple of unknown but exceptional antiquity at Abydos, is remarkably like some long known from pre-Incan Peru and Bolivia in Andean South America—the very continent nearest to Antarctica—and that the Osireion, like the Sphinx, is now believed to be a much older structure than the general 3300 B.C. date commonly awarded the beginning of the First Egyptian Dynasty, are collectively highly suggestive of common cultural links underscoring all these enigmatical wonders of the past.

Clow's acceptance of the Great Catastrophe that, as a benchmark event, separated a prediluvial from a postdiluvial world around 11,500 years ago, should henceforth serve prehistoric chronology well. Her reworking, within the resultant new chronological framework, of so many previously contentious aspects of prehistory permit the perception of exciting new perspectives. Likewise, her analyses of the crucial psychological aspects that have until now largely constricted the realization of a truer world picture are equally meritorious. Indeed, both unquestionably merit extended applause.

J. Bernard Delair
Oxford, December 2000

Introduction

Catastrophobia explores human evolution over the past 15,000 years based on the latest discoveries in archeology, mythology, and the earth sciences. A scientific global data convergence reveals a great cataclysm occurred only 11,500 years ago, which geology calls the Late Pleistocene Extinctions and theologians call the Flood or the Fall. This was followed by massive crustal adjustments and flooding for thousands of years, while human cultures struggled for survival. As this story comes forth, I can see that the majority of humanity believes that the end of the world is coming *soon* because this horrible trauma has not been processed. Many of us are afflicted with *catastrophobia,* an intense fear of catastrophes. This causes individuals and societies to think of the future in terms of a coming, potential disaster; thus, most people do not care for Earth and its inhabitants, which includes themselves and their families. Crippled by collective fear from the past earth changes—the racial memory of this geological paroxysm—our surface minds are filled with floating images of disaster, guilt, and suffering. We project these painful thoughts out of our inner minds, which creates a coming apocalypse as a self-fulfilling prophecy. However, *it already happened!* Because few people know this, our attention is riveted when preachers and New Age prophets make predictions, which *sound* true because they resonate with these disassociated inner images.

This book explores the probability that we have millions of years of peaceful evolution coming next, and right now—amid these examples of misplaced concreteness resulting in obsessional waiting for the End Times— we have begun a great spiritual and intellectual awakening. Today science is describing the real story of Earth's past. Based on geological, biological, paleontological, and archeological knowledge from carbon dating, ice-core drilling, ocean sediment cores, and computer-imaging technology, we know that a great cataclysm occurred in 9500 B.C. We also know a lot about the follow-up earth changes, such as the Black Sea Flood in 5600 B.C. In those terrible times, the planet was afflicted with floods, erupting volcanoes, earthquakes, and massive waves of death, and our species was reduced to bare survivalism. Now, as a result of more correct data, cross-cultural global mythology and settlement patterns suddenly make more sense. Archeological sites are coming alive because we know what happened, as well as when, and we even know how these mysterious places are connected.

Now that the date and the magnitude of the initial cataclysm are verified by science, we can see that it is a miracle anything survived, including ourselves. In my search for the key times in Earth's—and our species'—development, I went back thousands of years before the Cataclysm. I went back 20,000 years, because many researchers have discovered the remnants of an advanced global maritime culture from more than 12,000 years ago that vanished almost without a trace. Any fragments and traces of the lost world are incredibly significant, and I selected some to open your archaic or racial memory. Evidence for the lost world invites us to consider that a brilliant civilization existed not long ago on Earth that may have flourished for hundreds of thousands of years, and we probably have not yet approached these levels ourselves. I believe that this lost memory represents the 85 percent of our brains or the 97 percent of our DNA that scientists say we do not use.

Until very recently scientists investigated catastrophes that were comfortably distanced from us, such as the extinction of the dinosaurs 65 million years ago. Recently some scientists have been describing the magnitude of the more recent disaster, and their discoveries seem to have arrived just as a tidal wave of millennial fear and apocalyptical fanaticism has begun building in the world. As our species begins to awaken from collective amnesia, the more correct version of Earth's story seems to be stirring up repressed cataclysmic memories that lurk in our unconscious minds. The popular media taps in to this with films like *Asteroid*, while also fanning the Arab/Israeli time bomb. People feel cornered, as if there is no future. Scientifically speaking, although there are periodic asteroid and meteor impacts, glaciation, volcanoes, earthquakes, and severe climate changes, an event as great as the Cataclysm of 9500 B.C. occurs about *every 30 million years or more* in our solar system. Now that astronomy is exploring the Milky Way Galaxy, this long cycle has been discovered, and it is possible that nothing like it had *ever* happened before. It disarranged the whole solar system, which may have been a unique event. By order of magnitude, for the *solar system* this event was probably greater than the asteroid impact in the Gulf of Mexico off the Yucatan 65 million years ago that terminated the Cretaceous Period. The public mainly hears that there are recurrent cyclical disasters caused by fields of meteors and cycles in the solar system that influence Earth's climate. These things do happen, and they can cause big trouble. However, science seems to be infected with *scientific catastrophobia*—a big disaster is coming soon that could totally destroy the planet—and this terrifies the public. Of course, what the public hears is greatly managed by the planetary power brokers I call the Global Elite. Meanwhile, many politicians propose that we spend trillions to build weapons to shoot things out of the sky at a time when our species is poised for a great evolutionary advance and a spiritual awakening.

The data convergence described in this book is based on nearly incomprehensible amounts of work and exploration since A.D. 1600, which sped up exponentially 150 years ago and became a nuclear chain reaction 30 years ago. The flood of information is so huge that I'd like to explain how I got into this field. I began my visible career when I was thirty-eight; however, it was during my childhood that my Cherokee/Celtic grandfather educated me in the *real* story of Earth. In my early twenties, I became a student of catastrophism, which posits that Earth experiences long periods of peaceful evolution that are periodically punctured by cataclysms. During the 1960s and '70s, the uniformitarian mind-set—which posits that earth changes have been slow and gradual—was being questioned by many scientists. However, in school, uniformitarian theory and Social Darwinism—which posits that we are always evolving to a more advanced level by survival of the fittest—were the dogma of the day. All this totally contradicted my training by my grandfather, which he was careful to point out was a legacy from him that I was to offer to the world someday.

Suddenly, in the mid-1990s, my role as a successful author and a new paradigm publisher at Bear & Company made it possible for me to conceive of this book. Just the right mix of lucky encounters and opportunities occurred, and, in fact, the process has been magical.

I studied with Matthew Fox, the Dominican scholar, for a masters in creation-centered theology at Mundelein College during 1982 and 1983. Creation-centered theology celebrates our creative genius and deeply questions the guilt and obsession with personal salvation that is the result of the Fall, as described in Judeo-Christian doctrine. Because my education with my grandfather was a study of the ancient Cherokee Records, which are creation centered, I was fascinated with what belief in the Fall has done to our species; I was melding my early childhood training with theology. I became the acquisitions editor at Bear & Company (initially working with Fox) in 1983 until 1998, and my years in publishing are deeply reflected in this book. We published many healers and new paradigm authors. The real genesis of *Catastrophobia* came in 1996, when we decided to publish the 1997 American version of D. S. Allan and J. B. Delair's *Cataclysm! Compelling Evidence of a Cosmic Catastrophe in 9500 B.C.* My grandfather had said that the real story of Earth would be told once science discovered it, and suddenly I found a scientific book with the correct time line and scenario. This has enabled me to investigate how our consciousness has been altered and molded by earth changes, which is called Turtle Medicine in Cherokee tradition.

The wounding from earth changes and survivalism is the focus of other thinkers as well, such as the English writer Andrew Collins and the anthropologist Felicitas Goodman, and their work has greatly deepened this text. Because of the rapidity and intensity of the global data convergence in science, theology, and consciousness, the research for this book has been daunting. It is an analysis and synthesis of very well-researched books based on excellent primary sources. Outside of Plato, Egyptology, and Aegean archeological research, I used the secondary research of other writers, which is becoming a custom of new paradigm writers, especially in England. I have checked their sources carefully; however, I encourage readers to read some of the books I call out in "Suggested Reading," because I barely touched on their genius. This method made it possible to summarize and quote very recent arguments and theories that would have taken whole chapters of original writing. The new paradigm movement is an exciting field because it is like building things out of blocks, without having to first make each block. In that sense, this book is a selection of detail heavily sourced from about thirteen writers, plus my own research. When the text was nearly finished in 1998, my second child died in a tragic accident, and I missed reading *From the Ashes of Angels* and *The Gods of Eden* by Andrew Collins, a brilliant new paradigm writer who will soon be available in the United States. I finally read him a few months before this manuscript was finished, and it was as if Collins and I had visited the same library for years. Collins also follows earth changes to understand cultures and consciousness, which has intensified and clarified my own arguments. It so affirming to find another researcher who drew similar conclusions on material that orthodoxy has defined differently. Many of the new paradigm writers often feel like we are neck-in-neck in a horse race.

Two months before my deadline, I got a newly released copy of *The Stargate Conspiracy* by Lynn Picknett and Clive Prince, which is creating a firestorm of debates on the Internet because it investigates Global Elite manipulation in the New Age movement. Having been a publisher for twenty years, I was well aware of the Global Elite's infiltration of the New Age, and I had already written and lectured about it. The *Stargate* authors have written a whole book about it that brilliantly exposes how the Elite manipulates people by their beliefs and fears. I have summarized some of their research with my own thoughts, which invited me to assess my previous book, *The Pleiadian Agenda: A New Cosmology for the Age of Light*. The dimensional thesis of *The Pleiadian Agenda* offers much insight for healing, and the *Stargate* authors expose how the Elite works to corrupt these powerful teachings. Lastly, I have been studying with anthropologist Felicitas Goodman for seven years, and in the last stages of this book, suddenly I saw how her discoveries of how ordinary people can enter the alternate reality means of sacred ritual postures are of major importance for healing at this time.

Catastrophobia reverses everything we've been taught until recently in the earth sciences and archeology, and considering such radical new ideas is a great challenge in itself. The greater challenge is to integrate this knowledge through deep spiritual intention. To accomplish this, I based it on the greatest spiritual wisdom of the West. I was not able to include the wisdom of the East, because I am not trained in it. However, it seems to me that the West is the most in need of spiritual illumination. *Catastrophobia* is a call for a return of the spiritual basis of life, because scientific materialism—the theoretical basis of modern physics, paleontology, geology, astronomy, and biology—has never been proven. The spiritual realms have been denigrated by the materialistic premise, which has ruled culture for hundreds of years as belief in spirit waned. The first few chapters are a distillation of huge data banks that trace the movement back to spiritualism by many great thinkers. Pages could have been wasted on debates over Social Darwinism, old paradigm geology, and scientific materialism, but this book bypasses the arguments and is based on a perfectly credible premise: *Consciousness creates the material world.* The latest discoveries in cosmology, biology, geology, and psychology are considered from a spiritual perspective. The next few chapters are a revision of ancient history; through this revised view, there are then more chapters with in-depth studies of some truly incredible data banks that awaken very repressed memories. Some of them come from more than 12,000 years ago. Just breathe and absorb, because the theories concocted during the materialistic phase of science during the past 400 years are being expanded by a spiritual perspective. Science is the language of our times, and I cover new paradigm science to soften the endemic materialistic bias of scientific orthodoxy that is eroding human intelligence.

In its early stages, this book explored how the precession of the equinoxes has influenced human consciousness over the past 40,000 years. However, no matter how hard I looked, *I could not find any evidence for precession before 12,000 years ago,* and evidence for the Great Ages in human cultures and symbolism begins about 10,000 years ago. Finally, I came to believe that Earth and the solar system were profoundly altered 11,500 years ago, and J. B. Delair convinced me that the axis must have tilted then. Adopting this point of view has made sense of some really strange material in little-understood Egyptian sources, which evidence a literal obsession with axial tilting. However, the real reason I decided to use recent axial tilting as a working hypothesis is that the consciousness research I covered points to such profound changes in humanity 11,500 years ago. I discuss these arcane Egyptian sources and the consciousness changes. We seem to be integrating damage to the solar system, as well as earth changes, which is of interest to astrologers. I have written two books about the newly discovered planet, Chiron, which we astrologers say rules deep personal and species wounding complexes. Allan and Delair hypothesize that Chiron assumed its current orbit in 9500 B.C., and I hypothesize that the orbit of Chiron and the tilting axis is causing us to become much more emotionally complex, which I develop extensively. Chiron as the wounded healer is a major player in this book. This even took me by surprise, but I have always been amazed by the astrological potency of this little body in space. Chiron was the teacher of astrologers as long as 10,000 years ago, so he joins us in our journey through the story of Time.

1

Seizing the Cycles of the Stars

The Maya understood that human civilization cycles
from one extreme form of social organization to the other.
Out of this process of polariazation, or spiritual mitosis,
arises a new, greater being. Everytime the cosmic cell divides,
every 26,000 years, we are one step closer to the birth of
that vast higher being of which we are just cells.
—John Major Jenkins[1]

The Galactic Winter Solstice

As we enter the twenty-first century, Earth is being stirred by an extraordinary series of astronomical cycles that began only 11,500 years ago. As if new winter light is piercing the heart of the Galaxy, Earth is awakening to a new level of evolutionary potential. Our solar system is moving out of the Orion Arm into a dark region of the Milky Way Galaxy; Earth is precessing out of the Age of Pisces into the Age of Aquarius as Earth's North Celestial Pole moves to the star Polaris; and the intersection of the plane of our solar system and the plane of our Galaxy is in conjunction with the winter solstice Sun. During the 26,000-year-long precessional cycle, called the Great Year by the Greeks, this intersection line, the Galactic Axis, is closely aspected by the winter solstice Sun for 25 years from A.D. 1987 to 2012. The galactic alignment, the *Galactic Winter Solstice*, occurs while Earth enters the Age of Aquarius over the next few hundred years. The Galactic Winter Solstice is the nexus; it heralds the transfiguration of our species.

This Galactic Winter Solstice can be thought of as a stellar mystery play. The curtain rose on Harmonic Convergence—16 and 17 August

1987—an Earth celebration when millions of people meditated at sacred sites all over the world. The final act will be on 21 December 2012, the mysterious end date of the Mayan Calendar. As we approach A.D. 2012, as if there is a *strange time-attractor in the sky*, we feel this pull instinctively. Like caterpillars undergoing metamorphosis and eventually becoming butterflies, we may actually be time-coded to change into new forms. What could we become? Many of us have turned to the primordial wisdom for answers, because it contains many stories about other times when critical evolutionary leaps occurred on Earth. Guided by this primordial wisdom, I have discovered a collective malaise that I believe is insidiously limiting the potential of our species, which I call *catastrophobia*. In the midst of this amazing creative explosion, beliefs that we are coming to the end of humankind on Earth are simply wrong. The destruction of our species is not the meaning of the end of the mysterious long calendar of the Maya.

This book is a deep exploration of the past 15,000 years of human history. I am seeking earlier times when the ancient wisdom came forth to guide us. The book is inspired by my deep contemplation of Egyptology, which became the center of my intellectual journey when my grandfather introduced me to the Egyptian temple reliefs when I was five years old. Now Egyptology has become the center of the intellectual journeys of many seekers, and it is the focus of new insights coming from new paradigm research in archeoastronomy, geology, and archeology. After many journeys of my own in Egypt, I have integrated my Cherokee/Celtic grandfather's legacy—which I call Turtle Medicine—with Egyptology. Until recently, much of the information in this book was closely guarded knowledge only because it could not be understood yet. Now that the primordial wisdom is being sought and gained by millions worldwide, my grandfather's revelations can be shared. Many are seeking a new story of archaic human history, because the latest information suggests that human cultures were previously evolved and globally connected in some way. Our planet is littered with very old sites that have odd traces of lost technologies, such as Tiahuanaco in Peru, Osireion at Abydos in Egypt, and Baalbek in Lebanon. What happened to those people? We have a huge emotional barrier to break through because a long phase of our growth was literally shattered in a great cataclysm and our previous attainments were lost and forgotten until now. The latest discoveries suggest that archaic people once created a marvelous global civilization.

One thing is obvious about our ancestors: Their consciousness was deeply involved with the stars. They believed the cycles in heaven mirror the cycles on Earth. What were they watching for in the sky? According to my legacy and many indigenous traditions, the stage is set again in the sky for a big evolutionary breakthrough. This mystery play has actually already begun, and just like the old ones, we each can seize its creative potential and play our own roles. As in any drama, the sooner we get involved, put on our costumes, and learn our lines, the better. In myths and sacred teachings, the story of this awakening was very protected. What is this story? According to my legacy and the teachings of many sages, the new energy coming to Earth from the Galactic Center is enabling us to see that *we are a wounded species afflicted with global collective fear.* As we heal this fear, we remember the cosmic knowledge as the galactic cycles activate our brains.

Evolution occurs by cyclical time, not by clock time, which was invented about 500 years ago. There are more hidden and influential time cycles, such as the precession of the equinoxes, that emotionally guide human metamorphic processes. My astronomical discussions are mostly geocentric—viewing the cosmos from Earth—so simply allow your inner eye to contemplate these views. For thousands of years, early humans understood the sky very well without the complexities of modern scientific astronomy. In those days, the stars were living data banks of archetypal stories—stellar mythology—when the contemplation of stellar patterns and star emanations influenced cultural patterns on Earth. We are in the midst of a deep and wonderful changing right now because we've switched to raw instinct, which dominates humanity when one great age precesses into the next one. Everything moves so fast and changes so completely that we are forced to respond in the moment. According to science, 97 percent of our DNA is useless, the so-called junk DNA,[2] but I suspect this DNA is periodically stimulated by cosmic forces. I believe we are all hardwired to receive cosmic information, which activates latent brain capacity and may switch on the junk DNA. This is why the sages studied cycles by patterns in the sky.

Precession of the Equinoxes

Precession occurs because our axis is tilted—not vertical—as it travels around the Sun. From our vantage point on Earth, as we orbit the Sun, the Sun "eclipses" the stars behind itself, which is why the circle around the Sun is called the Ecliptic. Precession occurs because as Earth orbits the Sun, it turns on its axis tilted at an angle about 23 1/2 degrees from the true vertical and wobbles some. This results in a 26,000-year-long funnel motion that causes Earth's axis to trace an imaginary circle in the stars around the North and South Poles. If Earth's axis were vertical, the stars about the poles would circle eternally in the same places. Instead, the polar stars move like huge ancient serpents, and on today's horizon, the locations of the stars move 1 degree every 72 years. In this book, I explore the possibility that precession actually began 11,500 years ago, because some ancient texts suggest that long ago the stars moved through the night skies in unchanging circles. I present evidence that humans began tracking precession's slow movement on the horizon at the equinoxes 8,000 to 10,000 years ago, when there was a profound change in cultures that was brought on by seasonality. Equinoxes, by the way, are the only time of "balance" on Earth when the Sun is directly over the equator. Many others have suggested that precession may be a *post* cataclysmic phenomenon, and I'm going to follow this theory as a working hypothesis.[3] (See appendix D for more scientific and anthropological data on axial tilt.)

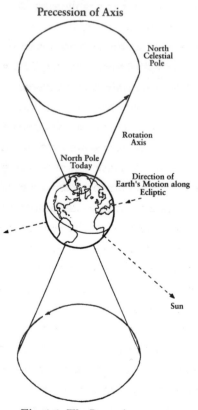

Precession of Axis

North Celestial Pole

Rotation Axis

North Pole Today

Direction of Earth's Motion along Ecliptic

Sun

Fig. 1.1. The Precession of the Equinoxes.

Precession is usually observed by tracking the Sun rising in specific zodiacal constellations at the spring equinox, the Vernal Point on the Ecliptic. For example, during the spring equinox 10,800 to 8,640 years ago—the Age of Cancer—the Vernal Point was in Cancer, thus the Sun

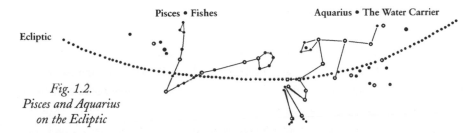

Pisces • Fishes   Aquarius • The Water Carrier

Ecliptic

Fig. 1.2.
Pisces and Aquarius
on the Ecliptic

"rose" in Cancer. In the year 2000, on the first day of spring, the Sun rose in the overlapping edges of the Pisces and Aquarius constellations, and thus people talk of the coming Age of Aquarius. Astrologers and astronomers give dates from A.D. 2100 to 2800 for the end of the Age of Pisces and the beginning of the Age of Aquarius. The Pisces constellation is a huge spread between stars seen as two fish. Pinpointing the exact time of the transition from one age to the next is arbitrary, because it is difficult to say when one constellation ends and another begins on the Ecliptic. Right now the Vernal Point is near the end of the second fish of Pisces, but the water that the Water Bearer pours is nearly flowing over the Vernal Point. Besides observing the Vernal Point in the constellations, the precessional influence is very clearly and simply described by the Platonic Great Year, a concept that was well defined by the early Greeks and exists in the Vedic scriptures. In the Great Year, the constellations are divided into twelve Great Ages or months that are each 2,160 years long. This is a very useful tool because the division of the constellations is otherwise arbitrary if done on a visual basis. Constellations rising at the spring equinox gradually give way to the next ones, so where is the end or beginning? And how many constellations are there on or near the Ecliptic? Thousands of years ago, astronomers used fewer constellations, whereas the Maya divided the sky into thirteen.

Orthodox history says precession was discovered by Hipparchus about 2,300 years ago. However, not only did Plato's Great Year and the Vedas—which describe precessional ages—predate Hipparchus, but numerous modern scholars have concluded that Hipparchus used much earlier Babylonian data that was based on precession.[4] In fact, precession has been tracked for many thousands of years, was of immense importance to early human societies, and many scholars have been exploring its influence. My primary focus, whether the axis first tilted 11,500 years ago or not, is that *this was a time when a radical shift occurred in human cultures.* For example, in D. S. Allan and J. B. Delair's *Cataclysm! Compelling Evidence of a Cosmic*

Catastrophe in 9500 B.C., Earth's axis was pulled into a tilt by fragments of a supernova in the Vela star system that blasted into our solar system in 9500 B.C.[5] According to these authors, before then Earth's axis was *vertical,* and we lived in the Golden Age. Many scholars have noted this distinctive shift in cultures 11,500 years ago when the Pleistocene epoch closed and the Holocene began. My working hypothesis is that the advent of precession in 9500 B.C. caused this cultural shift by fundamentally altering our experience of time. Suddenly humanity adopted agriculture in response to the new seasonality. Regardless, it is virtually certain that a great cataclysm changed everything on Earth 11,500 years ago.

Archeoastronomy

Archeoastronomy, a relatively new division of anthropology, dates ancient human sites by star positions according to precessional analysis. Archeoastronomers have proven that various stone constructions at archaic sites are aligned with the locations of stars at specific times in the precessional cycle; thus they are able to date these structures. These dates are often cross-verified when they agree with known history or other established dating systems, such as radiocarbon dating. They have established that the observable celestial effects of precession were being used for temple siting by ancient astronomers; however, the actual *mechanics* were probably not understood by archaic people.[6] This indicates that these cultures were more advanced than previously thought, which is also being established by others. For example, working with Egyptologist John Anthony West in 1991, geologist Robert Schoch established that the Sphinx is *at least 7,000 years old,* and West believes it is probably much older.[7] Based on precessional *symbolism,* which we know ancient people used, the Sphinx might be more than 11,000 years old. It has a lionlike body, and the lion is the symbol for the Age of Leo—10,960 to 8800 B.C. Most archeologists insist the Sphinx is only 5,000 years old, no matter what new evidence is offered to them, and they are losing their credibility with the public.

Ironically, the Sphinx is a great example of an artifact that can be dated by geology and archeoastronomy, but archeologists just assume it is the same age as the Giza pyramids. To top it off, the Valley Temple below the Sphinx is constructed very differently than the pyramids or other temples

Fig. 1.3. The Great Sphinx on the Giza Plateau.

built during the early Dynasties. The Sphinx and the Valley Temple may be older and venerated monuments that determined the sitings of the later pyramids, which also might have been built over very ancient constructions. Because Egyptian esoteric science is the basis of Masonic rituals and the Great Pyramid is on the American dollar, by refusing to integrate recent scientific challenges, Egyptologists are being accused of sinister cover-ups and power games. Such possibilities will be dealt with later in this book. For now, my focus is crafting a new story of Time, a term I will capitalize when it refers to the long cycles of Time as the emotional catalyst for human evolution.

The Sphinx is the central enigma. Most people who see it crouching on the Giza Plateau intuit that it must be the key into the ancient records— as if the ancient Egyptians created the Sphinx just so we'd keep asking questions about our past! Following the Cataclysm 11,500 years ago, assuming precession began, the lionlike Leo constellation was suddenly rising at the new Vernal Point as you looked at it from the Giza Plateau. This would have been quite an amazing sight to archaic stargazers! The Sphinx is the ideal symbol for the cataclysmic Age of Leo. J. B. Delair recently noted that hundreds of winged sphinxes from Sumerian and Egyptian through Roman times have lionlike bodies and women's heads, and that they represented "one of the lethal destructive 'dragons of chaos' accompanying Phaeton/ Marduk," the agency of the great Cataclycm.[8] The Sphinx reminds us subconsciously of the disaster and the long passage

15

of Time. The fact that sphinxes so often have female heads is compelling, because the Egyptian lion-goddess, Sekhmet, is the force that brings chaos to Earth when humans are out of balance.

Proceeding with my axial-tilt hypothesis, if precession began 11,500 years ago and the Sphinx was carved as long ago as 11,000 years, then the insights by Robert Bauval and Adrian Gilbert in *The Orion Mystery,* who describe the Giza Plateau as a starclock, are very close to mine, even though my dating differs slightly.[9] The new geological dating and Bauval and Gilbert's theories are creating a strong case for driving back the date of the original site plan of the Giza Plateau. Bauval's Orion Correlation,

Fig. 1.4. Sekhmet

which posits that the pyramids mirror the Orion star system, is very important because it correlates the Pyramid Texts with Giza Plateau technology. This connection greatly deepened my own contemplation of Egyptology, and I hope my indigenous knowledge will add a few insights to the exciting Great Work emerging from Giza. A Great Work is a new alchemy, a collection of insights that awakens new evolutionary potential.

Using precessional *symbolism* in conjunction with precise astronomical alignments helps decode extremely archaic monuments. This is true because key symbols express the qualities of each Great Age; for example, the bull for the Age of Taurus—4480 to 2320 B.C.—actually *was* the central symbol for temple/city cultures such as the Minoans, Egyptians, and Indians during that age. By knowing the dates of the Great Ages and their main symbols, which existed in ancient cultures all over the world, we can see how symbolic thoughtforms have directed cultures. There is much evidence that people have been greatly influenced by these changing archetypes expressed by symbolism for at least 10,000 years. *We are the ones who have forgotten how symbolism influences cultures,* yet Hapi pouring water out of the jar, the symbol of the annual Nile Inundation, is the symbol for the Aquarian Age. "For everything there is a season," which may be why the fascination with Egypt is building.

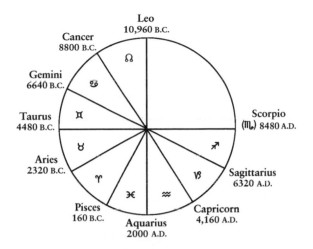

Fig. 1.5. The Platonic Great Year

The Platonic Great Year

The visual division between one constellation and the next on the Ecliptic is somewhat arbitrary, so to describe the long precessional cycles, the neo-Platonic Greeks devised the Platonic Great Year of twelve months and four seasons. This still helps us grasp long phases of Time. Many people thought of Time in this way until 2,000 years ago. In the Platonic Year, one "month" is 2,160 years, and one "season" is 6,480 years. The "year" thus totals 26,000 years. A key question is *where* does the 26,000-year-long Great Year begin? This book posits that the Platonic Great Year began only 11,500 years ago, but that still does not identify the beginning and end of this cycle, because it represents a moving orientation to the Milky Way. As you will see, it has only been possible to answer this question recently by knowing about the orientation of our solar system in the Galaxy. Some researchers—such as John Major Jenkins, Michio Kushi, Dan Giamario, and Nick Anthony Fiorenza—have concluded that the current alignment of the winter solstice Sun to the Galactic Axis is the opening of the whole Great Year, and I agree with them.[10] Assuming the whole cycle begins around A.D. 2000, then the four seasons of the Great Year begin with the fixed signs: Taurus, Leo, Scorpio, and Aquarius. This model totally synchronizes with astrology, which posits that the fixed signs are where energy *culminates.*

As we are poised to enter the Age of Aquarius, we can test this model by looking into what happened during the opening of the *previous season,*

17

the Age of Taurus, as the Vernal Point moves *backward* on the Ecliptic, as illustrated. If this model actually describes a process, this "season" would have been a phase when major cultural patterns flowered. In fact, around 4480 B.C. the Taurus constellation rose at the spring equinox, beginning a whole season, and the early groups, who later developed theocratic city cultures, appeared, such as the Sumerians, Egyptians, and Indians. A monumental shift in human culture began. Then, around 3500 B.C., highly advanced civilizations flowered with the bull as the central symbol! This "season" was when cities developed. According to the Platonic Great Year, a 6,480-year season is more foundational than the subsequent two 2,160-year ages, when the central issue of the fixed age matures. For example, during the Age of Aries—2320 to 160 B.C.—wars between the city cultures were the main theme. During the Age of Pisces, which is completing itself now, how people handle the emotional implications of city cultures has been the main theme. Of course, the beginning of the whole 26,000-year wheel—which we experienced in the year 2000—is the *most* foundational: We began a year, season, and Great Year simultaneously.

The Galactic Winter Solstice—2012—is the turning point of the whole Great Year; the winter solstice at 0 degrees Capricorn points directly to the Galactic Center at 27 degrees Sagittarius, which suggests that this energy is cosmic. Macrobiologist Michio Kushi, who also believes that Earth's axis shifted about 12,000 years ago, says about this phenomena, "When the earth's axis points directly through the Milky Way we receive much more energy radiation than we do when the earth's axis points away from the Milky Way."[11] *The Great Year describes how the Galactic Center influences Earth.* I would then ask: Where is the Sun in the Galaxy itself? Our solar system takes 200 to 250 million years to orbit the Galactic Center. According to indigenous traditions, for those of us on Earth, the Sun is our source of solar radiation (our biological fuel) and the Galactic Center is our source of cosmic radiation (our spiritual fuel). This awakening is spiritual because the alignment of the Galactic Axis to the center of the Galaxy greatly increases our connection with our spiritual center. This awakening is also biological because reptiles appeared on Earth approximately 200 to 250 million years ago. Now our solar system is in the same location in its orbit around the Galactic Center, and something truly

momentous is going on. Is the transfiguration of the human the final evolution of our reptilian intelligence, possibly the serpent in our spines?

According to galactic physics, this cyclical shift is an astronomical fact;
however, what does it mean? My previous book, *The Pleiadian Agenda: A
New Cosmology for the Age of Light,* contains some of the answers. In 1994
my brain was blasted open by nonphysical beings from the Pleiadian star
system, and I "channeled" the information. I think that this classic mystical
breakthrough must have been triggered by the building galactic alignment,
which I knew nothing about at the time. This kind of reception has often
been the source of the perennial wisdom; however, purely intuitional insights

deepen by conscious evaluation. As I've struggled to
assess this cosmology, I've found it very difficult to
understand galactic astronomy. Regarding the
Pleiades as a source for perennial wisdom, archeolo-
gist/astronomer F. C. Penrose has shown that the
Parthenon on the Acropolis in Athens was oriented
to the Pleiades rising in 1150 B.C.* In ancient lore, the
Pleiades are often associated with the goddesses of
wisdom—Athena of Greece and Neith of Egypt—
and the reemergence of the feminine is central to this
book. The Pleiades are part of our local Galaxy, and
perhaps the Galactic Winter Solstice alignment
makes it easier for people to receive information from
stellar realms in general. The influence from the
Pleiades may be the ultimate source for Time, because

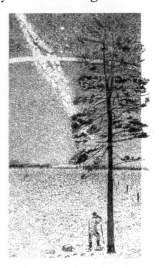

*Fig. 1.6. Observing the
Milky Way river of stars.*

the Platonic Great Year was initially called the Great Year of the Pleiades.[12]

A direct way to access these thoughtforms is to visualize the beautiful
stellar geometry forming in the skies and follow the cycles of the stars and
planets. For this book, it's not really necessary to understand astronomy
rationally, because celestial mechanics are very complex. After all, we live
on Earth and look at everything from our perspective anyway, and for
thousands of years people understood the patterns in the sky without

---

* Norman J. Lockyer, *The Dawn of Astronomy* (London: Macmillan, 1894), 413–24. Astute
readers will note that the Parthenon was constructed 600 years *after* this orientation.

knowing celestial mechanics. Ancient people were much more in touch with Earth by viewing the sky patterns in relation to monuments or topographic features located in their personal bioregions. To grasp celestial mechanics you may learn to visualiz complex patterns from many pespectives that cannot even be drawn to scale or seen from Earth. The Galactic Winter Solstice can be felt

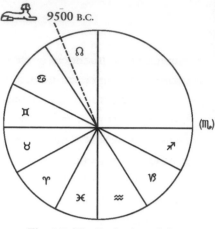

Fig. 1.7. The Beginning of the Great Ages in 9500 B.C.

by contemplating the River of Stars, which is the edge of the Milky Way, which often has a shamanic effect. As you observe the edge of the Galaxy shining in the dark night sky, the galactic plane and the Ecliptic cross at a near 60-degree angle, forming a sextile—the perfect harmonic. When you attune to these cycles, you might find yourself having mystical visions that carry you into other dimensions! Contemplation of Time and cycles is a psychedelic experience without any drugs, which is how I get high. We are going to explore the archaic mind experientially in this book, because that is how I've been able to enter it myself. It is important to consider that if the Great Ages first began only 11,500 years ago, then we are only just beginning to get used to this new process. Meanwhile, when you look for it, the influence of the Great Ages on human experience is very apparent for at least 10,000 years.

Before the Cataclysm, there is evidence that a global maritime civilization existed. Just as in the world today, many people often preferred living by the sea. For thousands of years after the disaster, the seas were rising, and we suffered great climatic, geophysical, and social instability. World civilization only became possible again during the Age of Taurus. After the Cataclysm, the Age of Leo was a partial age, but it was when *humans first mutated by Time through symbolic phases.* As is widely reported in mythology, the surviving people on the planet were assisted by sages who assumed great authority and saved civilization. Because of the desperate conditions on Earth, gods and kings emerged, and their symbol was and still is the lion. Then during the Age of Cancer—8800 to 6640 B.C.—people venerated the Goddess, because survival and birthing was critical in the struggle to repopulate Earth, and sexuality was of great import. The Mother Goddess is one of the most primordial archetypes in the human psyche that seems to recede back into the darkness of Time, and in fact she does. One symbol for this age is the Moon, which triggers memories of our rebirthing by monthly cycles. After this age ended and the Age of Gemini—6640 to 4480 B.C.—was in progress, a great flood in the Black Sea region decimated many people, and struggling survivors migrated to other lands.[13] The Age of Cancer balanced the power of woman with the Age of Leo realm of gods and kings. The winged sphinxes with lion bodies and the heads of women combined the symbology of both these ages, and then when the Age of Gemini began, cultures began exploring the meaning of Time. Fascinating sages, such as Zarathustra, appeared.

Individuation by Celestial Archetypal Forces

Regardless of when Time began, we are now ready to become conscious of how we have been individuating through the cycles and symbols of the Great Ages. Our orientation to the Milky Way and the Aquarian Age demands more consciousness about how archetypes inspire cultures. These archetypes, which we have been mostly unconscious of until recently, exist in the *collective unconscious,* as described by C. G. Jung, and within *racial memory,* as described by Sigmund Freud, which contains the memory of all human experience. We have arrived at a unique point: Many people are now realizing that they are influenced and manipulated by these archetypes, such as the cross of Christianity. We are *collectively questioning how we as humans affect Earth.* I don't think most people considered this until recently. The more perspective we have on this the better because the collective unconscious seems to be time-coded to respond by cycles. There is no reason that we cannot fully understand this process.

The story of how we lost our consciousness is wonderful: During the Age of Leo, we separated our identities into gods and men. During the Age of Cancer, we discovered that Earth's women are the goddesses of eternal birthing with their consorts. During the Age of Gemini, we identified order and Time. During the Age of Taurus, we organized ourselves in cities. During the Age of Aries, we fought over those cities and temples.

And during the Age of Pisces, we explored our lives through pain and heal-ing. All through these experiences, most of us worshiped gods while being controlled by their representatives. As we went through these phases, each issue was overlaid by the agenda of the next age, so now our collective unconscious is like a layer cake. Consider this: We rolled into the Age of Taurus imbued with our deep experiences with kings, the Mother Goddess, and the great Gemini sages, and this rich archetypal pool was deposited as a matrix in the great temples in the centers of commercial city cultures. Once the cities grew, they were like great organisms being fed by the sur-rounding fields in which the farmers toiled. Then, during the Arian Age, the cities warred with one another while the country people stayed out of the way as best they could. Finally, the people suffered and grew with each other during the Piscean Age and began to wonder about their emotions.

Just as the sacred king, goddess, and sage archetypes rolled into the Age of Taurus, we now roll into the Age of Aquarius, questioning whether we will use war, suffering, and emotional obsessions as the matrix for cyber-space. The fate of Earth causes us to question ourselves because religions claim God assigned us the stewardship of Earth. Meanwhile, as we go about our daily lives assuming that everything will go on as it always has, fewer people actually believe this and they nervously mark time. *During great seasonal shifts, such passivity is lethal.* To survive during rapid and chaotic change, to evolve at these moments, we must invent new ways of living that will sustain the new reality that is emerging. Furthermore, we must recover our precatastrophic ability to harmonize with Earth, an abil-ity we've been gradually losing since 9500 B.C. Michio Kushi says that with the new galactic orientation our mental images will begin to synchronize. "We think in terms of the whole planet united in a time of peace, creativ-ity and harmony by the descending (centripetal) energy which formed the galaxy, the solar system, and this earth."[14]

For thousands of years, we all lived more in darkness. The night sky was a fluid movie—star lore—that revealed our individual roles in the mythical story of Earth; it was the library of our thoughts. *The tilting axis has been causing us to discover ourselves in a field of great mythological dualities that have radically complicated our sense of self.* Various spiral patterns, such as the dra-matic rise and fall of the Orion star system and the undulating north polar serpent, Draco—brought on, perhaps, by the recent phenomenon of axial tilt—inspired great myths about sages, kings, mother goddesses, and family sagas. Luckily the Egyptians and other cultures who understood sacred science saved the stories that retain the stellar library. Ancient cultures *used storytelling to communicate the legends of the gods and great sages,* and because these memories exist eternally in the star libraries, suddenly the Galactic Winter Solstice is inciting many to remember their connections with these Time archetypes. For thousands of years before the Age of Reason, these nonordinary realms unfolded in a vast drama that played out in the skies. We had personal relationships with these worlds in Dreamtime, and these contacts are depicted in temple reliefs and sacred art, and described in mythology all over the planet. This relationship between Earth and sky got confused in A.D. 221, when the Synodic Vernal Point was fixed at 0 degrees Aries, because the constellations move by precession from Earth perspective. This needs to be noted here, because this fixing distorts geocentric viewing, and the planets are not located by the stars.

By losing connection with the stars because they are no longer a backdrop for planetary locations, human alienation has become progressively more profound. Because the planets rule primary psychology and the planetary influences are more emphasized when the stellar influences are removed, this alienation prompted the development of psychology, which enables us to observe and reflect on our own behavior. By mastering psychology, we are becoming aware of archetypal influences in our lives. For example, for thousands of years humans experienced the planets as archetypal forces that influence behavior, and today we have a resurgence in astrology. According to astrology, the planets exemplify the structural nature of our inner feelings. For example, Mars reflects our ability to use power, and Venus reflects our ability to express love and devotion. The planets mirror our own ecstasy and pain back to us, which makes it easier to recognize what is going on inside ourselves in relation to events outside ourselves. We now know that we do not act alone in this world. The planetary archetypes motivate us to evolve and understand our real purposes in life amid the collective passions of humanity. The fact is that this temporary alienation from the stars has brought a new facet of human awareness into being: self-reflective consciousness.

As the Age of Pisces ends, a keen awareness of astrology could be the ideal tool to use to get beyond being motivated by war and suffering. Mars rules war, but also personal mastery of power; Neptune rules Pisces, motivating suffering as well as personal mastery of compassion. The laws of astrology are based on the concept that the larger realm (macrocosm) mirrors our inner experience (microcosm). As already shown, the macrocosm is priming us to transfigure so that we might become enlightened in the microcosm. Understanding our urges by planetary archetypes helps us to objectify the personal morass we live in. This temporary stellar separation has enabled us to see how much we are being influenced by the archetypal realms, and we're beginning to wonder if there are puppeteers pulling our puppet strings. Yes, there are. We must identify control factors, lest we seek "aliens" out there, simply because we are alienated within. I suggest "control" instead of "influence," because I was a counseling astrologer for twenty-five years; the cycles of the planets *do* control those who are unaware of their influence. The precessional cycles also greatly motivate cultural patterns; thus they are great control tools for the powers-that-be, the Global Elite. I have been teaching how the planets influence collective humanity since 1988. I have become certain that the cycles of the planets are used by the Elite controllers, whose agenda is the New World Order for the Age of Aquarius. They have found it easy to manipulate people who are caught in war and suffering. As you will read later, manipulation by Time is how cultures are controlled, but astrology and precessional knowledge make it possible for *any* individual to attain freedom. Let's move back in time to search for a wider view.

Cataclysmic Theory

Scientists, of course, would not think of Time by means of the Platonic Great Year, but ironically, a new description of the past 15,000 years on Earth is being crafted that actually supports the time line of this book. Moving back a few hundred years, we were torn out of simple village life by the Industrial Revolution, and science came forth to describe human history. Previously, history had been the reserve of theologians, who pondered the cataclysms and the Flood in the Bible. Examining the evolution of the landscape—assuming that Earth is billions of years old—the newly emerging sciences invented a theory for Earth's evolution called *uniformitarianism*, which posits that geological and biological change is very slow and gradual. Lately, many scientists have shifted to *catastrophism*, which describes periodic instantaneous geological and biological change amid long periods of slow change. Then, during the mid-1990s, with the global data in place, science *converged*. The global survey reveals that Earth was nearly destroyed only 11,500 years ago, and there have been several very dramatic readjustments of the planet that followed. Concurrently, the galactic alignments seem to be flooding our minds with memories of previous advanced cultures and their horrific destructions. All of this is happening as the theocratic city culture of the past 6,000 years is imploding. Cataclysmic science, with its media soapbox system, is stirring up the potent stew of traumatic memories. For example, the film *Deep Impact* depicts an asteroid hitting Earth that turned the crust into jello. This triggered great unease, and viewers feared something terrible was coming soon. Then they were all primed for a Y2K technology crash, and Microsoft made billions. Now the Global Elite scientists are preparing the public for a weapons system that will shoot asteroids out of the sky.

Many people have become keenly aware in their daily lives of the control by archetypal forces that operate through schools, banks, governments, and other institutions. Many feel that humanity is being led down a road that few people want to travel, and people are passively accepting this because they do not realize that *the disaster is the past, not the future*. Because these disasters were not described by science until very recently, most people are deeply troubled by free-floating anxiety about the sky falling; they literally feel an apocalypse is coming soon. The sky *did* fall within recent memory, and then the recovery period from 9000 to 1500 B.C. was filled with periodic upheavals. These fearful memories will lurk in our subconscious minds until we remember this story, which I will help you to do in this book. *We are a wounded species on the verge of recovery, and we're poised to undertake the brave journey back to our previous brilliance.* We will cease cowering before the gods we have created out of our fear and soon be able to use our personal power.

In 1994 twenty-two fragments of the comet Shoemaker/Levy slammed into the viscous surface of Jupiter, which many people watched on television. Many remembered subliminally when Earth was slammed by similar monsters in the sky, and then other comets kept coming in. Many people reported they felt awe, dread, and sadness about Jupiter when they watched the impacts. Like adults who have unrecalled childhood abuse or trauma, we are deeply fearful, paranoid, and easily drawn into collective fear. We are easily incited by religious fanatics who intuitively know how to excite apocalyptical fear complexes because they are afflicted with catastrophobia themselves. Many truly believe the world is coming to an end, so they'd rather end it all right now. *This collective insanity could destroy human civilization.* The Cataclysm caused the Late Pleistocene extinctions, when woolly mammoths, saber-toothed tigers, and many other species—as well as many human clans—were decimated.[15] This massive wave of death lies deeply buried in the psyches of humans, and the cities have become massive economic machines fueled by people who desire material comfort at any cost. The fear of scarcity drove us to use nature by inventing agriculture, yet previously we *aligned* with nature as hunter-gatherers and horticulturalists. What has been accomplished materially since 9500 B.C. is amazing. We have proven that we can create almost anything; yet why are people so worried about the future? *We fear potential scarcity during this time of awesome plenty.* Anthropologists have demonstrated that cultures that retained their stories of origin do not want, need, care for, or use so many things. In comparison to modern Western culture, people in indigenous cultures often enjoy plenty of nonworking time. In our civilized, technological world of nanoseconds, we are all smothered in gadgets and garbage, we are all linked up and work constantly. What's next? I think we are on the threshold of a massive *dematerialization* after becoming more dense and material for 11,500 years, and I believe this will be the central theme of the Age of Aquarius. Yet *how* can we do this?

Generational Change and Dematerialization

How could we lighten up and do things differently? Seeking answers to this question, I have been hanging out with younger people, because they exhibit emerging characteristics of the new world to come. They will raise their families in the new times, and listening to what they are thinking about offers some clues about where we're headed amid the dizzying changes. Many people born since 1965 are experimenting with ways to

Fig. 1.8. The Osireion of Abydos.

live in a less material world. They know this is the only possible next step, because Earth cannot sustain the current level of technological overload. Meanwhile, based on precessional laws, we will become less materialistic anyway in the next cycle, because we will remember how to align with Earth's forces instead of merely *using* Earth. The remnants of cultures that have retained simple ways of life are suddenly being rediscovered and valued as critical resources, such as the precataclysmic cultures of the Australian Aborigines.

Precataclysmic cultures were using a currently unknown technology; nobody has figured out how they cut and moved huge stones. One of the best examples of this technology is the Osireion in Egypt, which has precisely cut and placed stones that weigh hundreds of tons. As a style these are called cyclopean stones, because they seem to have been forged by giants. Their forgotten builders must have known how to work in alignment with Earth's forces in ways that have now atrophied, yet there are ways to rediscover these forgotten skills. I've been studying for seven years with the anthropologist Felicitas Goodman, who has discovered how people in shamanic cultures gathered information to solve their problems for thousands of years. To do this, they went into trance while assuming very specific postures that helped them access spirits in the alternate reality for advice.[16] The alternate reality is a world that coexists with ordinary reality. These postures are an amazing tool for recovering archaic technologies and healing techniques. Maybe the spirits could explain how to build the Osireion or the Great Pyramid! I will report extensively on my work with Dr. Goodman throughout this book.

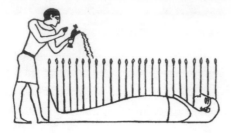

Fig. 1.9. Watering Osiris who Grows Corn in His Body from the Temple of Isis at Philae.

The most painful situation in this last stage of materialization is health and wellness. Many people, even many young people, are very ill in the midst of the rapid changing. It is good news that the Age of Aquarius promises to rejuvenate our bodies. The ruling planet of Aquarius is Uranus, which activates *kundalini energy,* the power that acupuncturists and healers stimulate and spiritual teachers awaken. In striking contrast to those who use alternative health only, people who depend on materialistic medicine are plagued by chronic disease; they are *nailed on the medical cross* as the suffering Age of Pisces closes. Newtonian physics has caused people to think of their bodies as machines, yet we are not just machines that need fixing. The health of people in modern Western countries has deteriorated, their kundalini energy is weak, and they are losing their life force and genetic integrity. Chemical and nuclear medicine toxify the environment and people's bodies, and we need the vibrational repatterning that comes with strong kundalini energy flow. Individuals with awakened kundalini are very psychic and energized, and as the Aquarian influence builds, many people are seeking healing methods that enhance kundalini flow to reduce the wave of chronic disease. For thousands of years before Western medicine, enhanced kundalini energy was used to revitalize people and repair our genes. These medicines are legacies from even *before* the Cataclysm, and the Aquarian energy is rebirthing them.

Growing up after the Second World War in Michigan, I watched the ecosystems around my childhood home deteriorate and the human cultures decline. According to my grandparents, these destructive traits were taking over because the people had forgotten their origins. My parents' generation—born between 1900 and 1930—did not think in terms of meaningful origins; they had lost hope in the future. They were depressed by the Great Depression and two world wars, and they were convinced they had only one life to live, which is one of the most lethal Christian dogmas. What a life! This life was their *only* life, in which they were battered by global and economic trauma. Earth was their torture chamber, and the term *Great Depression* caught on because it describes the psychological condition of this generation. My grandfather said the darkest hours on Earth for the past 10,000 years occurred during the Second World War, but the turn toward enlightenment also began. My parents' generation believed their one life was all they had, so they frantically pursued security, while their children—born between 1930 and 1960—watched Earth dying. Herded like sheep into concrete "shelters" during nuclear alerts and taken to the doctor to be inoculated with traces of disease, the children concluded the plan was to kill them as radioactive mushroom clouds exploded on the television. In light of such a tenuous future, the "war babies" dedicated themselves to facing and healing their own emotional scars, if only to avoid passing on negativity to their children. These children—born during the 1960s and '70s—are assuming roles in the world, and many of them possess great emotional strength.

Turtle Medicine

In the midst of the awesome death of life and culture after the Second World War, my grandparents gifted me with an unshakable vision of the future by exposing me to a wider perspective than the depressed view of my parents. Still in touch with their own origins and marvelously educated in Egyptology and other ancient cultures, they knew the great awakening would come after they were gone. They knew my parents would not live to see it happen, so they passed their legacies to me. Together we studied Plato and other classical sources, Egyptology, and Cherokee and Celtic stories. My Celtic grandmother taught me how to see the nature spirits in her garden and the spirits in the house, and my Cherokee/Celtic grandfather taught me how to hear the sounds of the stars in the wetlands, to see the spirits (Little People) in the forest, and to read the messages from animals and insects. They shared their knowledge of the long time cycles, and they taught me how to work with the Ancestors—unseen teachers who are symbiotic with Earth and who commune with all receptive humans. In this book, the Ancestors are also called the Elders, and sages are humans who

Fig. 1.10.
Turtle Medicine

29

work with the Ancestors and Elders. As a result of studying with Felicitas Goodman, I believe sages are humans who work *consciously* with Elders and Ancestors who inhabit the alternate reality. In my grandparents' home, modern culture was not thought of as enlightened or superior in any way. Instead, they explained that we are the descendants of an advanced culture that disappeared in a day. Plato saved the record of these days before the Flood, and my grandfather began supervising my study of Plato when I was eight years old. These long cycles of Time are in the Celtic myths, which my grandmother still remembered. In 1998, I decided to write their legacy in this book, which my grandfather called Turtle Medicine.

Turtle Medicine is about earth changes. Earth's surface is made of twenty great plates, like the skirt of twenty plates around the thirteen central plates on Turtle's back. Sometimes these plates move when Turtle walks, as do Earth's plates while we live on the surface influenced by the bodies in the heavens. The three stars in Orion's belt are Turtle's spine and the four outer stars—Saiph, Rigel, Betelguese, and Bellatrix—are Turtle's feet.[17] The way to be happy here on Earth is to contemplate these correspondences, which open pathways that connect us with our spiritual vehicles, the stars. *The stars are the home of our souls.* I was taught that Turtle's back is the home of my body—Earth—where I am assisted by the Cherokee Little People. Grandmother introduced me to the Faeries, who would always be around to tell us where to go if the sea were to rise and the land submerged. They taught me to trust Earth and her subtle realms. These subtle realms support everything that is material, yet they are invisible to us if we do not believe in them and trust Earth. My grandparents were symbiotic with these other worlds. Their house was filled with allies, many of whom still live with me today. Turtle Medicine means you exist intentionally and consciously in many worlds while you're alive; then life is never boring and there is no desire to make it more than it is. Grandfather also was a Mason who had attained a very high degree, which may be why he loved Egyptology. He helped me develop a living relationship with my *ba,* my body of consciousness that lives in the stars.

We *all* need to recover our connection with the stars, because we cannot exist on Earth if we conceive of ourselves as unloved creatures born to suffer through one life and die at the whim of avenging gods. Maya teachings are very similar to Cherokee knowledge, especially regarding Turtle Medicine, and the Maya legacy is their calendars. These teachings were graciously opened to me as an adult by Hunbatz Men of the Yucatan and Don Alejandro Oxlac of Guatemala, who helped me see how interconnected all the indigenous teachings are.* Maya calendars are weavings of thirteen days and twenty glyphs or modalities, because turtle shells are made of thirteen central plates that are edged by twenty smaller plates. The science of the twenty great plates that float in Earth's mantle is called *plate tectonics,* and during each solar year, the thirteen cycles of the Moon modulate human emotional patterns. Turtle Medicine expresses how these Time cycles create change. Besides using astrology as a tool for psychological maturity, we can also balance our emotional patterns by attuning with the twenty modalities that mature our emotions as we expand our consciousness and live in harmony with Moontime. If we develop these twenty aspects of our feelings and these thirteen lenses of time, we will harmonize with Earth. It is so important to realize that being *indigenous is a mind-set,* which is an intentional life of not being caught up in cultural definitions or clock time. Then you are not limited to ordinary reality—you can access the many dimensions of the alternate reality.

After the Cataclysm, which was reported accurately by indigenous people all over the world, we peered into the haze of the destroyed world and saw the faces and bodies of the leaders who had assumed authority roles; we believed they were gods. The priests said that they would punish us because we had not worshiped them correctly, and we must make sacrifices to them. In our stupor—banished from the primordial garden and saddened by the idea of an avenging deity—we got caught in Time. This is *the Fall,* and by this loss of grace, we became increasingly one dimensional and gradually lost our ability to feel the vibrations of Nature, the stars, and to see the spirits. This made us profoundly lonely, as the skies were changing. Fearing avenging gods and the sky, we adopted agriculture to harness Nature. Thousands of years would pass before we could wake up, while Earth bided her time. Earth knew a potent cosmic infusion of energy from the stars would cause us to begin to vibrate with Nature again, and we are.

---

* I am an International Maya Elder with the Mayoam Council of Chichén Itzá.

Sensing how deeply I grieved as I watched my parents and the amphibians, fish, plants, and mammals dying, my grandparents promised me my own children would be the first generation to walk into the primordial garden again. We would remember that long ago our whole solar system experienced a cosmic disaster and that *humanity was not punished by an avenging god.* It is time to laugh at that old, tired, and nasty male god who is all puffed up by our inner terror. The new scientific story is telling the real story of Earth, and finally we're hearing something that confirms our inner feelings. For postwar adults, it will be difficult to overcome a lifetime of false cultural beliefs; yet the new world can be seen in the eyes of the children. Thus, for now, many people born after 1940 are guardians of the dying material world in which the vibrational world is awakening. Many people do not trust that a new future is coming, and the current rate of chronic disease, genetic deterioration, and death reflects this lack of will to live. Never has it been more important to align with this cosmic energy flow.

Like gossamer tendrils of silicate light, the new wave comes from deep space as gamma rays, which trigger massive increases of photons that incite chaos and change. *During such intense change, you can avoid energy depletion by detecting the qualities of the new wave and participating in it.* These new energies are very intense, yet very subtle, and the only way to detect them is to play with them by noticing what excites or bores you. For example, I find that thinking of my body as a vibrational field that is directed by my mind free of charge is more empowering than thinking that my body is a car that must be tuned up by the doctor or repaired in the hospital—that is, if I have insurance and am a good girl and get to my appointment on time, I can sit and wait to get fixed. Each great age develops enduring qualities that will become significant foundations in the next one. During the past 2,000 years we have been exploring our feelings, and now courage, compassion, and devotion can be the foundations of the Age of Aquarius. With these powers, we can activate our energy bodies vibrationally and center that force in our *hearts.* We can be less material and more emotional—we already *are.* Merging these exquisite feelings in our awakened vibrational bodies, we will be self-aware in the awakened Earth. We will be able to see ourselves finally in Nature's vibrational field, because for the past 2,000 years we've become self-reflective and found our hearts.

2

The Great Cataclysm & the Fall

Precession took on an overpowering significance.
It became the vast impenetrable pattern of fate itself,
with one world-age succeeding another, as the invisible
pointer of the equinox slid along the signs, each age bringing
with it the rise and downfall of astral configurations
and rulerships, with their earthly consequences.
      —Hertha Von Dechend and Giorgio de Santillana[1]

Hamlet's Mill and the Precession of the Equinoxes

Precession of the equinoxes is an astronomical cycle that describes the timing and qualities of cultural patterns by symbolism, as introduced in chapter 1. This chapter investigates how this subtle symbolic force influences human cultures. The symbols are the key guides, as each Great Age is represented by a symbol that is derived from a constellation located on the Ecliptic. For example, the symbol for the Piscean Age, when Christianity was founded, was the fish, and the Pisces constellation is drawn as two interweaving fishes. These symbols go far back into prehistory; for example, the Taurus constellation is drawn as a great bull, and the Cancer constellation is a crab. The crab shares symbolic rulership with the Moon, which the sign Cancer rules. The temples of the times often have appropriate symbols for each Great Age, and sacred texts from these cultures describe ceremonies that were created to enhance the power of these symbols: Bull rituals during the Age of Taurus 6,000 years ago are carried on today as bullfights, and often women are thought of as crabs!

How might this symbolic weaving still influence us and even direct our lives? Even today, indigenous people identify themselves as members of clans by their animal totems, and isn't it mysterious that the zodiac is a circle of animals plus a few human images in the sky? The zodiac consists of the constellations on the Ecliptic—twelve out of eighty-eight constellations—and all eighty-eight star systems were thought of as spiritual influences. Are such totemic clans vestiges of precessional knowledge? Are bullfights lingering vestiges of the Age of Taurus? Besides the wonderful creative potential of these connections, does this subtle factor still direct the collective unconscious? If so, did the ancient people use these powers intentionally, and can we? Judging by the amount of work they put into building and maintaining their temples, we would be foolish *not* to consider whether the precessional factor actually affects us now. At the very least, we can understand the past better by understanding what these symbols meant to people in the past. Then we can investigate how precessional cycles influence human cultures now, whether anybody is aware of the moving circle in the sky or not. What if secret societies, such as the Masons, know all about these influences and noninitiated modern people are ignorant of them?

Traces of precessional influence are found in sacred scripture and mythology that have been passed down in the oral tradition for thousands of years and then were eventually written down. *Hamlet's Mill: An Essay on Myth and the Frame of Time* by famed scholars Hertha Von Dechend and Giorgio de Santillana is the penultimate study of mythology by precession. The authors determine that archaic mythology and art cannot be fathomed without understanding its underlying complex celestial basis—precession of the equinoxes—and I agree. *Hamlet's Mill* was initially labeled as a wild and radical tome that few could understand. It was widely read and discussed because it was written by two otherwise highly esteemed scholars. Lately it has become *the* foundational source for researchers who are investigating how archaic cultures understood precession. It explores how the core myths contain elements from earlier times layered over by later times, like a household of family antiquities mixed with new furniture. The archaic fragments are mixed in with more recent stories because the bards rescued them, even if they didn't know what they meant, just like treasured family heirlooms. This is what bards or keepers of the oral tradition did, showing that *Time is the essential structural format of myth*. Luckily, scholars can decode these factors, because myths have linguistic variations and archaic elements that reflect the layers of Time. Mythology is a veritable mathematics of consciousness. *Hamlet's Mill* examines the ancient sagas, stories, epics, and dramas and deciphers them by means of precessional cycles and symbolism. These stories often begin with phrases such as "Once upon a time," or "Once in the days long ago . . ." The core myths are filled with stories of origin that span extremely long cycles of Time in specific places. Often without even realizing it, we perceive events by Time. Try telling a story to somebody without using time and place.

In mythology, there is an archaic time-coded system that is a treasure hunt through thousands of years back into prehistory. Storytelling shows how people remembered and dealt with what happened to them over the Great Ages. In fact, there are extremely similar myths of the Flood in almost all ancient cultures. Possibly the tilting of Earth's axis led to the creation of postcatastrophic storytellers and astronomer-priests approximately 10,000 years ago, because they were obsessed with changes in the sky. An alteration in the cosmic order would have been very disturbing to them. They probably did not understand *why* precession began, but they came up with some very accurate mythic images, such as Atlas holding up the sky. They would have immediately noticed the radical change of star locations on the horizons, everyone would have noticed the new seasons, and eventually precessional movement was observed on the horizon or around the poles. Naturally, they also feared more disasters, and there *were* follow-up adjustments as Earth settled down. Archaic people offered sacrifices to the gods from earliest times hoping that the sky would not fall again.[2]

The possibility that precession began only 11,500 years ago is a radical hypothesis, which only can be *proven* by a very detailed analysis and synthesis of geological and paleontological records. More of this data is available in appendices B, C, and D. Astrophysicists would need to study the current orbits of bodies in the solar system to see if a new pattern began 11,500 years ago. This process has already been initiated by Allan and Delair in *Cataclysm!* Regardless of exactly when precession began, humans have been obsessed with Time for the past 10,000 years. There must be a reason, because tracking precession requires advanced astronomy and lots of leisure time. Many excellent technical books prove archaic people tracked precession, such as *The Dawn of Astronomy* by J. Norman Lockyer, *The Secret of the Incas* by William Sullivan, *Stonehenge* by John North, and *Maya Cosmogenesis 2012* by John Major Jenkins.[3] Later, I will discuss evidence from Çatal Hüyük in Turkey that archaic people were contemplating the precessional influence as long as *9,000 years ago* during the Age of Gemini—6640 to 4480 B.C. With a feeling for how far back this way of knowing reality may go, core myths and archeological sites are Time tunnels that open our eyes to see the brilliance and exquisite creativity of preliterate cultures. This is why they haunt and fascinate many people.

Hamlet's Mill posits that we need this system for guidance, because when the Great Ages shift, the transitions are extremely difficult. For example, the advent of warfare came when the Age of Aries began more than 4,000 years ago. Sometimes the shadow side of an age seems to take over nearly a whole 2,000-year Great Age. The Piscean Age's obsession has been suffering and salvation when it could have been an age of great spiritual enlightenment. Regarding *Hamlet's Mill*, the mill is a millstone, such as for grinding flour. The lost king, Hamlet, represents the tragic aspects of our lives during Great Age transitions, and a hamlet is a small village. The mill symbolizes the wheel of Time, the advent of agriculture, and the obsession with daily bread. These are perfect images for humanity caught on the wheel of Time, first by agriculture and then by being drawn out of our hamlets and trapped in cities and factories. Today, as cyberspace eliminates our opportunities to meet each other in person, perhaps we might want to ask before we all get absorbed into e-commerce: Did archaic people *want* to let go of gathering, horticulture, and village life?

The Cataclysm occurred in the middle of what became the first Great Age—Leo—so the shift into Aquarius is an entry into the sign that is *opposite* Leo. According to astrological principles, an oppositional phase is like the full Moon, which will bring to fruition all the things we've created since the Age of Leo and the Cataclysm. This *is* happening as archaic contents of the psyche trigger waves of barbaric warfare and personal psychosis, as if somebody had opened Pandora's Box and left it open. To integrate Aquarian energy with our true past, we must remember the Cataclysm. Who were we then? What happened to us?

The Terrible Days of Flood, Wind, and Fire

Cataclysm! Compelling Evidence for a Cosmic Catastrophe in 9500 B.C. describes the recent Cataclysm that disarranged our solar system and tilted the axis of Earth. Allan and Delair theorize that fragments of a supernova in the Vela star system crashed into our solar system 11,500 years ago and then approached Earth.* What follows is a replay of the day Earth nearly died based on *Cataclysm!*, and readers who question or respond powerfully to this description would be well advised to read this monumental work. My intention here is to awaken your own inner memory of this event because it exists deep within the subconscious minds of all people; it is the source of modern collective fear.

The Supernova fragments approached Earth, our atmosphere became electrically supercharged, and our waters and winds began to heat up. Earth was becoming hot and fetid, and a horror unfolded for all living things on Earth: Lurid monsters appeared in the sky that kept changing shape and color, which sometimes looked like a giant bird or a writhing serpent or dragon. Whatever it was, it was the most terrible thing that had ever appeared in the skies. It even seemed to be moving against the passage of the Sun through the sky, and people fell down on their knees in terror. The thrashing fire in the sky got bigger and bigger for

---

* D. S. Allan and J. B. Delair, *Cataclysm! Compelling Evidence of a Cosmic Catastrophe in 9500 B.C.* (Santa Fe: Bear & Company, 1997) 207–11. To summarize Allan and Delair's theories of the cause, they say on page 209, "Although it is impossible at this juncture to positively pinpoint Phaeton's (supernova) real identity, we can merely state what it was *not*." Then they list the "nots": meteors, asteroids, and conventional comets; satellites, such as moons; planets; passing stars; and giant interstellar comets. Finally, they offer details on the cloud of Aluminum-26 in space surrounding the solar system, which makes a supernova the likely candidate. According to astronomy, at least five supernovas have exploded near our solar system 15,000 to 11,500 years ago, and one of them—the Vela supernova—erupted 14,300 ago (D. K. Milne, "A New Catalogue of Galactic SNRs Corrected for Distance from the Galactic Plane," 32:83–92.) 11,000 years ago (G. R. Brackenridge, "Terrestrial Palaeoenvironmental Effects of a Late Quarternary-Age Supernova," *Icarus* 16:81–93). Of course, they say "it is impossible at this juncture to positively pinpoint Phaeton's real identity."

many days, and as it came closer, it looked like it would pass over the North Pole as it moved inside the Moon. Then terrible sucking winds came as Earth began to tip toward the chimera in the sky.* There was a deafening explosion in the vault of the sky and Earth shuddered.† Within hours, blocks of ice, hail, and gigantic masses of water pummeled our planet.‡ What was coming? What could it be? asked all who stared at the frightening sky.

The atmosphere imploded and all living things were terrified of the deafening sound. Great electromagnetic storms overwhelmed the bioelectric fields of animals, humans, plants, and even rocks. On that day, fear was so deeply imprinted in human consciousness that ever since our minds have tried to suppress and deny this memory. Chaos reigned next as volcanos exploded and spewed, as the oceans and lakes boiled, as Earth shuddered and cracked insanely.

The following extract contains more details of this story from *Cataclysm!* The authors use Ovid's Phaeton to represent the fragments of the supernova and Kingu (a moon of a destroyed planet, Tiamat, from the

---

* Allan and Delair, *Cataclysm!* 250–54. The authors comment on page 250 that the Persian legends report that this phenomenon went on for many days, and the weird shapes must have been caused by the electromagnetic activity and changing positions within the fragments and debris. On page 252, they say "Earth/Moon gravitation now begins to affect the course of the intruders, while Earth, tilting axially away from the vertical, starts to align itself toward Phaeton and Kingu."

† Allan and Delair, *Cataclysm!*, 254. The authors speculate that Kingu (a moon of Tiamat that is a destroyed planet in the asteroid belt) disintegrated in Earth's Roche Limit, the area around Earth that will expel or destroy objects approaching the planet.

‡ Allan and Delair, *Cataclysm!*, 281–89. Judging by the swarms of craterlike depressions in the Atlantic Coastal Plain, the Carolina bays the craterlike shallow depressions in the Alaskan permafrost near Point Barrow, and other such formations in Bolivia and the Netherlands, the authors constructed a global schema and map of this falling matter that seems to indicate by the debris that Phaeton was passing over the North Pole and opposite Earth's rotation. On page 221, they speculate that the fragments could have ruptured the Kuiper Belt, a belt of tiny planetoid objects that orbit around the solar system or occasionally inside of Pluto's orbit. Decaying Aluminum-26 surrounds the solar system in this general region. If the fragments did shatter the Kuiper Belt, on Earth there would have been visual effects of an explosion but no sound. My sense that the solar system would vibrate like a bell comes from some of the findings science garnered from research on Supernova 1987A. For example, according to astronomer Alfred K. Mann, "During the 12 seconds, SN 1987A generated an amount of power in the form of neutrinos that dwarfed all power production on Earth by about 34 powers of 10" (*Shadow of a Star: The Neutrino Story of Supernova 1987A* [New York: W. H. Freeman and Company, 1997], 103).

Akkadian epic, the *Enuma Elish*) to name the mass that moved along with the supernova fragments toward Earth.

The combined separation of Kingu from Phaeton and the stopping or slowing of Earth's axial spin caused terrible havoc on Earth. The waters of the world's rivers, lakes, and oceans were drained from their original basins and drawn gravitationally to the point on Earth nearest (opposite) Kingu and Phaeton. Worldwide traditions remember the awesome effect.

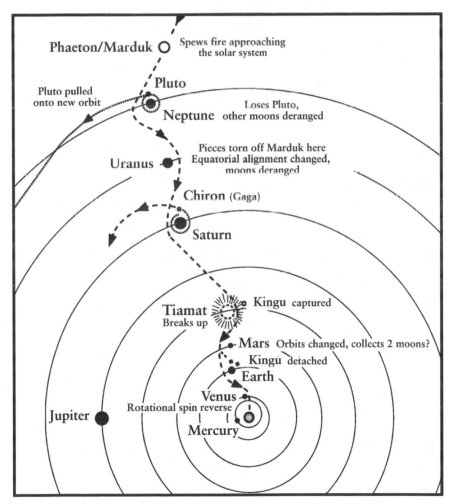

Fig. 2.1. The Great Cataclysm in 9500 B.C. Figure 4.13 of
Cataclysm! Compelling Evidence of a Cosmic Catastrophe in 9500 B.C.

The retarding of Earth's rotation also resulted in the world's winds blowing with a ferocity and intensity never experienced by modern people—winds which flattened whole forests, whipped ocean billows to mountainous heights, moved giant rocks and removed incalculable volumes of loose surface materials to very great distances. It was, in fact, remembered as a veritable diluvium venti.

Meanwhile, the internal magma tides continued to flow below the tormented terrestial crust. Through the united gravitational influence of Kingu and Phaeton, they will have been slowly pulled towards that aspect of Earth nearest those celestial bodies. This inevitably resulted in geoidal deformation, huge portions of the lithosphere buckling, fracturing, subducting, collapsing, or overriding one another as simultaneously numerous mountain ranges were up-heaved. Rivers of molten lava, rains of red-hot ash, and vast clouds of volcanic dust and gas swirled over enormous regions. Elsewhere rampant fires will have consumed all living things in their path.

*At some localities volcanic gas clouds—*nues ardentes—*transported large boulders many miles, scored rock surfaces with striae closely resembling those often ascribed elsewhere to glacial action, and, in company with high pressure grit-charged steam, polished and carved rock surfaces, and excavated entire valleys. Concomitantly, avalanches of boiling mud ejected from volcanic vents and fissures poured down hillsides and along valleys transporting more boulders and producing further rock striations.[4]*

Crustal Shifting Models

Science historian D. S. Allan and geologist/anthropologist J. B. Delair drew their description of the Cataclysm from a comprehensive analysis of worldwide accounts of the disaster in the voluminous geopaleontological and astronomical data. It seems impossible that a disaster of such magnitude as they describe could have *ever* happened, much less only 11,500 years ago, yet the scientific records of Earth and the solar system confirm this, as do the ancient legends. Modern science is only putting all this together now. Meanwhile, this memory was kept by indigenous people all over the world; their cross-cultural records that tell the same story verify modern cataclysmic theory.[5]

The magnitude of the Cataclysm calls for serious consideration of new theoretical geological mechanisms, such as crustal shifting, which are discussed extensively in this book. For example, scientific data indicate that the *topography of Earth was almost completely rearranged.* "The former dis-

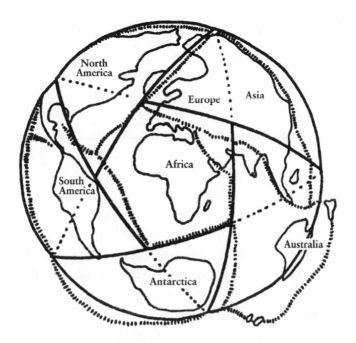

Fig. 2.2. Icosahedral Earth. Figure 5.9 of Cataclysm!
Compelling Evidence of a Cosmic Catastrophe in 9500 B.C.

position of land and sea was changed, a new world mountain system came into being, the number of active volcanoes was augmented enormously, a legacy of seismic activity was bequeathed which is far from over, a new land drainage pattern was instituted, and completely different oceanic and atmospheric circulatory regimes were established."[6] Ocean basins collapsed and global rift valleys and fracture complexes formed that can only be explained by plate tectonics—the movements of Earth's crustal plates— that *dislocated Earth's lithosphere both vertically and horizontally.*[7]

The major tectonic plates of Earth are divided by great faults, such as the San Andreas Fault in California, where Earth's crust has actually fractured. A popular theory for the presence of these great seismically active faults has been Wegener's continental drift theory.[8] However, recently some researchers have begun to question continental drift as the only factor in the formation of these major tectonic plates. Allan and Delair point out that the global *pattern* of tectonic plates is actually icosahedral— a polyhedron of twenty faces—suggesting that *Earth expanded hemispherically very recently,* "cracking apart like the shell of an overheated egg."[9] The authors give voluminous evidence that this incredible geometrical faulting had to have been caused by a uniformly exerted *external* stress, such as

41

Phaeton, and the pattern of the faulting indicates that this stress markedly slowed the speed of Earth's rotation and caused longer days.[10] "The sudden slowing of Earth's rotation, therefore, inevitably caused severe crustal fracturing worldwide. The continued rotation of the semi-molten magma below Earth's halted or decelerated crust resulted in vastly increased thermal energy and, not improbably, in temporary geoidal deformation."[11] In a letter, J. B. Delair commented that "the plates formed more or less simultaneously and suddenly under violent conditions."*

This geological mechanism may be the only possible explanation for what happened so recently to our planet. After consideration of various radical catastrophic geological mechanisms, such as Rand and Rose Flem-Ath's crustal-shifting theory in *When the Sky Fell* and Charles Hapgood's theories in *Path of the Pole*, I've adopted Allan and Delair's model.[12] Astute readers will realize how mind-bending their theory is, and a description of some other cataclysmic theories are in appendix A. Because Allan and Delair have thoroughly catalogued the worldwide Late Pleistocene data, considered the forces required for such great destruction, and then found a logical candidate for the mechanism, their theory calls for serious consideration. The remarkable convergence of 200 years of physical evidence of the recent Cataclysm is throwing science into great turmoil, because their theoretical models just don't work for the past 20,000 years. Tired of being pigeonholed in specific fields and denied an overview, many young scientists are looking at new mechanisms for cataclysmic change. The existing theories do not make sense now in light of the magnitude of the obviously recent disaster, and even the Holy Grail of geology, the Geological Column, is being reconsidered.

The Geological Column

Scientific analysis of layers of rocks—stratigraphy—assumes that these layers were created by gradual processes over millions of years. Allan and Delair also suggest that gigantic and geologically very rapid *relocation and*

---

* J. B. Delair, letter to the author, 3 August 1999. He also noted that the plates would *not* have moved as a single unit as once advocated by Charles Hapgood, and Hapgood admitted this to him during conversations in London a few years before he died.

reconstitution of many rocks has occurred by *crustal shifting*, a mechanism that is not even under consideration by orthodox geologists, at least officially. For a geologist, discussing crustal-shifting theory is anathema, like a historian discussing Atlantis or an archeologist redating the age of the Sphinx. Of course, it is extremely difficult to imagine the crust of Earth being pressed, rolled, liquefied, upthrusted/downthrusted, or pushed up sideways in an instant, and it is hard to know with sea levels whether they change because the land raised or lowered. It is even harder to think of this as a relatively recent event. However, in light of Allan and Delair's research, *all geological descriptions of the landscape based on noncatastrophic models must be recon-*

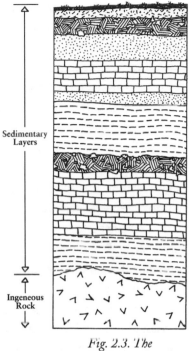

Fig. 2.3. The Geological Column.

sidered, including the Geological Column, which correlates and dates rock and coal layers and alluvial deposits. This column is used to date sedimentary rocks in all the earth sciences, and it was invented by uniformitarian science. Supposedly, these sequential layers represent millions of years of geological deposits found all over the planet. It is the basis for the *global geological timeline:* The lower layers are older, the upper levels are more recent, and the thickness of the layers represent specific lengths of time. Then the fossils found in the sedimentary layers can be dated whenever they are found in layers that are datable according to the Geological Column.

Another theory that seriously calls the Geological Column into question is from French geologist Guy Berthault. The new paradigm science reporter Richard Milton examined his research. He reports that in 1985, Berthault conducted an experiment that seriously challenges sedimentation theory and the validity of the Geological Column. He crumbled samples of rocks and reduced them to their original constituent particles. Then he sorted and colored them for identification purposes, and he mixed them all together and flowed them into a tank, first in a dry state, and later into water. Berthault found that *when the sediments settled on the bottom they re-created the appearance of the original rocks from which they had come.* According to Richard Milton, Berthault said in summary, "These experiments contradict the idea of the slow buildup of one layer followed by another. The time scale is reduced from hundreds of millions of years to one or more cataclysms producing almost instantaneous laminae (layers)."[13] That is exactly what happens during crustal shifting and massive flooding. What if the Geological Column is a record of how soil usually deposits when its constituent particles settle out over millions of years, but also is a record of how they settle instantaneously after they've been broken down by water? This would more accurately explain some features of the landscape that settled out after massive flooding 11,500 years ago.

No matter how this theoretical turmoil works out, we have been educated by—and are still being educated by—flawed geological theory. This makes it very difficult to consider new theoretical geological mechanisms or reconsider the age of the landscape. Meanwhile, whether orthodoxy ignores the intensifying challenge or not, there is mounting evidence that something is wrong with the Geological Column. Berthault's experiments suggest that crustal shifting and floods periodically reconstitute the layers of rock. Considering the magnitude of the devastation 11,500 years ago, crustal shifting and global flooding is the most likely mechanism, unless geologists can come up with ideas that explain the nature of the Late Pleistocene deposits, which *contain the remains of plants and animals from a spectrum of 29 million years ago to the Cataclysm.*[14] As mentioned above, the stratified layers are dated by the ages of the fossils deposited in them, so this fact also calls the Geological Column into serious question. What matters here is to open the possibility that *most of Earth's present topography is only 11,500 years old!* Of course, Earth's rocks are millions and billions of years old, but the *layers* of rock, especially those in the areas of the planet that were the most massively devastated, may not be a datable record at all. The next question that arises in light of the awesome magnitude of the destruction: What was the world like *before* the Cataclysm?

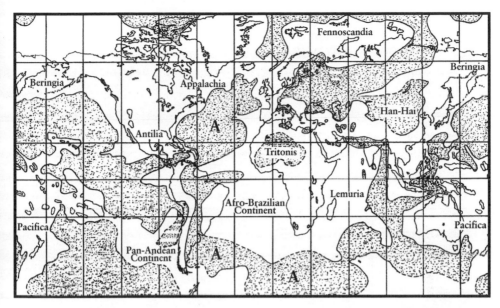

Fig. 2.4. Tentative Reconstruction of the Prediluvial World. Map 2A of Cataclysm!

The Prediluvial Landscape

The world before the Cataclysm is often referred to as the *prediluvial world*—Earth before the biblical Flood or Cataclysm. It is very difficult to imagine what the world was like before it was nearly destroyed; however, Allan and Delair examined the global fauna and flora and the geological data and have proposed a tentative precataclysmic map of the world. Also using the rare fragments in myths that describe the world before the Flood, Allan and Delair hypothesize that before the Cataclysm: (1) Earth must have been a stable planet over a long span of geological time; (2) the disposition of land and sea must have been very different; (3) mountains were fewer and lower, and deserts were less extensive and seas shallower; and (4) polar ice caps, if they existed at all, would have been of modest size. They surmise that there was more carbon dioxide and oxygen in the atmosphere; storms were infrequent and modest; humidity was high with mostly dew instead of rain; and vegetation was luxuriant.[15] In those days, some writers have alleged that Earth was perpetually springlike when we were "in the prime of life, with no aging or senility."[16] Based on his analysis of very old Japanese documents, Michio Kushi says the prediluvial world had a system of global transportation—boats as well as airplanes—and natural agriculture based on the idea that Earth would produce all that

Table 1A: The Tertiary and Quaternary Periods

*The conventional subdivisions of the **Tertiary** and **Quaternary** periods with their estimated duration shown in parentheses. Not to scale.*

Period	Epoch			Millions of Years
Quaternary	Holocene			**.011**
	Pleistocene	Upper	Ice Ages	**2**
		Middle		
		Lower		
Tertiary	Pliocene	(10,000,000 years)		**12**
	Miocene	(17,000,000 years)		**29**
	Oligocene	(12,000,000 years)		**41**
	Eocene	(10,000,000 years)		**51**
	Palaeocene	(9,000,000 years)		**60**

Table 2C: *Revised chronology for the **Tertiary** and **Quaternary** periods in the light of the Phaeton disaster.*

Eras:	Period	Epoch	Stages	General Conditions	Approx Dates (in years BP)
CAENOZOIC	**Quaternary**	Holocene *(Later)*	Historic	As at present	2300–today
			Sub-Atlantic	Dry mild	2700–2300
			Atlantic	Wet mild	3450–2700
			Boreal	Dry cold winters Warm summers	5500–4900
				Glaciers Melt	
		Holocene *(Earlier)*	Pre-Boreal	Dry cold	8000–7500
			Sub-Arctic	Wet cold	11,400
			Pleistocene	Severe. Rapid development of glaciers	11,500
	PHAETON DISASTER				
	Tertiary	Pliocene		Equable	14,000,000
		Miocene		Equable	29,000,000

Fig. 2.5. Revised Chronology of the Euro–American Quaternary Subdivisions. Tables 1A and 2C of Cataclysm! Compelling Evidence of a Cosmic Catastrophe in 9500 B.C.

was needed if it was "untouched." He says, "People in Paradise had freedom without the concept of freedom, health without any idea what health was, happiness without the need to speak of happiness."[17] This was *the Garden of Eden during the Golden Age,* a utopia that lives in the subconscious minds of many people along with the memory of the time when this primeval earthly paradise was abruptly destroyed.

Allan and Delair have catalogued worldwide sources that indicate Earth's axis changed from vertical to a significant tilt—about 23½ degrees—since the Cataclysm. Before the axial tilt, during the Golden Age, there was little seasonality, and through the year the stars revolved in a *tholiform* manner—always on the same horizontal plane as Earth's spin. The stars rose and set in the same location on the horizon, making a perfect circle around the vertical celestial poles in a day.* With no axial tilt, there would have been no equinoxes or solstices, and this alteration in the sky explains humanity's virtual obsession with the sky after 9500 B.C. During the early years after the Cataclysm, the stars—especially the prominent Orion star system—rose and set seasonally in the heavens. Such alterations in the sky and the new seasonality affected our consciousness in ways that still influence us today and are explored throughout this book.

The Holocene Epoch: Earth after the Cataclysm

The period after the Cataclysm is the Holocene epoch, according to the Euro-American quaternary subdivisions, which vaguely divide the Upper Pleistocene and Holocene at about 9000 B.C.[18] Allan and Delair call for a *Revised Chronology* that says the Pleistocene epoch was a short transition phase between the end of the Pliocene and the beginning of the Holocene to emphasize *exactly* when the disaster occurred and its magnitude. This emphasizes how different the world was during the chaotic early Holocene epoch, when there was rapid glaciation and deglaciation and crustal settling. They call for this correction because the *cataclysmic debris found all over the planet from 11,500 years ago contains Miocene, Pliocene, and Pleistocene epoch deposits.*[19] They conclude from this that "extraordinary speed, huge scale,

---

* Allan and Delair, *Cataclysm!,* 14. Delair noted in a 13 August 1999 letter to me that the star groups before the deluge were not the ones familiar to us now and that the zodiac was lunar.

great violence and indiscriminate action are therefore equally prominent factors in *both* the geological and biological records of the period under review."[20] These biological remains or *drift* are easily datable because they are organic, and they show that the drift deposited 11,500 years ago contains plants and animals from all three epochs—Pleistocene, Pliocene, and Miocene—over 29 million years. These plants and animals were still alive 11,500 years ago, which suggests a tranquil and peaceful world for 29 million years until then. Readers must read *Cataclysm!* to consider the magnitude as well as the accuracy of these staggering conclusions. Readers also may wonder why I decided to write about their research, given that I am not a scientist. I have been a student of catastrophic theory for forty years, and Allan and Delair's theory is the first satisfactory theory I've ever found to explain the Late Pleistocene drift deposits. Both the Pliocene and Miocene epochs were very favorable for the development of life-forms, which thrived until the sudden end 11,500 years ago, and this era is called the Cenozoic. Allan and Delair posit that the Pleistocene is better used as a very brief cataclysmic *stage* in the beginning of the Early Holocene, not as a real epoch between the Pliocene and the Holocene.[21] This revision makes more sense of the Early Holocene archeological sites and the Pleistocene drift deposits. We next need to look at the Holocene epoch itself.

In the beginning of the Holocene, survivors emerged and attempted to comprehend the destroyed landscape and shifting sky. There is much evidence that we were *more* advanced at the end of the Pliocene epoch (using the Revised Chronology), and we had significantly *de*evolved at the beginning of the Holocene. Of course, neo-Darwinian dogma posits that humankind has been progressively evolving from apehood to modern computer man. A major alternative source on the Holocene times is cartographer Charles Hapgood's 1967 book, *Maps of the Ancient Sea Kings: Evidence of Advanced Civilization in the Ice Age* (often referred to as *Maps* because it is the key source), which is an analysis of thirty maps that are thousands of years old.[22] Hapgood proved that the maps he examined were the tools of a *scientifically advanced global civilization that sailed the oceans more than 6,000 years ago.*[23] He got the cold shoulder from academia, but he built an airtight case, which is receiving wide attention now. Regarding who the mapmakers were, J. B. Delair suggested that they were "all-know-ing culture-heroes who helped stricken mankind to begin again."*

Mapmaking requires mathematical expertise and global assessment. *Maps* has essential information on Earth's geography during the Early Holocene, a period that is difficult to assess because Earth's crust was con-tinually readjusting and the seas were rising. Without Hapgood's research, all we have from 11,500 to approximately 6,000 years ago are scattered archeological sites, mythological fragments, and big gaps in the records everywhere. Of course, any suggestion that there were mapmakers who charted the planet globally before 6,000 years ago absolutely destroys all conventional historical models! Graham Hancock comments on the rising seas and Hapgood's research: "The combined effect of the Piri Re'is, Oronteus Finaeus, Mercator and Bauche Maps is the strong, though dis-turbing, impression that Antarctica may have been continuously surveyed over a period of several thousands of years as the ice-cap gradually spread outwards from the interior (of Antarctica), increasing its grip with every passing millennium but not engulfing all the coasts of the southern conti-nent until about 4000 B.C."[24]

Hapgood concludes that *the various maps "argue for both the vast anti-quity of the maps and for the displacement of the earth's crust."*[25] About the mapmakers themselves, he says, "In geodesy, nautical science, and map-making, it [the global maritime civilization] was more advanced than any known culture before the 18th century of the Christian Era."[26] Along with cyclopean monument sites, such as Tiahuanaco in Bolivia and the Giza Plateau in Egypt, these maps are evidence for a scientifically advanced lost culture, a culture with a technology *that we are just beginning to discover ourselves!* Rand and Rose Flem-Ath in *When the Sky Fell* make a very good case that the Atlantean city described by Plato has not been found because Earth's crust underwent a monumental shifting approximately 11,600 years ago, and then ice grew over Antarctica. They believe that the city

---

* J. B. Delair, letter to author, 3 August 1999. Hapgood's map research is being revived by Allan and Delair, Graham Hancock, Rand and Rose Flem-Ath, and many other new-paradigm scholars. It is interesting to note that Hapgood's earlier book, *Earth's Shifting Crust*, recently rereleased as *Path of the Pole*, was first introduced by Albert Einstein.

exists under this ice.[27] This theory may solve the biggest problem in Atlantology: The large and civilized island has not been found. Atlantis will be discussed later, because it obviously existed in the prediluvial world, and its descendants were still around during the Holocene epoch.

When the Sky Fell and *Cataclysm!* both describe the same scenario that is the basis of this work: *The Earth cracked, undulated, and groaned when an intense paroxysm ended the Golden Age.* The trauma was repeated during massive flooding in the Mediterranean and Black Sea regions. On the continental shelves around the world, communities were swallowed when the land sank or the seas rose. In more recent memory, the volcano on Santorini in the Aegean erupted, which triggered a minor crustal adjustment when "a world-wide geological upheaval took place, and this was the final readjustment of the earth's outer shell to its new position after its last displacement."[28] This last major displacement caused subsistence in the Aegean and western Mediterranean, north and equatorial Atlantic, and East Indies; while Siberia, India, the southwestern United States, the Caribbean, Peru, and Bolivia uplifted.[29] Regarding these reverberating disasters, it is wise to differentiate between the great Cataclysm and the major disasters that occurred afterward. The event in 9500 B.C. terminated a whole geological era and ushered in a new one, which is why Allan and Delair devised a new chronology.[30]

No matter how all the details wash out, *we are a multitraumatized species.* Motivated and driven by fear, mass culture is profoundly disconnected from the past. My grandparents taught me that mass global warfare in the twentieth century was triggered by these unrecognized inner fears. Now as these catastrophic memories boil to the surface, people do anything to avoid inner darkness. They park their awareness in the media and cyberspace and ignore the ecological and emotional damage the cyber revolution is causing. Unresolved inner trauma is projected out of their vacated subconscious minds as the outer world becomes the theater for human-caused cataclysms. Wars and obscene killings are rampant as *outside events re-create images that lie deep in the collective unconscious.* Our current situation has all the elements of the end of an age, yet the new paradigm is on the verge of supplanting the old one, and it heralds the possibility of peace returning to Earth.

A deeply connective river of inner knowledge flows within us. I call it the *inner stellar chronometer,* a perceptual faculty that links humanity with the flowing river of Time. This chronometer cannot properly function on an incorrect database, which scrambles our brains as if we are programs that cannot access the computer's hard drive. Allan and Delair's Revised Chronology awakens archaic intelligence because it actually explains what really happened to us during a very short and recent time; it activates the inner stellar chronometer. We are time-coded by precession, which I believe is even altering our anatomy. Anatomically, this inner stellar chronometer would be the source of the Choroid Pulse, a waveform that pulses cerebrospinal fluid throughout our bodies.* The inner stellar chronometer resonates with the correct time line by the Choroid Pulses, which resonate with Earth. Ironically, *computer technology is waking up the inner chronometer* because computer data banks are time-coded by pulsing quartz crystals. Our consciousness resonates by Choroid Pulses, and Earth's crystals vibrate by hertz frequencies in the iron-core crystal in Earth's center, which resonates to stellar vibrations.† *These waves enable us to feel whether what we're told about past times is correct.*

Our inner time sense is scrambled by the incorrect historical time line. The old paradigm data bank makes us stupid, whereas the new chronology is exciting. Professors and scientists had better revise the scientific paradigm because kids won't go to school and memorize false data much longer. *As Time converges with the winter solstice Sun crossing the Galactic Axis, the real time line is taking over in the minds of many people.* The galactic cycles are making it possible to imagine the next stage of evolution. The Revised Chronology makes it easier to get in touch with the peaceful Pliocene and Miocene epochs, yet the horror of the recent global destruction is in the way. The next chapter explores the possibility that the Cataclysm actually altered our brain function, because there is evidence for cranial narrowing in the Holocene epoch.

---

* John Beaulieu, from a presentation at the Biosonic Repatterning Training at Beaulieu's Stone Ridge (New York) workshop, 11 October 1999.

† Quartz resonates to 4,068 hertz waves, and so the more we interact with quartz, the more we get activated by very high frequencies.

3

The Bicameral Brain & the Sphinx

Some say he bid his Angels turne ascance
The Poles of Earth twice ten degrees and more
From the Sun's Axle; they with labour push'd
Oblique the Centric Globe ...

... to bring in change
Of Seasons to each Clime: else had the Spring
Perpetual smil'd on Earth with vernant Flours,
Equal in Days and Nights, except to those
Beyond the Polar Circles ...

　　　　　　　　—John Milton[1]

The Breakdown of the Bicameral Brain

In *The Origin of Consciousness in the Breakdown of the Bicameral Mind,* neurologist Julian Jaynes hypothesizes that consciousness is a learned skill that has emerged out of an archaic hallucinatory mentality. For as far back as 12,000 years, human consciousness has been radically altered by catastrophic trauma, and he explores in detail historical and mythological sources for these changes that occurred over more than 6,000 years. In early literature, the gods spoke in our heads as if they *occupied our brains,* and they broadcasted from a relatively dormant area of the right brain, Wernicke's area.[2] In those days, we were bicameral, or split in two, with an "executive" part called god and a "follower" part called man.[3] We lost this facility as our left brains became increasingly dominant as we became "conscious." I prefer the term *self-reflective* to *conscious,* because using *conscious* suggests that archaic people were *not* conscious. Archaic people seem to have been very conscious, albeit more so of Nature, spirits, and community, whereas they seem to have been less *self*-conscious or separate from the alternate reality, very much like the rare vestiges of undisturbed indigenous people living on Earth today.

Jaynes characterizes this process of becoming conscious as an evolutionary advance. I would argue it was a *perceptual narrowing* that began during the Cataclysm and accelerated during repeated cataclysms that followed. (See appendix B for more detail on these cataclysms.) However, just as we developed psychology while losing access to the stars, we *have* attained self-reflection during the past 2,500 years. Armed with a new sense of the separate "I," our left brains have matured. Yet the fullest range of human intelligence—the right brain—is extremely dormant in most modern people. Jaynes traces the breakdown of the bicameral brain in detail, especially since 1500 B.C., when earth changes in the Mediterranean repeatedly traumatized humanity. This is a great counterpoint to *Catastrophobia*, because we both explore the same data bank from differing points of view. For Jaynes, consciousness is located in the left brain; but in my experience, consciousness emerges out of the right brain, and then the left brain organizes its data. The left brain is merely a tool, like a computer, whereas the right brain accesses intelligence from many dimensions. Naturally, orthodoxy adopted Jaynes as their golden boy because his book is based on the premise that we are evolving out of a primitive mentality to a higher level. We have become more rational, but is that such an advance? In Jaynes's book, people with bicameral brain skills—artists, channels, and prophets—come off like nutty skulls loaded with babbling gods.

Armed with neurological skills, Jaynes shows how the human mind has been mutating during the past 12,000 years. Probing mythology and early literature, he detects great perceptual alterations in humans, which are evocative and thought provoking. While reading him, I realized that I had inadvertently reactivated my own bicameral brain during 100 hypnotic sessions I undertook to research my trilogy, *The Mind Chronicles.** Maybe this is because these past-life regressions under hypnosis sessions are *experien-*

---

* There is no need to presume that past lives are real for this therapy; however, the idea seems to facilitate the process. After investigating this field for twenty years, I am certain of one thing: It is possible to travel into the minds of people in the past.

tial; clients move their consciousness fully into real live bodies of past people, which is described in detail in chapter 9. Melding into these individuals with my full perceptual powers turned on, I awakened archaic intelligence in my current self. Of course, I live during a time when I am not compelled to obey orders of the gods occupying Wernicke's area of my brain, and my experience of the inner voices was vastly different than it was for someone 4,000 years ago. I didn't get stuck in archaic mentalities, yet I was able to access amazing data. For example, I can now make sense of very ancient symbolism and art, as if archaic "brain maps" have awakened that access dormant perceptual systems from past times.[4] The inner stellar chronometer described in the previous chapter is the *timekeeper* of these dormant brain maps, which can cause a whole phase in the past to come alive like an old movie.

Bicameral skills seem to be reactivating in many people, yet they remain self-reflective, which suggests some form of *super*consciousness is activating. This might enable us to balance our species with planetary ecology. Accessing people from Paleolithic times, who respected the supportive powers of Nature, might enable us to *release Nature from human control*. Remnants from Paleolithic times, such as Magdalenian cave art, suggest that in those days we were immersed, fused with, and totally enlivened by Nature in the primordial Garden of Eden. I found verification for this when I traveled far back in Time; the numinousness or light infusion in Nature was awesome. Archaic humans must have experienced symbiosis with other life-forms, which may be essential for balance in Nature's systems. I've come to suspect that long ago, *phosphorescent in the waters of the Garden, our brains were open lenses to all of Nature's intelligence.*

Reawakening the Bicameral Brain

As science currently understands it, human perceptual access lies within the Visible Light Spectrum (VLS) of the Electromagnetic Spectrum. Access to wider vibratory fields, such as seeing infrared or ultraviolet light, is probably what enables people to see and hear things that people normally are not aware of, such as hearing the voices of gods or seeing auras. Considering Jaynes's analysis of human perceptual abilities over thousands of years, as our left brains have matured, our psychic skills have atrophied.

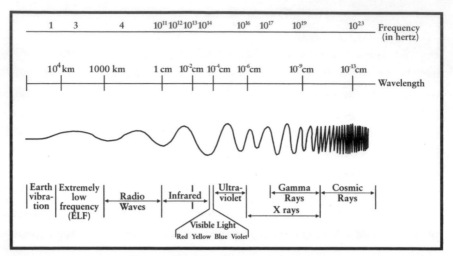

Fig. 3.1. The Electromagnetic Spectrum.

Human access range in the Electromagnetic Spectrum has narrowed. Prophets, artists, schizophrenics, and channels are bicameral, so this process of becoming superconscious may be why the times we are living in are intense and chaotic. Instead of supporting the great perceptual activation, doctors prescribe mood-altering drugs to shut people down. These drugs disable reality-check mechanisms, and many people wander around in insane worlds as if they are not at home in their bodies. Since Prozac was introduced in the 1980s, approximately 85 percent of the random killings have been committed by people on antidepressants, the Columbine massacre in Colorado being just one recent example.* Meanwhile, regardless of how much anybody tries to stop it, human perceptual range is widening beyond the VLS. The airwaves are saturated with a great range of vibrational frequencies emitted by microwaves, radio and television waves, and cellular towers. Modern wave technology stimulates latent cranial potential beyond the VLS. People are said to be bipolar, but it would be more correct to say they are bicameral.

When Plato wrote the *Timaeus* and *Critias* approximately 2,500 years ago, humans were losing the last vestiges of the bicameral brain.[5] Plato valued the more expanded mind, and he saved sources that reflect this mentality. Archeological researcher Mary Settegast examines Plato's rich

---

*See Linda Mounts, "Brave New World of Antidepressants," *After Dark Magazine*, July (1999): 4–6, 15; Julian Whitaker, "The Scourge of Prozac," *Health and Healing Magazine*, September (1999): 1–6. Prozac may alter our range on the Electromagnetic Spectrum.

sources from the archaic period in her monumental *Plato Prehistorian: 10,000 to 5000 B.C.—Myth, Religion, Archaeology.*[6] She argues that cultures of the Old Stone Age (Paleolithic)—35,000 to 11,500 years ago—were *more advanced than human cultures of the early Neolithic Age* (Holocene)— 11,500 to 10,000 years ago.* We have *regressed*. As an example, when Plato wrote the *Timaeus* and the *Critias,* his Greek contemporaries didn't even know that the earlier Aegean people had written languages, Linear A and B. Their memories may have been erased by the earth changes circa 1500 B.C. Just as personal memory can be erased during electroshock therapy, cultural amnesia can be caused by massive earth disturbances. Approximately 100 years ago, the discovery of Troy and the Minoan palace, Knossos, established that Greek myths are often, possibly always, historically based. In recent times, many archaic sources that were labeled mere myths have turned out to be real history, such as the worldwide myths that describe great floods and cataclysms. The Social Darwinian model—we are always evolving to a more complex level—is simply wrong.

According to Social Darwinism, modern rational culture is the most highly evolved, but this chauvinistic model cloaks hidden trauma. People got thrown into mental institutions in the 1950s for hearing voices in their heads. Now the looney bins have mostly closed down, and people are given drugs. However, unresolved trauma from past cataclysms lurks in their subconscious minds ready to erupt. Lately, cataclysmic popular science has been making people feel very nervous, which actually may be a good thing. Just like therapy for early childhood abuse, the real story of Time that is coming forth encourages people to recognize their inner fears. The more that people realize that archaic people attained abilities that we have not yet achieved in modern times, the more they become suspicious of the prevailing historical orthodoxy. The media, like a gigantic memory-fogging machine programmed by the Flintstones, repeats and repeats the false story of Time. However, *we are at the end of the progressive narrowing of human perceptual lenses.* Jaynes's study of human brain function over the past 12,000 years explains why more and more people—not just psychics

---

* Mary Settegast, *Plato Prehistorian: 10,000 to 5000 B.C.—Myth, Religion, Archaeology* (Hudson, N.Y.: Lindisfarne Press, 1990), introduction. Her dates for the beginning of the Neolithic are approximately 12,000 to 10,000 B.P., which I altered to 11,500 to 10,000 years ago for clarity.

and prophets—are seeing, hearing, or feeling frequencies beyond the VLS. The airwaves are filled with frequencies beyond the VLS, consensus reality is increasingly chaotic, and old patterns break down while the new vision of the deep past is changing belief patterns.

Redating the Sphinx sheds new light on other mysteries. Çatal Hüyük in Turkey is an incredibly sophisticated archeological site that dates back at least *9,000 years*. Back in the 1960s only a small part of it—4 percent—was excavated, and then the funding of its discoverer, esteemed archeologist James Mellaart, was terminated, and it was reburied! Advanced cultures in Turkey from 9,000 years ago support the greater antiquity of Egypt, especially the Sphinx. Meanwhile, what happened to the people who built Çatal Hüyük and the Sphinx? As you will see, that question *can* be answered. As it turns out, Çatal Hüyük is a precursor of the Minoan culture, which was merely a myth until a hundred years ago. *We know more about the ancient world than people knew for thousands of years!* A whole new story is waking up in our world, and it is important to fight for the correct interpretation of these sites and artifacts. This exciting heritage must be totally available to the public. No one even knew these sites existed for thousands of years. So, based on limited data, it is not surprising that an incorrect time line was concocted a few hundred years ago. Suddenly stories that were merely myths for thousands of years are history. Mythology is a Time tunnel in the middle of this mass revelation; shining light down this tunnel illuminates artifacts, sacred texts, mythology, and ancient sites. Lost worlds emerge like the images of forgotten places on undeveloped film. It is exciting to remember who we were in the days long ago, and new theories about Egypt are excellent examples of how this process is working.

The Orion Correlation and the Riddle of the Sphinx

Redating the Sphinx must be the starting point of all discussions about ancient Egypt, because recent geological opinions contradict old paradigm Egyptology. The greater antiquity of the Sphinx supports those Egyptologists who thought the mysterious Pyramid Texts were already very old when they were first discovered. Carved on the granite walls of the Pyramid of Unas 4,300 years ago, according to highly respected Egyptologist Wallis Budge, these texts were composed long *before* the reign of the First Dynasty Pharaoh Menes 5,300 years ago.[7] Were the writers of the Pyramid Texts from the same culture that carved the Sphinx more than 7,000 years ago? What happened to the people who wrote the Pyramid Texts and built the Sphinx?

Robert Bauval and Adrian Gilbert's controversial astronomical decoding of the Pyramid Texts in *The Orion Mystery* correlates the texts with the Giza Plateau complex, which they believe was developed in some form more than 12,500 years ago.[8] These texts, as well as others—such as the Turin Papyrus from 1400 B.C.—describe the "First Time," or Zep Tepi, from which Dynastic Egypt was derived. The leaders of Zep Tepi, the Shemsu Hor, were semidivine sages who ruled Egypt for thousands of years before the Dynastic times. Throughout all of Dynastic history, Egyptians said that *all* of their rituals and ways of kingship derived from the Shemsu Hor.* Manetho, who was an initiated Egyptian priest and scribe 300 years after Plato, was said to have recorded 36,525 years—dating back to *39,000 B.C.!*—for the duration of Egyptian civilization.[9] (See appendix A for an Egyptian time line.) Manetho's history did not survive, but it was extensively quoted by others, and it was a common source in the ancient world. Manetho's dates are of the same magnitude as the Turin Papyrus, which says that the time before Menes went back at least 36,620 years.[10] The quotes and summaries by other scholars out of Manetho's history all cross-check, signaling that these dates came from him.[11] There is no reason to doubt Manetho's veracity, because his historical chronology has been consistently verified by archeology. Yet Egyptologists ignore Manetho's huge spans of early time while they use his Dynastic record! Graham Hancock says about this absurdity, "What is the logic of accepting thirty 'historical' dynasties from him and rejecting all that he has to say about earlier epochs?"[12] The fact is that Manetho described a First Time more than *40,000 years ago*, when semidivine rulers led Egypt. When Solon visited the Egyptian temples and libraries 2,500 years ago, the

---

* Robert Bauval and Adrian Gilbert, *The Orion Mystery: Unlocking the Secrets of the Pyramids* (New York: Crown Publishers, 1994), 179–93; Robert Bauval and Graham Hancock, *Keeper of Genesis: A Quest for the Hidden Legacy of Mankind* (London: Heinemann, 1996), 13, 193–94. All of these writers base this on R. T. Rundle Clark, *Myth and Symbol in Ancient Egypt* (London: Thames and Hudson, 1991), 246–63.

priests still retained the records of Zep Tepi. Solon passed this same information to Plato, who was privy to secret Egyptian temple information himself.[13] The Giza Plateau is the place to search for the abode of the Shemsu Hor of Zep Tepi, now that the age of the Sphinx has been pushed back at least 4,000 years before Menes's First Dynasty.

We will search for the ancient Egyptians of the First Time based on orthodox Egyptology and the new-paradigm researchers. Also, the Giza Plateau has been the focus of strange conspiracy theories for the past 50 years, which I will discuss in chapter 8. I will not waste time here describing the explorations and measurements of the Great Pyramid, because this has already been done so many times; nor will I discuss the pyramids-as-tombs theory, because this is just dogma that has never been proven. Readers can consult *Secrets of the Great Pyramid* by Peter Tompkins or *The Riddle of the Pyramids* by Kurt Mendelssohn regarding these issues.[14] It is patently obvious that usage as tombs was not the only or main purpose of the pyramids, if at all. Yet this claim is repeatedly thrown at readers, who end up bored and exhausted with little energy left for thinking about the real functions of the pyramids. There are much more important issues to investigate, such as the mysterious Blank.

Fig. 3.2. The Valley Temple of Giza.

Cyclopean Nonincised Stone Monuments

Based on extensive archeological digs near the Nile, there are no complex pharoanic sites from 12,500 years ago to approximately 6,000 years ago, a period known as the Blank.[15] The official story is that the Unification of Upper and Lower Egypt occurred under Menes 5,300 years ago, when the First Dynasty entered history as a totally complex theocratic culture with hieroglyphics, a pantheon, pharaohs, complex burials, and exquisite art. Egyptologists say this *instant-flowering model* just dropped out of thin air, as if they believe in magic! Recently ecologists and archeologists have discovered many reasons for the Blank. Who's more right? According to the instant-flowering model, the Giza Pyramids, Valley Temples, the Sphinx, and the Osireion of Abydos are no more than 5,300 years old. They date these monuments by nearby Dynastic constructions that are dated by cartouches at the sites. Nonincised cyclopean stone monuments, such as the Valley Temple, are constructed by similar methods as cyclopean monuments around the world, which are known to be much older.* The fact is that *the oldest nonincised structures located at the major sites on the Nile have never been dated.* For example, Abydos Temple was built during Seti I's reign about 3,300 years ago, and then the same date was assigned to the adjacent Osireion, which is *50 feet lower.*† It is constructed of huge nonincised cyclopean stones, except for Seti I's cartouche, which marks his restoration. John Anthony West argues that the Osireion and the Valley Temple below the Sphinx were both significantly weathered by the heavy rains that occurred more than 10,500 years ago.[16]

An examination of these temples with Nile ecology in mind indicates that they were heavily weathered by rain during the Neolithic Subpluvial, a period of heavy rain 9,000 to 6,000 years ago. These temples are at least 6,000 years old, and at least some of them may

Fig 3.3. Sacsayhuaman Temple in Peru.

be more than 11,500 years old. To avoid such contradictions to orthodoxy, Egyptologists simply ignore the monuments that are radically different from the incised temples that have been dated by pharaonic cartouches. Meanwhile, while visiting the Osireion or the Valley Temple, anyone who has studied Nile ecology and has seen other cyclopean temples—such as Sacsayhuaman in Peru, which is constructed with similar cyclopean

---

* Graham Hancock, *Fingerprints of the Gods* (New York: Crown, 1995), 62–92. Examples are the cyclopean monuments in Bolivia and Peru.

† Hancock, *Fingerprints of the Gods,* 400–407. Hancock does a very good job of criticizing the excavation of the Osireion by archeologist Henri Frankfort from 1925 to 1930.

interlocking-stone construction—concludes that the nonincised temples are much older. It would seem the most logical that Seti I built Abydos Temple to venerate the already-ancient Osireion, a sacred temple from the First Time. The rooms in Abydos Temple that contain the King List and reliefs depicting the birth of Horus from Isis and Osiris lead right out to the Osireion. Like other cyclopean sites, the Osireion is one of Earth's great mysteries.

If archeologists cannot find reasons why the Osireion is 50 feet below the most sacred corner of Seti I's temple and is of such radically different con-

Fig. 3.4.
The Osireion of Abydos.

struction, the instant-flowering model collapses. The truth is, Egyptian sites were used selectively to support a scenario concocted during the nineteenth century by British, French, German, and American archeologists who were beholden to their patrons: museums and wealthy individuals. Precious remains have been lost or misunderstood because they were not correctly identified and valued. For example, the Osireion is filling up with water and sinking from seepage caused by the Aswan Dam. The silt that flowed down river during the Inundation lined the Nile bed and prevented water seepage into the layers of the limestone beneath. The silt no longer comes with the Inundation, so the water runs between these layers and threatens the Osireion. Now that many ancient sites are endangered, it is time for indigenous Egyptologists to critique the foreign archeologists who destroyed the earliest evidence at the main sites while they looted Dynastic remains and stocked their museums with artifacts selected to support their faulty paradigm.

The past is history. It is time to rethink the key sites based on the latest findings of Nile ecoarcheology and geoarcheology. Comparisons of construction styles of worldwide archaic structures are needed, as well as the latest correlations between sacred texts and history. Hard science is being offered a golden opportunity: Egypt has so many remnants of texts and wall reliefs from Dynastic Egypt that the Dynastic Egyptians said reflect much earlier times. This claim was even reported to early visitors, such as Solon, who brought this information back to Greece according to Plato, who himself had a direct linkage with the Egyptian temple teachers. Plato says in the *Timaeus* that in his day (2,500 years ago) *complete records* of Egyptian institutions went back *8,000 years,* which of course is right after the Cataclysm.* Using *all* of Manetho's history, the Turin Papyrus, and Plato's report, the undated cyclopean monuments must have been constructed thousands of years earlier by the Shemsu Hor during Zep Tepi. That is, *cyclopean temples in Egypt are from the First Time.* The Osireion must have been buried by the Flood or by the Neolithic Subpluvial rains or both. To properly venerate the Osireion, Seti I dug it up, restored it, and located the rooms with the King List of Abydos in the hallway that leads to it. The Osireion is probably at least 10,000 years older than Seti's temple, which was known as "The House of a Million Years"— this name must refer to the Osireion.[17] Maybe it goes back 40,000 years. One thing is certain: The Osireion is much older than Seti I's temple, just as the Sphinx is older than the First Dynasty.

Assuming that there was an exceedingly advanced civilization on the Nile more than 12,000 years ago, that still does not explain the Blank, which stands right in the way of crafting a new time line. The fact is that outside of the obvious implications of the cyclopean stone remnants and ancient reports just discussed, there still is a serious lack of archeological evidence for civilization from 12,500 to approximately 6,000 years ago in comparison with the Dynastic sites. Regarding this gap, archeologist Michael Hoffman says, "The Epipaleolithic-Predynastic Gap remains one of the least known and most important research problems facing prehistorians and archaeologists working in northeastern Africa."[18] I've come to realize that the Blank is the reason why most Egyptologists *genuinely* believe that Egypt was in a primitive state until 6,000 years ago, and then civilization suddenly flowered. Until ecologists recently surveyed the Nile as a complex alluvial river system, this problem could not be solved. Where

---

* Plato, *Timaeus and Critias,* trans. Desmond Lee (London: Penguin, 1965). This statement further verifies my contention that precession began in 9500 B.C. The Egyptian sources mentioned by Plato are the temple records once precession or Time began. The period before that is the First Time, for which the Egyptians even had some records.

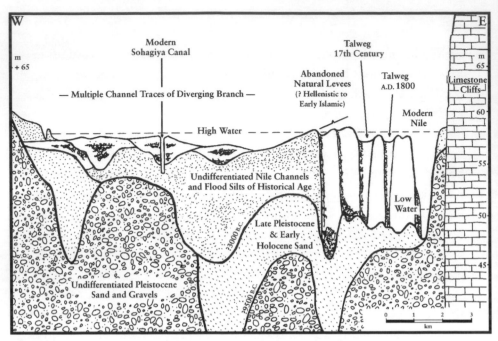

Fig. 3.5. Nile Valley Cross-Section Near Tahta, adapted from figure 1 of Early Hydraulic Civilization in Egypt.

are all the cities, villages, temple complexes, and tombs from this earlier civilization on the scale of protodynastic and early Dynastic remains from 5,000 to 6,000 years ago? Even if there was a high civilization in Egypt *before* the Cataclysm, considering the Blank, how could Dynastic Egypt just appear more than 5,000 years ago? Well, based on the recent findings of Nile ecologists, there was a precursor culture on the Nile that moved back to the current riverbed after they abandoned sites when the heavy rains ceased.

The Mysterious Blank Phase and Nile Ecology

During the Neolithic Subpluvial (9,000 to 6,000 years ago), the Nile basin was very rainy. Because of so much flooding, either the precursor sites of protodynastic Egypt are buried in deep silt or hidden in terraces far away from the current river, or the Egyptians went far away for thousands of years and returned. The Nile changed its course after the Cataclysm and after the rainy phase. The Nile flows from Lake Tana and Lake Victoria in central Africa down to the sea, and the volume of rain in Africa greatly affects Egypt. Ecoarcheologist Karl Butzer says, "Major segments of ancient Egyptian history may be unintelligible without recourse to an ecological perspective."[19] Just like in Egypt today, stone temples, mud-brick villages, and tombs were located close to the Nile, away from the fierce aridity and heat of the desert. If the volume of the river decreases or the level of the Mediterranean drops, the water then cuts down through its old silt level, which *leaves the previous shores high and dry as terraces above its new course.* Therefore, generally the highest terraces are the oldest, and the lowest are the most recent.[20] Approximately 13,000 years ago, the Nile was extremely full and wide, and then it cut down deeper, becoming less wide after 11,500 years ago.* It is extremely doubtful that the Nile course is in the same place now, as can be seen in figure 3.5, and precursor sites must be buried in terraces way out in the western desert or in silt. About early Dynastic times, Karl Butzer says, "The axis of the Nile ran far west of its present course between Akhmim (north of Denderah temple) and Cairo."[21] One thing is certain: When the level and location of the Nile changes, people move to the new shores.

More can be understood about the moving and changing sites by studying records of how this process worked during protodynastic and early Dynastic times, which Butzer covers in detail. The Abydos region is rich in layers from very early sites, because it is a huge alluvial valley between the mountains, where the river can shift or lakes can form. For example, today Abydos is located far away from a great curve of the Nile, but during wetter times, the Osireion was closer to the river. Another moist interval ended about 2900 B.C., which caused the abandonment of desert-nomad sites like Abydos and Hierakonpolis.[22] The Osireion seems to have been designed for water to flow into it during the Inundation, because it contained inner pools. The ancient Egyptians built sophisticated systems for channeling the Inundation to the fields, lakes, and temples, such as the Osireion.[23] Legends describe the fabled Mound of Creation, where Osiris was born when it rose out of the waters after the Flood. The birth of Horus is depicted on the walls in Abydos Temple, and by its very name it is a temple of Osiris. Hence, the Osireion may very well

---

* Michael Hoffman, *Egypt before the Pharoahs: The Prehistoric Foundations of Egyptian Civilization* (New York: Dorset Press, 1979), 83–90. This phase is called the Sahaba-Darau Agradation, from 13,000 to 10,000 B.C. The later phase was a time of massive flooding.

be the sacred Mound temple. The Mound would reappear in the Osireion when the Nile receded after the Inundation, and probably a statue of Osiris was set on top. This was an important yearly ritual; once the river channel moved, the early Dynastic Egyptians cut a canal to it from the Nile, and water continued flowing into it. This temple was literally the rebirthing center for Osiris. For thousands of years, they built other temples and tombs near it because it was so sacred, yet they abandoned the site, most likely around 2900 B.C. Then Seti I revived the region again. Butzer shows in great detail how the abundant and lean times described in history are directly correlated with the varying volume of the Inundations.

This continual rebuilding caused by changes in the bed of the Nile can be seen all along the river even today. The Valley Temples of the Sphinx and the second Pyramid were once closer to the Nile; later the Nile dropped down, most likely after the moist interval around 2900 B.C.[24] Great limestone causeways that still exist were built to create new access to the Nile. Regarding these kinds of constructions, Butzer found the stone revetments, large piers, and extensive artificial basins—*harbor installations*—on the edge of the desert near Abusir and Abu Garob to be of great interest, and so have I when I've visited them.* *It's amazing to think of what must lie buried under the shifting sands of Egypt.* Saqqara, which now is high above and away from the Nile, has been extensively excavated and restored. It is possible to walk on the limestone causeways that once reached the Nile, which have mysterious deep pits next to them that once contained large cedar boats. In 1991, twelve 5,000-year-old large wooden boats were discovered buried in brick pits near a funerary enclosure for a First Dynasty Pharaoh, Djer, at Abydos, 12 miles from the Nile.[25] This discovery supports the likelihood that the Nile dropped after the 2900 B.C. moist interval, as if their boats were left high and dry!

In *Egypt before the Pharaohs,* Michael Hoffman explored the ecological approach of Karl Butzer and others, and he notes that conventional archeological opinion is gradually moving again in the direction of locating the

---

* Karl W. Butzer, *Early Hydraulic Civilization In Egypt: A Study in Cultural Ecology* (Chicago: University of Chicago Press, 1976), 45. Abdel Hakim and I visited this area in March 1996, and the only possible conclusion is that these massive constructions are a harbor.

Fig. 3.6.
Round Head Art from
Tassili n'Ajjer with inset
of Osiris and Nut in the
Primeval Waters. Round
head art is adapted from
figure 59 of Plato
Prehistorian, *and Osiris*
and Nut is from
Twentieth Dynasty Tomb
of Rameses VI.

Old Nile.[26] *Ecoarcheology is putting Egyptology to shame, yet their findings rarely get to the public.* I've had reservations about covering so much of this material in detail; however, *Nile ecologists are driving the dates further back.* By studying the overall context of sites, attention shifts to the whole Nile basin and away from just the known sites on the present river. Considering the Cataclysm 11,500 years ago and in search of a better time line, the course of the Nile would have changed radically during the crustal shifting and flooding. Later, people lived farther out in the desert for quite a while after the Neolithic Subpluvial ended about 6,000 years ago. They then moved much closer to the river again, and Egyptians who had gone to other places may have returned. After 2900 B.C., people migrated north out of Abydos, and the pharaohs became more organized. Nile ecology explains the absence of complex sites before 6,000 years ago, which is far superior to the instant-flowering model. Will Egyptologists continue to use the Blank as a hammer for nailing down their pet theories, even as Nile ecologists prove them wrong? As the hard sciences come up with much better ideas, maybe Egyptologists hope that the public won't have the patience for detailed scientific analysis.

The bed of the Nile downcutted and shifted dramatically 11,500 years ago, and it continued to downcut and move until the rains decreased 6,000 years ago. Predynastic civilization arrived seemingly out of nowhere, yet in fact a whole culture relocated its temples and villages, nome by nome, closer to the Nile. *Many sites from 15,000 to 6,000 years ago must be out in the western desert.* How far west? Settegast examines Egyptian influences in Tassili n'Ajjer artwork from 10,500 to 6000 B.C. that was found in the central Sahara. Regarding the Blank, she comments, "One of the many puzzles presented by the Tassili collection is how, at a time when the Nile valley seems almost deserted, so many of the Round Head compositions could show what appears to be an 'Egyptian' influence."²⁷ The central Sahara was wetter during the Neolithic Subpluvial, and remnants of the Shemsu Hor probably sojourned there. The Nile might have even been totally flooded then, and imagine the volume of silt and debris that came down from Central Africa after the Cataclysm! Butzer says, "The Nile floodplain and delta are free-draining, seasonally inundated alluvial surfaces that have marked the focus of human settlement since Paleolithic times."* There is no reason *not* to accept Manetho's report of Egypt being ruled by the Shemsu Hor for at least 25,000 years before the Cataclysm. There is no reason *not* to consider the possibility that the Sphinx, Osireion, and Valley Temple are more than 12,000 years old and are relics from the First Time. There may be many sites buried in the desert that are different from Dynastic sites because the survivors would have been rebuilding their cultural models. Just as this book was completed, a British team of archeologists released news of a 6,000-year-old treasure trove of sophisticated carvings in the desert east of the Nile. Egyptologist Toby Wilkinson calls it "the Sistine Chapel of Predynastic Egypt" because the depictions of boats and representations of gods have all the elements of later Egyptian art and pharaonic culture.²⁸ Maybe the culture of the First Time could only be regenerated in full flower on the sacred river, the Nile.

On a much more speculative note, I'd like to offer two assessments of some new paradigm theories and discoveries that might assist the process of sifting out the really great ideas coming forth these days. Let's rule out that extraterrestials have ever had anything to do with Egyptian civilization. I do not believe the Sirians came to Earth and gave the Dogon in the central Sahara their ritual system. I find nothing in Dogon, Egyptian, or

---

* Butzer, *Early Hydraulic Civilization in Egypt*, 106. Some scholars suggest that the early Dynastic Egyptians appeared in full flower because they were influenced by the Sumerians. However, these two cultures differ radically, and what influence there is comes from periods when people from the fertile crescent periodically sojourned in Egypt. Such speculations often come from those who assume that the indigenous Egyptians could not have just evolved themselves. See Hoffman, *Egypt before the Pharaohs*, 298–344.

Sumerian culture that could not have been accomplished by shamanic traveling in the sky and in the Dreamtime. The archaic Egyptians were masters at visiting other worlds whenever they wanted to. The Sirius star system is one of those worlds, yet anybody can go there now with their consciousness. Of course, Sirians or other extraterrestrials *could* come to Earth. I just think there are plenty of better earth candidates for the Shemsu Hor; they were an indigenous flowering on the Nile, and when the stellar and environmental conditions were exactly right, their culture reformulated. They may have left the Nile circa 10,000 B.C., and returned circa 4000 B.C., which is discussed in chapter 7. The idea that Egypt's wisdom *had* to have been delivered by spacemen denigrates their obviously extraordinary innate abilities. Second, another theory that clouds the minds of otherwise rational men is the search for secret chambers and the "Hall of Records," beliefs coming from the "Sleeping Prophet," Edgar Cayce. Although I admire Edgar Cayce's skills as an intuitive healer and medical diagnostician, I have never found his channelings about Egypt to be accurate or very interesting. I have experienced many of these sessions myself and researched their contents. I have found that such input is best evaluated by constant reality checks. Now that most of Cayce's prophecies have failed, it is time to stop looking for hidden rooms in Egypt as the source for enlightenment. With these reservations clearly stated, now let's explore some of the *credible* theories from the new Egyptologists.

The Giza Plateau as a Cosmic Clock

The Giza Plateau is the geographic center of Earth's landmasses. It is probably more stable during geological cataclysms, which is exactly what the temple priests told Solon. Butzer says that the Nile alluviated (created silt barriers) rapidly between 7000 and 4000 B.C. to compensate for rising seas and marine incursion from the Mediterranean.[29] These are reasons why monuments on the Plateau could be much older. Robert Bauval theorizes that the site plan of the pyramids was laid out in 10,450 B.C., but his evidence for that exact date is not convincing. Strangely, it is the same as Edgar Cayce's date for the supposed high Atlantean civilization in Egypt, which Bauval even notes.[30] As for my own thoughts on this dating, I think the Giza site plan was designed right *after* the Cataclysm as one of the *earliest*

precessional clocks. Taking the oldest Egyptian records seriously, the Giza Plateau and the Delta would have been major habitation sites during the Paleolithic as long ago as 20,000 years before the Cataclysm. Once Earth's axis tilted and survivors recovered enough to look at the sky, *the Leo constellation would have been rising at the new Vernal Point on the Giza Plateau.* The site plan may mark *the advent of Time.* Wooden posts going back to 8000 B.C. have been discovered by the side of Stonehenge, which are early evidence for a solstitial and equinoctial system that evolved into Stonehenge.*
These may be early remnants of devices invented to figure out the altered

sky and the Sun's new journey on the horizon. I agree with Robert Bauval that divine kingship *began* during the Age of Leo. The double lions that support the Pharaoh's throne in Dynastic times suggest this, and a very archaic double-lion symbol, Aker, may symbolize the Ecliptic.

Fig. 3.7.
Tutankhamen's Throne and the Aker, on the arms of the throne, adapted from a photo of the throne.

I think the Giza Plateau is an observatory for the new astronomy. Bauval and his coauthor Adrian Gilbert have built a very solid case that the main pyramids by the Nile mirror the Orion constellation by the Milky Way Galaxy in 9000 to 10,000 B.C. Factoring in Egyptian records, the Osireion, and ecoarcheology, the site plan and the Sphinx probably are part of a site layered with tens of thousands of years of settlement. The site plan was probably built as a system of mounds that mirror the Orion star system at its low-rising point approximately 11,000 years ago.† The 9500 B.C. date for the Cataclysm is very solid, so I think the site plan was

---

* Christopher Knight and Robert Lomas, *Uriel's Machine: The Prehistoric Technology that Survived the Flood* (Boston: Element, 1999), 149–82. Readers are advised to check out this book for a really wild and fascinating theory about Stonehenge and other megalithic sites in the British Isles. Their theory is too recent and advanced for me to integrate before publication.

† Bauval and Gilbert, *The Orion Mystery,* 192. Orion's declination would have been about 48 degrees, 53 minutes and its altitude at meridian about 11 degrees, 8 minutes in 10,450 B.C. In 9500 B.C., it would have been about 48 degrees, 20 minutes and its altitude at meridian about 11 degrees, 40 minutes. *Giza: The Truth* (Ian Lawton and Chris Ogilvie-Herald [London: Virgin Publishing, 2000]) notes on 350–52 that the vertical placement of the Orion system circa 12,000 to 9000 B.C. does not change much.

built very soon thereafter because (1) the Orion constellation does not change its vertical angle much when it is reaching its low-rising point in the sky; (2) the mounds were covered by the later pyramids, making it difficult to pinpoint their exact original locations; (3) if there was no precession before 9500 B.C., there would have been no reason for the site plan, which highlights the Sphinx as a marker of the new seasonal points; and (4) the first postholes at Stonehenge were placed soon after the Cataclysm, and then the stone version was built in stages later like the mounds and pyramids. The Shemsu Hor selected the spectacular Orion system to mark the effects of the new cycles because it is right above the equator, and at Giza, Orion's high and low-risings are extreme during the 26,000-year cycle. As with the Osireion, if the Sphinx *predates* the Cataclysm, it would have been restored afterward when the silt that buried it weathered away. Close to the geodetic center of Earth, the Sphinx would have been the perfect mythological symbol for the Cataclysm during the Age of Leo; my intuition tells me it was built soon after the Cataclysm, and then the people left. They might have built it to find their way back.

Bauval and Gilbert argue that the pyramids that exist today were built on the site plan mounds in 2550 B.C., when the shafts into the King's Chamber of the Great Pyramid were aligned to key star positions, an idea first posited by Egyptologist Dr. Alexander Badawy.[31] The authors of *Giza: The Truth*, Ian Lawton and Chris Ogilvie-Herald, discount the shaft-alignment theory because the shafts curve, as viewed from above.[32] That is, starlight would not be sighted through them, which Norman Lockyer demonstrated was a key part of Egyptian stellar technology.[33] I leave this to be argued over by others, but it is important because the shaft-alignment theory supports the traditional construction date for the pyramids, circa 2500 B.C. Regardless of exactly when the site plan was first constructed by the Nile or when the pyramids were actually built, the Giza Plateau may mirror the Orion star system by the Milky Way Galaxy approximately 11,000 years ago. If this is true, it would have been the ideal system for marking when precession began and was noticed. The Sphinx marks the constellations that rise on the spring equinox, the four sides of the Great Pyramid dramatically emphasize the four cardinal directions, and the high and low rising of Orion emphatically marks Earth's new galactic alignment.

Fig. 3.8.
The Solar System
between the Orion
Star System and the
Galactic Center.

Robert Bauval and Graham Hancock move in this direction regarding the precession of the equinoxes, and the astrological ages were "believed to have begun to unfold after a kind of spiritual and cultural 'Big Bang' known as Zep Tepi—the 'First Time' of the Gods."[34] If the Giza Plateau complex is a sophisticated precessional clock, when was the Big Bang?

In the Pyramid Texts, the oldest sacred texts in the world, the Pharaoh is guided to travel out in the sky to the Orion star system; that is, *he was star traveling!*[35] This idea really struck me, because in Maya and Cherokee traditions, attunement with Orion is an essential doorway to cosmic consciousness. The ridges on the spine of Turtle's Back are the three central stars of Orion that correspond to the three Giza pyramids, and the outer four stars are Turtle's feet.* Assuming the Pharaoh was actually star traveling, then *why* would a high priest want to move the Pharaoh out through the Orion star system? Why not the Ecliptic? The answer is *astronomical:* Our solar system is located between the Orion system and the Galactic Center. If you were in the Galactic Center and you looked out to this solar system, you would see the Orion star system way out beyond our solar system in the Orion Galactic Arm. That is, from Earth's perspective, regardless of precession, the center of the Galaxy is always in one direction and the Orion constellation is in the exact opposite. Then, once the axis of Earth tilted, from the Giza Plateau, during the solar year, this "stargate"

---

* Graham Hancock and Santha Faiia, *Heaven's Mirror: Quest for the Lost Civilization* (New York: Crown, 1998), 35–37; John Major Jenkins, *Maya Cosmogenesis 2012* (Santa Fe; Bear & Company, 1998), 116. During Maya Initiatic 1995 at Uxmal in the Yucatan, Alberto Ruz Buenfil and I confirmed this issue at El Templo de Tortuga. My grandfather, Gilbert Hand, said the same about Orion as the turtle constellation.

exhibited a wild serpentine movement on the horizon, changing its position in the sky from summer to winter, as it still does today.

According to modern science, the Orion star system is where the greatest number of new stars are being born; it is the nursery of stellar intelligence.[36] Bauval and Gilbert have shown that the Pyramid Texts describe the Pharaoh becoming a star by ascending to Orion, which makes his intelligence eternally available to Egypt as a cosmic data bank. The archaic Egyptians found *another dimension or alternative reality populated by their ancestors.* As long as the Pharaoh could go there for guidance about how to maintain a balanced and peaceful culture by the Nile—Maat—the stargate was open. I think the complex stellar technology of the Pyramid Texts explains this system, and a way to visit this world in our times is described in chapter 9, which also suggests that the Pharaoh took this journey during his life as well. Maybe the advent of precession made it more difficult to access the other reality? As you will see later, that is true. Regardless of the few differences I have with Robert Bauval and Adrian Gilbert on dates, he has shown that the Pyramid Texts are about the Pharaoh's ascension to Orion. Other highly respected researchers, such as Egyptologist Jane Sellers, have come to the same conclusion.[37] In some way, ascension to Orion linked the Dynastic pharaohs with Zep Tepi. Maybe the Pharaoh's stargate initially deconstructed because of axial tilting and access was lost to Zep Tepi. Then the Dynastic Egyptians rebuilt this access to the utopia by reinstating the rituals from Zep Tepi once the sacred river was habitable again. Temples were built again for the Shemsu Hor, just as indigenous people living in sacred cultures build them today.

Numinousness and Stellar Genius

Norman Lockyer catalogues complex star alignments of Egyptian temples from *6400 B.C. to 700 B.C.* that were constructed to capture the light of key stars. Yet because the stars were moving as a result of precession, they had to be constantly reconstructed.[38] This must have been a system for visiting the other reality as far back as 6400 B.C. Other systems for capturing stellar, lunar, and solar light exist all over the planet, as if these ancient astronomers believed the reception of starlight was critical for humans, possibly to maintain direct links to other worlds. Maybe they found a way to "read" stellar frequencies and developed some form of cosmic telepathy? This is not crazy, because these systems existed worldwide for thousands of years. I realize Lockyer's dates contradict the Blank, especially his findings at Karnak.

The Egyptian records say that there was a radically different *quality* of time during Zep Tepi that was unlike Dynastic and predynastic Egypt. They say Zep Tepi was a formless eternity that was ruled by gods, not mortals, when the Egyptians were very happy. Later the pharaohs assiduously maintained a *kingship covenant* by their words and deeds, and Osiris and Horus connected Dynastic pharaohs to the Shemsu Hor.[39] *Hamlet's Mill* portrays archaic myths as a code language based on highly technical astronomical knowledge, as already discussed. Based on sixty years of research as an Egyptologist, Jane Sellers offers impressive evidence that the Egyptians tracked precessional changes *as far back as 7300 B.C.*, during the Age of Cancer.* Because she goes back so far, Sellers is a significant source for Axial Tilt Theory. Regarding the Unification of Upper and Lower Egypt under Horus, Sellers concludes, "It was an account constructed to explain the altered sky, and solve the consequent problems that the alterations posed."[†] This suggests that the rebirth of an order from the First Time by the Unification was designed to deal with the changes caused by the tilt, which is explored in depth in chapter 5. Sellers's statement suggests that Zep Tepi was a time before the axis tilted, and she contrasts the earlier and later periods by noting that during the First Time, "the skies had a magnificent balance," and during the later historical period, myths were created "to deal with distressing alterations in the sky."[40] The Pyramid Texts tell the story of Sekhmet, the lion goddess, who unleashed the Flood in

---

* Jane B. Sellers, *The Death of the Gods of Ancient Egypt* (London: Penguin Books, 1992), 93. Bauval and Hancock, *Keeper of Genesis*, 222 and 336, say that Sellers goes back this far with precession because she locates the Golden Age between 7300 to 6700 B.C., the beginning and end of Orion's rising at spring equinox. I would suggest that this period represents the first time they could measure this after the Cataclysm, and I think they were measuring Orion on the eastern horizon. Hertha Von Dechend and Giorgio de Santillana in *Hamlet's Mill: An Essay on Myth and the Frame of Time* (Boston: David R. Godine, 1977), page 63, says that men and gods could meet during the Golden Age at Time Zero about 5000 B.C.

† Sellers, *The Death of the Gods*, 94. Note that the Unification in this case is *before* Menes, which was a predynastic union, as is evidenced by the Narmer Palette from Nekhen.

*Fig. 3.9.
Seti I erecting the
Djed pillar from
Abydos Temple in
the Osiris Hall.*

a rage and nearly obliterated Earth during the Age of Leo.[41] Then the
Dynastic Egyptians even created a ceremony that involved rebalancing the
skies, the erection of the Djed Pillar.

Maat and the Djed Pillar

The Egyptian line of descent was through the mother, so it was shocking
when a female goddess, Sekhmet, created catastrophes on Earth. The
sought-after order on Earth, Maat, was lost, which was a profound shattering. The sacred balance and access to the stargate had to be found again,
so the Dynasties were established to maintain order versus chaos by the
Nile. A Dynastic foundational ritual was the Djed Ceremony, which
involved erecting a pillar to connect Earth and sky. This maintained the
power of the Pharaoh because *it gave him access to the sky.* In the reliefs of
Abydos Temple, the Pharaoh or sometimes a neter (carrier of divine principles) is shown holding a tilting pillar that is capped by four sections,
which means the Djed Pillar is a classic cosmic vertical axis. The Djed
Pillar is depicted initially tilting about 20 to 25 degrees off vertical, *the
same as the axial tilt angle of Earth!* Then it is erected to a vertical position,
as if making Earth perpendicular to its orbital plane around the Sun. The
Djed Ceremony may be a memory of the vertical axis during Zep Tepi,
and it shows that the Dynasties were founded to reerect the pillar to the
sky to rebalance Egyptian culture and reestablish Maat. Because of its central geodetic location, the land of Egypt—Khemet—is divine for the
world; it is the bridge to the stars that holds the dimensions in place. Maat
had to be reestablished after the axis tilted, because balance is essential for

human happiness. Notice that the four sections on the top of the Djed Pillar are ideal symbols for the equinoxes and solstices. These four quarters of the solar year forced everyone to learn to live with Earth in a new way, because agriculture was invented to deal with seasonality. The Djed Ceremony of Abydos shows the New Kingdom Pharaoh, Seti I, reestablishing Maat, as Plato in his time protected the ancient wisdom. In light of the Djed Ceremony as a way to access the divine world, the Giza Plateau complex as a technology for pharaonic ascension through the Orion stargate is not as far-fetched as it may seem. Possibly unusual cosmic infusions came to Earth when Orion was at its low-rising cycle approximately 11,500 years ago.

Possibly the Dynastic Egyptians completed the early site plan to access vibrations from key stars more than 11,000 years ago, and then the time came to build the Great Pyramid, around 4000 to 3500 B.C., as a *multidimensional technological device*. Engineer Chris Dunn has written a very challenging book, *The Giza Power Plant*, which argues that the Great Pyramid and certain other pyramids were *sonic power plants that harvested the wave powers of Earth*.[42] After building a strong case that advanced power tools were used in Egypt at least 5,000 years ago, Dunn asked, where's the power source? Could Chris Dunn be right? If so, how can Chris Dunn's theory coexist with Robert Bauval and Adrian Gilbert's Orion Correlation? How could the Great Pyramid be both a power plant and a device that is initiatic, as well as a place that enhances human intelligence?

According to *The Pleiadian Agenda*, nine dimensions of consciousness are available to humans while they are in physical bodies. The Heliopolitan Mystery School, one of three ancient Egyptian theological schools, also taught that humans can attain these nine multidimensional levels.[43] As we've seen, during the past 3,000 years our perceptual range has become so limited that we perceive only this dimension—linear space and time. This has made us so left-brain dominant that people think Egyptian sacred science is arcane nonsense. Based on vibrational resonance, many other dimensions exist whether people tune in to them or not as described by advanced mathematics. *The Pleiadian Agenda* describes how modern humans detect these vibrations, just as the Heliopolitan Mystery Schools described how the ancient Egyptians accessed many dimensions. In my system, the higher dimensions—the fifth through ninth—all vibrate to stellar frequencies; the lower dimensions—the first and second—are the vibration of Earth; and the middle dimensions—the third and fourth— vibrate by hertz frequency ranges that most people detect. The third dimension is linear space and time, and the fourth dimension is the aggregate of human emotions, which is fundamentally out of balance, possibly because of axial tilt or left-brain domination. I will discuss Chris Dunn more later, but for now the base of the Pyramid is a harmonic integer of Earth that taps Earth energy. This is the same as tapping the second dimension in my system, which many people can feel as deep Earth vibrations.[44] The Electromagnetic Spectrum maps the field of vibrational frequencies from the lower frequencies that map all the way up to stellar frequencies, which are all potentially detectable by humans aided by technology. Now that we are inventing vibrational technologies such as ultrasound and microwaves, we can see that the ancient Egyptians could have attained such technological expertise as well.* Chris Dunn is actually demonstrating that *sacred*

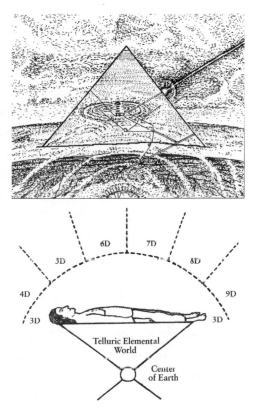

Fig. 3.10. The Pyramid as a Power Plant and the Pleiadian Agenda Energy Model. The pyramid as a power plant is adapted from The Giza Power Plant *and the energy model is from figure 10 of* The Pleiadian Agenda.

science is technological as well as multidimensional. One dimension does not cancel out another one—they all can coexist in structures and bodies.

---

* Some new paradigm researchers have been citing Chris Dunn's research on Egyptian machinery, but they do not want to follow him to the key question: If they were using machinery, where's the power to run the machinery?

Stretch your minds! *The Pyramid is a device that links lower and higher vibrational frequencies by tapping the vibrations of Earth, which broadcasts stellar frequencies.* That is why it was built on the geodetic center of our planet.

As more and more intense galactic particles penetrate Earth, such as gamma rays, more people are realizing that everything is vibrational. A specific range of frequencies causes physicality, such as massive stone pyramids or your body, but all the other frequencies also exist in physicality. *We are simultaneously material and vibrational.* Like a pharaoh, we can travel in space and also establish the other world on Earth, which is what our technology would be if it was based on harmonic resonance. Few modern people can imagine a device (much less their own bodies) that can exist in many dimensions simultaneously and also be a material technology, yet that is alchemy. The severe lack of imagination in modern science causes scientists to theorize that the soul is a ghost in the machine. But, *the soul manifests the physical body.* Chris Dunn has come up with a great theory for the material usage of the Great Pyramid, which merits serious consideration along with Bauval and Gilbert's theories about higher dimensional star traveling by the Pharaoh. In my mind, the Great Pyramid can be both a power plant and a Giza Plateau star clock. We'd better consider how the Pharaoh traveled out to Orion, because new stars—thermonuclear universes—are being birthed there right now. In *The Pleaidian Agenda,* the eighth dimension is the Orion star system. It is the abode of the Elders and the Ancestors, and sages are able to tap in to its wisdom. The Pharaoh would want to go there after death so that he could continually advise the living Egyptians. We are trapped in our physical bodies on Earth unless we develop multidimensional access powers. Like the Pyramid, we have a physical form that vibrates with Earth and accesses higher frequencies while we live our daily lives. We have forgotten we exist in the divine world: our human bodies.

4

The Story of the Prediluvial World

The racial memory of a species is a matter of fact:
It tells a wild creature how to build its nest, how to provide
food, how to find a mate for procreation, how to survive
in open spaces or in a long winter; but the most devastating
experiences are also the most deeply buried and their
reawakening is accompanied by a sensation of terror.
                                        —Immanuel Velikovsky[1]

Science Brings Back a Lost World

The great Cataclysm in recent memory destroyed a highly advanced civilization in a paroxysm of massive crustal shifting and global flooding. Our ancestors struggled to rebuild their cultures as the continents and seas kept changing amid more disasters. Earth was a sea of change for thousands of years. These memories lurk in the deepest recesses of the human brain, and science is resurrecting them. Psychoanalyst Immanuel Velikovsky, who was one of the early analysts who studied with Freud, became widely known as a cosmologist and ancient historian. He rebirthed catastrophic theory in the 1950s with his bestselling book, *Worlds in Collision,* and he was shocked by the intense reactions to his theories. The scientific establishment was irate and attacked his publisher, Macmillan, because *uniformitarianism*—everything happens by slow change—was the official paradigm. The senior editor at Macmillan, who accepted the manuscript, was sacked, as well as the director of the Hayden Planetarium, who had proposed a display of Velikovsky's cataclysmic theory. Many scientists refused interviews with Macmillan representatives for their upcoming books.[2]

At the end of his life, after publishing many other books that sold millions of copies, Velikovsky attempted to comprehend the weird response to his work by writing *Mankind in Amnesia*. This time, using his analytical skills, he assessed the hidden springs of human irrationality in both the minds of his detractors and readers. From his practice, he had come to the conclusion that we all have inherited unconscious memory, or *racial memory*, which means we were actually present in the horrible cataclysmic scenes amid unchained elements. Regarding this memory, "All ascendancy reaches back to the same generation that was exposed to the trauma."[3] That is, as the memory of the Cataclysm is coming back, we are participating in the recovery of a collective terror, and Velikovsky's graphic descriptions of the unchained elements caused a big reaction. Quite on my own, while under hypnosis, I experienced the same instinctual fear, and I felt profoundly verified by Velikovsky's findings. He believes we need to recover the originating memories to move beyond the fear, as I do. According to indigenous people all over the world, we need to know our stories to value life. Our lives become shared journeys with Earth, and collective survival is valued over individual agendas. We focus on sharing instead of acquiring and hoarding, creativity instead of violence; and we respond to life with courage instead of fear.

Mythology has stories of life in the global maritime civilization, but they have been hard to understand until geology and archeology shed more light on them. Recent discoveries of archaic sacred sites that date back 9,000 years, such as Çatal Hüyük in Turkey, reveal that some extremely old cultures were very advanced. Plato saved some historical accounts of global maritime cultures, such as Atlantis, Egypt, Greece, and the Magdalenians, and Charles Hapgood's *Maps of the Ancient Sea Kings* provides a cartography of the lost world. In Plato's day, 2,500 years ago, only scattered stones and memory fragments of the lost world still existed, and Aristotle said Plato was the last person in the ancient world who truly understood mythology. As if he knew how important these fragments would be someday, Plato carefully wrote these records down, even though many of his contemporaries could not believe they were true.* During the

---

* Ralph Ellis, *Thoth: Architect of the Universe* (Dorset, England: Edfu Books, 1997), 205. The philosopher Crantor, who was a contemporary of Aristotle and wrote the first commentaries on Plato's dialogues, went to Egypt to confirm Plato's report, and he actually saw the column of hieroglyphs that is described in the summary.

Golden Age of Greece 2,500 years ago, the Alexandrian Library of Egypt was a repository for at least 10,000 years of the records of the leading minds of the ancient world. Many of them believed that Atlantis existed. The library was partially burned by Julius Caesar in 48 B.C., later by Christian fanatics, and then closed when the Arabs destroyed Alexandria in A.D. 642. The Roman Empire was sacked by the Vandals in A.D. 455, Graeco-Roman culture died, and memory of the old world sank into the gloom of the Dark Ages. If Plato's accounts had not survived, the Western world might have totally forgotten the prediluvial world. The memory was also retained worldwide by indigenous people in the Western Hemisphere for thousands of years, but they were conquered, and the stories of their origins were nearly destroyed during the "Age of Reason." Because the mythology of these indigenous people was remarkably similar to the stories of origin in the Bible, that mythology had to be eliminated be able to characterize them as mere savages and murder them. Now the cataclysmic scenario is coming forth as a result of the new scientific paradigm caused by 200 years of data collection. Amazingly, the cross-cultural global records of indigenous people are actually being verified by science.* *We are poised to remember Earth as a global maritime civilization more than 12,000 years ago.*

This recovery of historical taproots excites us, yet we exist in a cultural field called Social Darwinism—an intellectual elite who says that archaic people were nonverbal primitives and humanity has been ever advancing since the past. How can one appreciate the Lascaux cave painters if they are thought of as grunting hairy oafs with clubs who drag their skin-clad women around by the hair? How can one relate to the indigenous inhabitants of the Americas when they are described as wild hordes of vicious hunters armed with sharp Clovis points who roared down from Beringia to Tierra del Fuego 11,500 years ago? By being educated on such half-baked ideas, humanity has almost lost its ability to correctly reconstruct the past. As the new paradigm researchers find the evidence for highly

---

* Gregory Benford, *Deep Time: How Humanity Communicates Across Millennia* (N.Y.; HarperCollins, 2000), 8. Folk memory lives a long time. For example, Australian Aborigines have described the locations of hidden 8,000-year-old landmarks with such precision that modern divers have found them.

advanced archaic cultures, more and more people wonder why modern culture is so degenerate if we've always been advancing. Casting aside this infantile conditioning, many are going on passionate treasure hunts to find the lost parts of our ancestry. Even if the new paradigm searchers seem like excessive romantics seeking Arthur and the Grail, they are rebooting the hard drive that crashed inside our skulls. You may feel angry when you realize we've been led by fools with superiority complexes who aim to rule the world by controlling access to the past, but it is the truth.

After 300 years of scientific research, we are seeing Earth with fresh eyes. Still, much of the record of the deep past is lost. Globally mapping the previous world is like working on a 1,000-piece puzzle with only 50 of the pieces and without the finished puzzle picture on the cover. We must accurately date, identify, and establish locations for every fragment from the prediluvial world as a basis. Plato reports that Atlantis was only one among many of the leading cultures in the maritime civilization. They probably came through the Cataclysm in better condition than the inhabitants of many other cultures because they were a seafaring culture that had already been migrating when the intense earth changes occurred. They probably were very influential during the early Holocene epoch, when widely separated survival legends report that Atlanteans helped people survive and start over. Regarding this time, Rand and Rose Flem-Ath say, "The Atlanteans now ruled over the ruins of a world humbled by the earth's fearful and widespread desolation."[4] Another task for the new paradigm researchers is to seek cases in which the old paradigm archeologists and anthropologists actually hid data. For example, wanting to control the story of the peopling of the Americas, the Smithsonian in 1911 took control of all previous claims that human beings were in the Americas during the Pleistocene epoch—2.4 million to 11,500 years ago by conventional chronology.[5] Allan and Delair's Revised Chronology (figure 2.5) shortens the Pleistocene to a brief period between the end of the Pliocene epoch and the beginning of the Holocene, which would suggest that most of the original people in the Americas perished, and many new people came in after 9000 B.C.

Rand and Rose Flem-Ath argue that the Aymara language of Peru, which is still spoken by 2.5 million descendants, must have survived from Atlantis. Bolivian mathematician Ivan Guzman Rojas used Aymara as the basic interpretive basis for computer software that translates English simultaneously into other languages. "Aymara is rigorous and simple— which means that its syntactical rules always apply, and can be written out concisely in the sort of algebraic shorthand that computers understand. Indeed, such is its purity that some historians think it did not just evolve like other languages, but was actually constructed from scratch."[6] The Flem-Aths wonder, "Could it have been the survivors of the lost island paradise who gave the Aymara a language so precise, so grammatically pure, that it would become a tool for the most advanced technology of our own century?"[7] Peru and Bolivia are two of the most likely places for such a survival, because incredible cyclopean monuments *13,000 feet above sea level* still exist on the Altiplano, which drastically uplifted only 11,500 years ago.[8] As we have only recently found that Aymara works as a computer language, the value of realizing the levels of our previous attainments is self-explanatory. If the Peruvians derive from Atlantis, what was it like on the original island? Let us take a closer look at Plato's story.

Plato's Description of Atlantis in the *Critias* and the *Timaeus*

Mary Settegast says that Plato's story is "our most reliable guide to the Epi-Paleolithic World."[9] Existing in the *Critias* and part of the *Timaeus*, his story is the source for almost all speculations about Atlantis—*atlantology*.

What follows is my own synopsis of Plato's description of Atlantis from the *Critias*, a story that was told to Plato by Critias, who claimed he got it while visiting Sais, Egypt, from Solon, a Greek statesman, in the early sixth century B.C.

The city of Atlantis where Poseidon seeded Cleito was constructed of great concentric circles around a center island. There were two great circles of land around the island, and three great circles of water around the land. The central island had two gushing springs of pure water—one hot and one cold—which were channeled throughout the island for growing abundant produce.

*Fig. 4.1.
The Atlantean Seal
created from Plato's
description in the* Critias.

The ten children of Poseidon and Cleito lived in districts around the temples in this central complex. The island had its own abundant mineral resources and received many imports as duty. There were plentiful trees, domesticated and wild animals, and all crops, roots, herbs, and drink were produced by the island in the sun in rich profusion. This was its natural endowment.

The Atlanteans built temples, palaces, harbors, and docks, and they bridged the great concentric circles of water built by Poseidon by digging a canal 300 feet wide and 100 feet deep from the sea to the outside ring. They made channels through the rings of land at the bridges, which they roofed over. The bridge to the central island led to an exquisite palace, and each successive king added to its beauty, because it was the home of the original Ancestors. The center of the palace was a sacred shrine to Poseidon and Cleito surrounded by a golden wall, and entry was forbidden. Here there was a temple of Poseidon, which was covered with silver; and the pediments were graced with gold figures, which contained a statue of Poseidon in a chariot drawn by six winged horses. There were other altars inside, and hot and cold springs flowed through fountains into basins and baths, and the springs flowed into Poseidon's grove of tall trees. Then the water was channeled to the outer ring islands by means of aqueducts over the bridges. The middle island had a special course for horse racing and barracks for the king's bodyguard. The city was densely built up around a circular wall around the outer ring of the palace, and beyond the city were numerous villages with a wealthy population sprinkled amid rivers, lakes, pastures, and woodlands.

Each of the ten kings of Atlantis had the power in his own region. All ten assembled in the Temple of Poseidon every fifth or sixth year to exchange mutual pledges and deal with mutual interests. Bulls roamed at large in the central palace, and each king entered alone with clubs and nooses to hunt a bull. When a king caught one, he cut the bull's throat over the central pillar, which was engraved with the laws and curses on those who disobeyed the law; the blood flowed over these inscriptions. The kings dropped a clot of blood from each bull they'd slain into a bowl of wine and mixed it. After cleansing the pillar and burning the rest of the blood, they drew wine from the bowl in golden cups, poured a libation over the fire, swore their oaths to the laws and themselves, and drank of this cup. After this they donned their deep-blue ceremonial robes, remained by the fire as it died out, and gave and submitted to judgments. They

*Fig. 4.2. The Sacrifice of the Bull in the Temple
of Poseidon created from Plato's description in the* Critias.

*promised to never make war on each other but come to each other's aid if any one
of them might lose his royal power. They would consult each other about affairs,
and the house of Atlas was leader; but even the king of that house could not put
any of his mutual fellows to death without the consent of the majority of ten.**

Prediluvial Cultures

This story of Atlantis is the oldest *historical* description of precatastrophic
civilization. Plato repeatedly insisted on its total veracity, and because of
his stature as a scholar, there is no reason to assume he made it up. As with
the Egyptian records, we need *to seriously* consider all the parts of these
ancient sources and cease picking the parts that fit with preconceived
notions. However, any academic who takes this story seriously is called an
irrational fool. Still, many have gone on a search for the actual remains of

---

* Plato, *Timaeus and Critias,* trans. Desmond Lee (London: Penguin, 1965) 136–44. The *Critias*
actually starts out in the *Timaeus,* which is a dialogue about human origins from the cosmic
realms. Once humans emerge on Earth, Plato tells the story of Atlantis. The way Plato linked
these issues is very similar to how the Egyptians linked Zep Tepi to the Shemsu Hor. This suggests that both concepts represent the same time period more than 11,500 years ago. By ana-
log, Plato's description of the cosmic time may be right out of the Egyptian temple records.

advanced civilizations from more than 12,000 years ago. This is a daunting search because the rising sea levels from 17,000 to 10,000 years ago must have totally obliterated the sites of the global maritime ports and cities such as Atlantis. Rand and Rose Flem-Ath build a strong theory that the remnants of Poseidon's Island are under the ice of Lesser Antarctica, which could be true based on Hapgood's research of a map that shows ice-free sections of Antarctica.[10] The search for prediluvial civilization has tended to focus on finding Atlantis; however, Plato said Atlantis was one civilization among many 11,500 years ago. Hapgood's *Maps of the Ancient Sea Kings* greatly widens the view to a global maritime civilization, and other scholars who widen the focus will be discussed. Prediluvial remains are still being discovered; for example, a major cyclopean monument 150 feet below sea level near Yonaguni Island east of Taiwan is being surveyed. Books on this site will probably be released around the publication time of this book, and this will widen the search for the seafaring civilizations of more than 12,000 years ago on the continental shelves worldwide.

Maps provides ample evidence for a global maritime civilization that was trading all over the world from 17,000 to 6,000 years ago. This shows that *Atlantis is only one advanced culture among many that existed more than 6,000 years ago*. Earth hosted a global maritime civilization of seacoast cities that are mostly underwater, and their boats would have rotted because they were wooden. On the land, hunter-gatherers and horticulturists used caves for rituals, such as Lascaux Cave, and their tools and monuments were made of stone. When you start to look, signs of the archaic seafaring culture show up everywhere. For example, some of the most amazing artifacts left by the early Dynastic Egyptians are boats of "an advanced design capable of riding out the most powerful waves and the worst weather of the open seas" that were buried at Saqqara and the Giza Plateau.[11] The wall paintings of Akrotiri, a buried city on Santorini Island, depict astonishing fleets of large ships that are very similar to the Egyptian boats. These murals hearken back to the global maritime civilization, and the oldest layers of Minoan sites are at least 7,000 years old. The ancient Egyptian boats are really intriguing, because on the Giza Plateau these boats were found resting in their own special stone tombs next to the sides of pyramids, as if they are venerated relics of the seafaring culture or replicas built during the early Dynasties. Even today primitive cultures exist on the planet with advanced societies. More evidence of primitive cultures is found after cataclysms because they used stone implements, whereas the remains of more advanced cultures are often totally destroyed.

Plato describes a war between the Atlanteans, Greeks, and Egyptians, who were all sailing the Mediterranean and the Atlantic 11,000 years ago. Plato's war attracts less interest than his description of Atlantis, yet it sheds light on the *politics* of the seafarers. Later, Egypt and Greece entered history, but Atlantis did not, although many indigenous people claim Atlantean descent, such as the Mayas. According to Plato, Atlantis controlled the Magdalenian region (southwestern Europe). Mary Settegast's *Plato Prehistorian* explores this riveting clue in detail, and it is a bridge to cultures that flourished from *30,000 to 11,500 years ago* that have left traces of themselves.* The famous Magdalenian cave artists of southwestern Europe depict the main elements of Plato's description of Atlantis: the key Atlantean animals (bull, horse, and lion). Many have wondered why the Magdalenian artists just disappeared from the face of Earth as if they never existed, like the fall of Atlantis! Where were the Magdalenians during the war? *Plato Prehistorian* analyzes the *Timaeus* based on the assumption that it is an accurate description of Mediterranean politics more than 11,000 years ago, which creates a bridge to the mysterious cave painters.

Atlantis as the Primal Root
of the Magdalenian Culture

From 20,000 to 12,000 years ago, southwestern Europe was dominated by the Magdalenian culture. Their remnants have been found in caves on or near rivers that empty into the Atlantic in present-day Spain and France, such as the Lascaux Cave. Deep within these caves are exquisite, world-renowned paintings of bulls and horses—Poseidon's animals—and many have commented on their artistic sophistication and eerie beauty. In

---

* Mary Settegast, *Plato Prehistorian: 10,000 to 5000 B.C.—Myth, Religion, Archaeology* (Hudson, N.Y.: Lindisfarne Press, 1990), 21–34. Plato says in the *Timaeus,* paragraph 25, that the Atlanteans controlled the populations inside Mediterranean "Libya up to the borders of Egypt and Europe as far as Tyrrhenia (Italy)." Cultures in the Magdalenian area have other labels, such as Solutrean, but for simplicity I am using Magdalenian.

Fig. 4.3. Paleolithic Bridled Horses adapted from figure 9a of Plato Prehistorian.

popular Greek mythology, Poseidon was the first to tame the horse.

Evidence exists that the Magdalenians tamed horses—for example, 15,000-year-old drawings of horses with bridles can be found on the cave walls.* The Atlanteans must have had a written language, because Plato said the central pillar was engraved with the laws and curses. The connections between the Magdalenians and the Altanteans in language, art, and symbolism are major. Anthropologist Richard Rudgley finds many similarities between the Old European script from the Vinca culture (likely derived from the Magdalenians) and Linear A of the Cretans.[12] Regarding Poseidon's pillar, Settegast compares known Paleolithic signs with early Indus Valley, Greek, and Runic signs and concludes that they all derived from Upper Paleolithic signs. Atlantis may be the inspiration for Magdalenian art, as there was a remarkable regional uniformity in widely separated cave art over a long phase of time. This uniformity has always puzzled scholars. Settegast suspects "that the original source and conservor of the Magdalenian canon lay elsewhere."† There are other Atlantean elements in the cave that are even more spectacular than horse training, linguistic roots, and symbolic derivations; Settegast believes she has actually uncovered the primal/generative ritual source of Atlantis in the famed Lascaux Cave painting of the bird-headed man. Her astonishing interpretation of the Lascaux ritual cave as a root of early Indo-European mythology is presented here in detail because it is also a core issue for the healing of our modern world.

---

* Settegast, *Plato Prehistorian*, 27. See her text for information on various archeologists who have concluded that paintings of horses in the caves St. Michel d'Arudy, Grotte de Marsoulas, and La Marche are wearing harnesses or bridles.

† Settegast, *Plato Prehistorian*, 28–29. Settegast notes that Magdalenian cave art shows "virtually no regional differentiation" and in southwest Europe "a uniform style is recognizable in the art, and whenever the style changed, it changed everywhere."

"First Man and the Primordial Bull"
Summarized from *Plato Prehistorian*

The 16-foot-deep shaft in Lascaux Cave drops down to a small chamber at the bottom, where there is a 6-foot-long painted panel that depicts a bird-headed or masked ithyphallic man suspended at an angle. A bird perched below the man on a pole, a wounded bison hovers above the suspended man, and a rhinoceros is behind the man and moving away. Judging by the worn-away condition of the shaft, as well as deposits of bone points is and small stone lamps, this was the main ritual cave of Lascaux.[13] Many scholars believe this painting is the death of the divine twin when the world was created, and Settegast builds on their ideas, because twin kingship is a core shamanic archetype in world mythology. This mythological zone is

Fig. 4.4. First Man and the Primordial Bull from Lascaux Cave.

very rich, and a review of Settegast's thoughts on the archetype is needed first. She believes that the Indo-European peoples remembered the Golden Age when the twins were born. She notes that the main hero/twin kings of Indo-European culture—Yima of Persian history, Yama in the *Rig Veda*, and Ymir of Scandinavian myth—are all derived from the same Indo-European root, *yemo,* or "twin."[14] When Yima lost his kingly power and glory, it fled from him in the form of a bird; the ithyphallic man is bird-headed and seems to have dropped his bird-topped staff. Also, stories of Yima losing his power are involved with bull sacrifice, the central ritual in the gatherings of the Atlantean kings.[15] An early version of the myth is the story of Gayomart and the Primordial Bull, which Settegast examines as the inspiration for the Lascaux painting.*

---

* Settegast, Plato Prehistorian, 109. This myth is from the Persian Bundahishn.

Anthropologist Felicitas Goodman was intrigued by the angle of First Man as well as the odd position of his arms, and she thought it could be a ritual posture. She compares it with a similar Dynastic depiction of Osiris with the same angle and arm positions, which depicts Osiris rising toward the heavens, most likely to Orion. Goodman also links this painting with divine twinship mythology, and by linking the Lascaux painting with Dynastic Egypt through posture analysis, she spans *12,000 years and links the prediluvial world with Dynastic Egypt.* Osiris was dismembered by his twin brother, Seth; he was put back together again by Isis so he could procreate and ascend; and his son, Horus, is bird-headed. To test this hypothesis, Goodman constructed boards to hold students at the same angle (37$^1/2$ degrees). She had them assume the same arm postures, she rattled and put them into trance, and they ascended to the sky world!* This link between Dynastic Egypt and the Magdalanean culture is also supported by the research of Dr. Stephen Oppenheimer. Oppenheimer is a physician who has traced Southeast Asian migratory patterns by hemoglobin defects, which he describes in *Eden in the East: The Drowned Continent of Southeast Asia.* He constructs a link between the universal stories of Southeast Asian twin kingship and the story of Osiris and Seth in the Pyramid Texts, which places the twin myths of Southeast Asian sea-faring cultures back more than 5,000 years.[16]

Most researchers believe the Indo-Europeans lost their unity and power approximately 11,000 years ago, about the same time as Plato's date for the fall of Atlantis. Regarding the global environment again, the seas rose (and the land sank in various places) approximately 300 feet during the flowering of Magdalenian culture and approximately 150 feet during the Early Holocene. The global maritime people would have built their cities on the seacoasts and rivers, just as we still prefer today; yet these areas are currently hundreds of feet under the sea. How the sea affected these cultures was dramatically emphasized in 1991, when an undisturbed cave from 27,000

---

* Felicitas D. Goodman, *Where Spirits Ride the Wind: Trance Journeys and Other Ecstatic Experiences* (Bloomington, Ind.: Indiana University Press, 1990) 20–23, 58–60; and see Belinda Gore, *Ecstatic Body Postures: An Alternative Reality Workbook* (Santa Fe: Bear & Company, 1995). The first experiment took place at Denison University in 1977.

Fig. 4.5. Prediluvial Global Maritime City. An imaginary city that might have existed more than 12,000 years ago near Cosquer Cave, which is now 300 feet below sea level on the Mediterranean coast of France.

to 18,500 years ago, Cosquer Cave, was discovered near Marseille by divers 137 feet below the sea's surface. The 137 feet reflects the Holocene rise, and the earlier 300-foot rise would put the cave quite far above the shore.[17] Somebody, either the seafarers or the people who lived on the land, used sacred caves for rituals. The Magdalenian cave painters left records of themselves in the caves, even though the more advanced ruins of seafarers lie more deeply submerged on the continental shelves. To assist readers in imagining the seacoast cities more than 12,000 years ago, the illustrator took the Cosquer Cave site based on a rendition of its extended continental shelf 27,000 years ago, and he drew an imaginary global maritime city on the coast and below the sacred cave (figure 4.5). Revealing little about how the people lived at these times, these caves do offer clues about their mythology and rituals. Cosquer Cave has paintings from 17,500 to 27,000 years ago, and Allan and Delair's Revised Chronology in figure 2.5 makes more sense in light of such vast spans of time, as if these painters were living during the finishing stages of 29 million years of relatively peaceful evolution.

Returning to the discussion of Lascaux Cave, Settegast believes that the Lascaux ritual painting depicts the mythical or ancestral roots of the original Lascaux group and that it is also a portrayal of one of the mythical twins of Atlantis.[18] She says, "The scene portrayed here may find its closest surviving counterpart in Indo-European cosmogony. The composition in the Lascaux Shaft bears a provocative resemblance to the world-creating death of Gayomart (the Iranian First Man) and the Primordial Bull . . . Gayomart and the bull lived in a state of divine bliss until the evil principle broke into the world, causing the death of the pair. When the bull died, its marrow flowed forth to create all the nourishing and healing plants; its semen was borne to the moon for purification and thence to the creation of the species of all animals. From Gayomart's body came the metals, from his own seed, purified in the sun, sprang the ten species of men."* Gayomart and the bull have their counterparts in Scandinavian and Vedic mythology, and the Iranian version (the one that is thought to be the original version) is the one that is the most faithful to the Lascaux Shaft. Of course, this indicates that Atlantean influence reached all the way to Scandinavia, and Hapgood's analysis of the Zeno map supports this possibility.[19] The similarity of the Lascaux Cave posture to the Osiris postures compared by Goodman emphasizes the global nature and age of the myth. Oppenheimer traces the movement of the story of twin brothers, Kulabob and Manub, from central Southeast Asia to South America more than 5,000 years ago. He believes that this story is the source of the story of Cain and Abel and that the mark of Cain is a common reptilian tattoo that is found in Southeast Asia.[20]

The links between Plato's description of the Atlantean bull ritual, the Lascaux painting, the ascension of Osiris, the originating Iranian creation

---

* Settegast, *Plato Prehistorian*, 109. Settegast credits A. Laming-Emperaire, *Lascaux* (Harmondsworth: Pelican, 1959) for much of this insight.

story, and Southeast Asian mythology are mind boggling, but there is even more, according to Settegast. The rhinoceros embodies the principle of evil in Eurafrican mythology. This has the elements of the Persian myth of Gayomart in the *Bundahishn,* in which "the bull lived in divine bliss until the evil principle broke into the world, causing the death of the pair."[21] According to mythologist Brian Clark, "Ultrasound technology has revealed that many twin pregnancies result in a single birth, and that one of the twins is either absorbed into the body of the other twin or expelled, unnoticed by the mother . . . *the vanishing twin syndrome.*"[22] These core twinship myths may even be *biological.* The erect phallus of the man may represent his seed that generated the ten species of men, and the large bull balls may represent the flow of the bull's semen that created the plants and animals.* Settegast comments, "The slaying of the First Man and the Primordial Bull—the cosmogonic act itself—would have been an eminently appropriate subject for portrayal in the depths of the sanctuary at Lascaux."[23] Man-bison themes have been found at three other Magdalenian sites dating from 19,000 to 14,000 years ago, and Cosquer Cave has a similarly depicted bird-man being killed.

Imagine the ancestors of the Indo-Europeans sliding down a rope carrying torches into the depths of Lascaux Cave thousands of years ago to ritualize the slaying of the First Man and the Primordial Bull. Once Goodman discovered that postures took people into specific experiences while in trance, she experimented with them in 1977, and the Lascaux Cave posture caused the group to embark on a spirit journey. She realized that they were rediscovering "a system of signals to the nervous system, a complex strategy capable of shaping the amorphous trance into a religious experience." They had "taken the step from the physical change of the trance to the experience of ecstasy, they had passed from the secular to the sacred."[24] Possibly 17,000 years ago, initiates were taken to see the depiction of the bird man, and possibly they were taken into the larger area of

---

* Settegast, *Plato Prehistorian,* 109. In *Where The Spirits Ride the Wind,* Goodman says on page 23 that the erect phallus of the Birdman of Lascaux is proof that a ritual posture is being depicted because this posture causes modern people to become very excited, and the energy converges in the genitals. The large bull balls may be entrails.

the cave, assumed the posture, a rattler or drummer put them into trance, and they took a spirit journey. Did we lose this ability because of the earth changes? Julian Jaynes suggests that consciousness emerged out of a cataclysm more than 10,000 years ago.

Regardless, these mysterious caves draw us way back in time when life simply sprang forth from the semen of the First Man and the entrails of the Primordial Bull. Because Cosquer Cave exhibits such long time sequences, it seems that *we've been deeply separated from direct contact with spirit realms by the cataclysmic rift.* Goodman has found a way for modern people to connect with archaic consciousness by means of assuming the postures while in trance, because these postures were used by shamanic cultures for thousands of years. There is much evidence that shamanic cultures experienced great freedom and timelessness during their lives. Velikovsky says that we inherit racial memory and instinct. Animals inherit instinctual ways of life in their habitats, and if their habitats are destroyed, they cannot function. As we are thinkers, *what if human habitat is fields of energy that sacred and magical cultures can access and develop?* The bird-men may have been depicted all over the world for many thousands of years so that people could remember how to ascend to the spirits or stars, such as Osiris ascending to Orion. I have found, working with Goodman, that spirit journeys are available in modern times just by using the postures. We will go back to Plato's war to seek more understanding about our loss of primordial memory.

A Three-Part "Fall of Atlantis" Scenario

By Plato's account, the Atlanteans attacked the Athenians, who were allies of the Egyptians, just before the Cataclysm.* The pole shift and rising seas

---

* Settegast, *Plato Prehistorian,* 15–74, and 55–68. Settegast dates this war to circa 8500 B.C. based on extensive carbon dating of battle remnants. The Catalcysm would have obliterated most evidence for Plato's war. The Cataclysm occurred 1,000 years before 8500 B.C., so these battle remnants are most likely evidence for maritime raiding and stress among wandering people in the Mediterranean (1,000 years of resettlement chaos). Plato says the war occurred before 9600 B.C., and I think the cataclysm Plato describes is the same one as described in *Cataclysm! Compelling Evidence of a Cosmic Catastrophe in 9500 B.C.* Early art at Tassili n'Ajjer and Acacus in the central Sahara may reflect the war *before* the Cataclysm. See *Plato Prehistorian,* 97–103.

may be why the Atlanteans were having such severe political problems. According to Hapgood, from 17,000 to approximately 12,000 years ago, *the magnetic North Pole shifted from the middle of Hudson Bay in Canada to its present location*, and Antarctica relocated over the South Pole.* This movement of the magnetic pole would have created dramatic temperature changes at and near the poles.† Then if we add Rand and Rose Flem-Ath's theory—Poseidon's island is Antarctica—then many Atlantean controversies can be revived. Desmond Lee, who translated the *Timaeus* and the *Critias*, commented, "The idea of a lost world or continent is an invitation to let the imagination run riot." [25] Atlantis has driven thousands of scholars crazy, but now we have enough scientific and archeological data to begin to clarify the real story. The main issues are: (1) If Plato's island sank, *where* is it now? (2) Is Plato's date of 9500 B.C. correct? and (3) If Atlantis is the originating culture for many world cultures, how did it pass down its knowledge? These are big issues because orthodoxy dumps out the

---

* Hapgood, *Maps of the Ancient Sea Kings: Evidence of Advanced Civilization in the Ice Age* (London: Turnstone Books, 1966), 175. Hapgood says on the same page, "According to my interpretation of much radiocarbon and other evidence, a great shift of the Earth's crust began about 17,000 years ago. It was of course a slow movement, requiring perhaps as much as 5,000 years for its completion. North America was shifted southward, and with it the whole western hemisphere, while the eastern hemisphere was shifted northward. The effect was to cause the melting of the great ice cap in North America, while placing Northern Siberia in deep freeze." Astute readers will notice that Hapgood suggests a gradual crustal shifting, whereas Allan and Delair *(Cataclysm!)* suggest an instantaneous shift in 9500 B.C. J. B. Delair helped me clarify this issue by noting in a letter dated 3 August 1999 that during a conversation he had with Hapgood about this in London a few years before he died, Hapgood admitted the crust would not slip as a single unit as described above.

† Hapgood, *Maps of the Ancient Sea Kings*, 177. Rand and Rose Flem-Ath are in agreement with Hapgood that a crustal displacement occurred, but they feel it was more sudden and was triggered by the astronomical cycles. Regarding crustal shifting and astronomical theory, the Flem-Aths say in *When the Sky Fell: In Search of Atlantis* (New York: St. Martin's Press) on page 46, "We suggest that if the shape of the earth's orbit deviates from a perfect circle by more than 1 percent, the gravitational influence of the sun increases because its path is narrower at points. The sun exercises more pull upon the planet and its massive ice sheets. Their ponderous weight alternately pushes and pulls against the crust and this immense pressure, combined with the greater incline in the earth's tilt and the sun's increased gravitational pull, forces the crust to shift."

already-proven existence of the global maritime civilization by debunking Atlantis. What follows is my own highly speculative scenario of the history of cultures during the Atlantean times. I incorporate the Flem-Ath Antarctica theory because their case is excellent. This is a working concept, because new data is flooding in so fast that few can keep up with it.

According to conventional science, Antarctica and northern Europe were getting colder and freezing up 17,000 to 11,500 years ago, and North America was warming as the polar ice melted.* Cambridge geologist Tjeerd H. Van Andel says the end of the glacial maximum 18,000 to 12,000 years ago was totally untypical of previous glacial phases and that ice cores indicate a sharp cold phase 10,500 years ago (Younger Dryas) that caused very rapid climate changes.[26] Almost all habitation sites were destroyed 11,500 years ago; therefore, I can only speculate on what people were doing in this environment. But I will offer some working images. Because of climate changes and rising seas, approximately 15,000 years ago people began moving from one place to another. Because of rising water and intensifying cold, between 14,000 to 12,000 years ago the Atlantean kings in Poseidon's city on Antarctica would have been forced to move. Various early sources say that they arrived at islands in the Atlantic that were accessible to the Straits of Gibraltar. For example, Plato says these islands were Atlantean colonies or trading partners for thousands of years. The secondary location in the Atlantic is probably Plato's island (or islands) that sank beneath the mud.† The Atlanteans would have needed easy trading access to the Mediterranean colonies, such as the Magdalenians. Secondary location could have been the landmass that encompassed all of the Cape Verde, Canary, Madeira, or the Azores Islands, as well as the mysterious equatorial island ("93") that can still be seen in the Piri Re'is map, which is at least 8,000 years old accord-

---

* For example, ancient maps of the north show glaciers farther south than Sweden, and the level of the Mediterranean was much lower than today. According to Hapgood in *Maps of the Ancient Sea Kings* on pages 124–50, that actually *was* the case 15,000 years ago, but nobody knew that 500 years ago. J. B. Delair commented to me in a 3 August 1999 letter that seismic activity was rare or nonexistent before 9500 B.C. Polar movement could have caused the climate to change from 17,000 to 11,500 years ago.

† Plato, *Timaeus and Critias*, 131–32; parentheses are mine.

ing to Hapgood.* They might have been in the Caribbean, the Bimini region, Central America, or much of the whole region. Andrew Collins proposes that the Bahamian and Caribbean archipelagos and Cuba were the landmasses that were sunk by a "comet impact in the West Atlantic Basin at the end of the Pleistocene epoch."†

The Monte Verde site in Chile and the most recent archeological finds in Brazil are decimating the old paradigm "peopling-of-the-Americas" theory, which theorizes that Mongoloid people wandered across Beringia—the land bridge between Russia and Alaska—approximately 11,500 years ago and then migrated into the Americas in only 400 years. Recently, archeologist Thomas Dillehay's Monte Verde site in southern Chile has furnished incontrovertible evidence for human habitation 12,500 years ago. So who were they?[27] Anthropologist Walter Neves has presented the skull of a young woman, "Luzia," who wandered the south-central savannah of Brazil 11,500 years ago, and she has Negroid rather than Mongoloid features. According to Neves, "Luzia belonged to a nomadic people who began arriving in the New World as early as 15,000 years ago."[28] The discoveries in Brazil are the basis of a 1999 BBC documentary called *Ancient Voices*. It posits that the first settlers in the New World were from Australia, because skulls in Brazil thought to be 12,000 years old match those of Australians living about *60,000 years ago*. Artifacts in northeastern Brazil indicate human habitation as long as 50,000 years ago. Neves has also measured hundreds of skulls that are between 7,000 and 9,000 years old, and these skulls go from exclusively Australian to Mongoloid.[29] South America must have been already populated before 11,500 years ago, and then was repopulated after the devastation by people immigrating from Central and North America. The rising seas were

---

* Hapgood, *Maps of the Ancient Sea Kings*, 4–68, and 177–81. Hapgood discusses the Pluvial Period, approximately 10,000 to 6,000 years ago, which was a very rainy period, and then points out that the Piri Re'is map reflects this period or even an earlier time.

† Andrew Collins, *Gateway to Atlantis: The Search for the Source of a Lost Civilization* (London: Headline, 2000), 288–89. Ivar Zapp and George Erikson in *Atlantis in America: Navigators of the Ancient World,* (Stele, Ill.: Adventures Unlimited Press, 1998) explores Atlantean remnants in Costa Rica and the Americas. Their theory, as well as theories on other locations for Atlantis, actually is resolved when the global maritime civilization is recognized as a global culture before 11,500 years ago.

inundating the Asian continental shelves, and Far Eastern seafarers traveled east to South America, west to India, and even to the Fertile Crescent. Because Antarctica is so close to Australia, southern Chile, and East Asia, the Monte Verde site may be part of the massive migrations thousands of years ago.[30] The theory that Atlantis was once located on Lesser Antarctica helps explain the great age of the Australian aboriginal culture and the likelihood of a similar situation in Brazil.

Without extensive archeological investigations on Lesser Antarctica, it is impossible to prove it was the location of Poseidon's Island. Hapgood reports that Ross Sea cores on Antarctica show it was ice free from 15,000 to 6,000 years ago.[31] Regardless, Plato's report of the island that sank must be of secondary locations that sank 11,500 years ago. The early fall of Atlantis occurred in two main phases: (1) migrations out of Antarctica 14,000 to 12,500 years ago, and (2) the sinking of secondary sites 11,500 years ago during the Cataclysm. Cultures around the world would have been exceedingly challenged by the Atlantean dispersal to warmer Atlantic Islands before the big crustal shifting. There is much evidence that the secondary cultures that may have been Atlantean colonies sank, which is why other locations, such as the Caribbean region, are thought of as sunken parts of Atlantis. One thing is very likely: In regions such as the Caribbean, Sundaland in the Far East, the Mediterranean, Egypt (buried because the Nile moved), and Lake Tritonis in Africa, seafaring people were very active in the latter days before the Cataclysm and during the Early Holocene. (See appendices B and C for more detail on these global changes.)

The third phase is the early Holocene, when Atlanteans provided assistance amid rising seas and continual great crustal adjustments. Some regions experienced further cataclysms that became confused in the myths with the 9500 B.C. disaster. For example, the Far East, North America, and the Black Sea regions experienced crustal uplifting or suppression, flooded continental shelves, and flooded-lake problems. Viewing the demise of Atlantis in the midst of the other global maritime cultures offers a better scenario. For example, Plato's war suggests that the Atlanteans pressured other surviving cultures: They attacked the Athenians because they wanted to occupy the Mediterranean. Looking at it from the Egyptian and Athenian point of view, *suddenly the Atlanteans just showed up ready for war,* exactly as Plato said. If we use our modern experience, this makes a lot of sense: Wars happen when cultures are stressed by climate changes, seismic activity, and migrations. Plato's war occurred just *before* the crust shifted, which probably ended the war. Putting it all together, this war is a sad story of the Atlanteans seeking new territory, and eventually losing the battle. I believe that this war and its lingering mythology is the genesis of such global issues as modern war, excessive economic and political control tendencies, wandering peoples, and obsession with scarcity. The breakup of the global maritime civilization may be why the New World Order is coming up these days as a subconscious return to an ancient archetype. With persistent rumors of Global Elite secret power bases on Antarctica, perhaps the original New World Order has already found Poseidon's Island?

Allan and Delair's Revised Chronology really straightens out the historical emergence of human cultures after the Cataclysm; there is a literal before-and-after point once the prediluvial world ended. This explains the latest archeological digs in Brazil, and it may assist in the reappraisals of cultural dispersals, such as Oppenheimer's Sundaland hypothesis. By using 9500 B.C. as a focal point, we begin to make sense of dispersal patterns, resettlement, and rebuilding of cultures. An advanced global civilization ended abruptly 11,500 years ago, and then people began again in the early Holocene amid a field of chaotic earth changes that did not settle down until 6,000 years ago. Faulty sequencing scrambles our brains because *time relates events*. Using Allan and Delair's chronology, the Pleistocene as a cataclysmic division between the Holocene epoch and the Pliocene and Miocene epochs explains why it seems that archaic humans were stone cultures—little else survived the destruction. Judging by new Brazilian, Australian, and Asian time lines, the global maritime civilization may have achieved *50,000 years* of human evolution when the Cataclysm occurred, which is verified by the Egyptian temple records. The Vela supernova event that caused the Cataclysm was a rare event in Earth's history; normally earth changes are not so dire.

The Goddesses Neith and Athena

Returning to Plato's description of Atlantis, male kingship, control, and bull sacrifice were the basis of the politics, society, and rituals, and these

Fig. 4.6. Neith and Athena.

elements still exist today. Plato said that the original Athenians were a wise and judicious people who were great seafarers and venerated the Goddess. The Egyptians of Plato's time said that they shared their ancestral records with the Greeks because both venerated the same goddess of wisdom— Neith in Egypt and Athena in Athens.[32] According to the description of Atlantis in the beginning of this chapter, the Atlanteans were the descendants of the sea god Poseidon and the Earth-born woman Cleito, who bore Poseidon five sets of male twins. Like a queen bee, Cleito was kept in the center of the Atlantean complex, and all power emitted from that center. Cleito was grabbed and raped by Poseidon, and the Atlanteans discuss no goddess of wisdom.[33] The Egyptian and Greek pantheons have *balanced* proportions of male and female deities. Archeologist Marija Gimbutas points out that when archaic cultures worshiped the Goddess, they lived in peace for thousands of years.[34] The Egyptians said that they shared their knowledge with the Greeks in 600 B.C. because the Greeks lost their records during recurrent catastrophes; they needed these records so that they could recover their memories.[35] In the *Dawn of Astronomy,* J. Norman Lockyer identifies Neith, or Nit, and Athena as goddesses of the Pleiades, and in both cultures, major temples were dedicated to them, such as the Parthenon in Greece.[36] These goddesses were equated with wisdom and good memory, and later you will see that they are very archaic and hearken back to the time before the axis tilted. The Pleiades were known as the Seven Sisters by indigenous people in North America, Siberia, and Australia, and this common heritage means they were described more than 40,000 years ago.[37] We must remember our records according to indigenous people, which is why the Goddess must be venerated: *She is the protector of wisdom and memory.*

By contrast, the Atlantean culture venerated Poseidon, who used an Earth-born woman as a birthing machine for the five sets of twin kings. Then the sons claimed the right to take what they wanted and eliminate anyone who got in their way; they started to war with their neighbors. The Greeks and the Egyptians won that battle. After the Cataclysm, the Greeks, Egyptians, and Atlanteans re-created their civilizations during the Age of Cancer—8800 to 6640 B.C.—which I theorize was the *first complete precessional age,* the time of the goddess, because Cancer is ruled by the Moon. Thus Moontime is a source code for wisdom. The Greeks and Egyptians highly valued the arts of the Goddess—wisdom, cosmology, healing, and divination—which, as you will see in chapter 7, are called the *forbidden* arts by Christianity.[38] The Atlanteans invented trade, mapmaking, weights and measures, autocracy, ritual power-bonding, and the birthing of sons to colonize the planet. Both approaches are essential cultural ways, and when the planet is balanced, both gods and goddesses influence humanity. We must learn to live again by the magical and initiatic arts of the Goddess, or the New World Order will totally control the world. Each one of us born on Earth has the ability to use these powers by working with Nature. How? There is an ancient science called geomancy—Earth divination—that is being recovered now that cosmic energy is flowing into our solar system. In the next chapter, we will explore ways to work with these powers to reattain harmony with Earth.

5

Geomancy &
Primordial Memory

*The Goddess in all her manifestations was a symbol
of the unity of all life in Nature. Her power was in water
and stone, in tomb and cave, in animals and birds,
in snakes and fish, hills, trees, and flowers. Hence
the holistic and mythopoetic perceptions of the sacredness
and mystery of all there is on Earth.*

—*Marija Gimbutas*[1]

Geomancy and Sacred Sites

Geomancy is the study of Earth's energy and how humans have interacted with its subtle but measurable forces; it is a science for living harmoniously with Earth. Vestiges of this science can be found in megalithic sites all over the world, because geomancy was used long ago by archaic people to detect Earth energy and to locate sacred sites where contact with the divine is especially available. English sacred-sites researcher John Michell says we cannot penetrate the megalithic world until we see that their stone monuments are "the instruments of their science."[2] Megalithic standing stones, ancient springs and water temples, barrows, dolmens, straight tracks, and gigantic geometrical forms are old treasure maps to other times or dimensions. When we assume one of the Sacred Postures, our body moves into a form that can access certain energetic forms. Sacred sites and temples create a form that access specific energies to that place. During the past 200 years, people have begun to study these markings and monuments, which exhibit similar patterns around the world. They were planned and measured by similar systems, and local legends often say they were built by giants.[3] Geomancy has established that megalithic and cyclopean structures often mark *vortexes*, or places where powerful telluric or inner Earth forces circulate and respond to cosmic cycles, but nobody really knows why they did this.

In modern times, geomancers often use *dowsing* as a tool to determine where the energies exist at sacred sites because it detects electromagnetic forces that lead to the vortexes.[4] Holding two metal rods that respond to the connection between the energy of their bodies and the water or minerals in the earth, dowsers follow the electromagnetic forces by taking the direction the rods point to. Water courses and minerals are always strong forces at sacred sites, and dowsing is one of the most popular methods for detecting unusual Earth energy. Many books already exist that detail the *construction* of sacred sites. I will focus on the *forces* available in these places, because geomancy often adds insight to the astronomical, archeological, and mythological data of sites. When studying the archeological and mythological data on a sacred site, I usually get much deeper insights if I have already gone there and tuned into the geomancy first. The sites often have unusual telluric forces as well as alignments to the stars and seasons, and sacred architecture was used to enhance these forces. Some researchers have even discovered linkages between the sites and the originating myths of the people who inhabited the land where they are located. For some mysterious reason, accessing telluric and stellar forces was very important to our ancestors, and their sacred sites were often technologically advanced in this regard. They created things we can barely imagine building today, and now we are in the early stages of comprehending what our ancestors were really doing in these places.[5] Just like the data convergence in the earth sciences, sacred-sites research has also matured. Geomancers have uncovered a global network of sacred sites, and now many writers are homing in on exactly what people might have been doing there. Also, sacred sites can often be used to trace the wanderings of cultural groups, because each culture has specific geomantic laws they superimpose on their new temples.

Most archeologists and historians are not open to the idea that these sites were constructed by advanced scientific skills. However, the findings of archeoastronomers are making it difficult to deny that archaic people were involved in a monumental global work of art. I think this clash will eventually be resolved when people see that megalithic science was advanced but *radically* different from modern science, and the precata-

Fig. 5.1. Callanish Stone Circle on the Isle of Lewis, Scotland.

clysmic cyclopean technology differed radically from the megalithic. Often when modern science "discovers" a new technology, they can suddenly see that archaic people had already been using it. For example, sonics technology was probably used to levitate huge stones, as is discussed later. Meanwhile, the public is very curious about sacred sites and unusual Earth energies, and the popular media are exploiting this interest by offering programs about the *ancient mysteries*. Millions have heard that archaic sacred sites are astronomically aligned and located in places known to access potent Earth forces. People who visit these sites find they can easily feel the energetic difference between the sacred and the profane as *numinousness,* that magical moment when we fill with light. Visiting these places also often activates very deep and dark emotions, and many people are disturbed by these forces when they have unresolved emotional conflicts, such as catastrophobia. The forces of the dark and the light intersect in places where geomantic energy is strong, and most people report a wide range of emotional responses to this.

According to geomancy, lines of energy—*leys*—run everywhere beneath Earth's surface, and sacred sites were built and rebuilt where they intersect. These crossings create channels or conduits of energy that draw water, which is why dowsers can detect them. John Michell notes that geomancers agree that "all megalithic sites, every stone, mound, and earthworks, are located over or beside a buried spring or well or at the junction of an underground stream."[6] Built above these energy streams, the sites were designed to enhance them, generating strong electromagnetic fields that we can feel, especially because we are mostly water ourselves. Sacred sites are located all over Earth as a patterned global network of electromagnetic fields.[7] Within this mysterious network, electromagnetic energy flows more strongly during equinoxes, solstices, and new and full moons (especially during eclipses), and scientific tests have detected enhanced electromagnetic fields during such times. Yet, on ordinary days, often there is little energy.[8]

This mapping of *Earth's circulatory system* exists all over the planet, and archaic people put stupendous effort into building it. Whether archeologists and scientists choose to test or ignore this system, geomancers, archeoastronomers, and new paradigm researchers are studying it. It may even be perilous to ignore the implications of this system. Indigenous people have always believed that the enhanced electromagnetic fields are the basis of a strong life force, which surely was the same for people thousands of years ago. Like those who go to spas today, people went to sacred temples during important times of the year to enhance their health and well-being. Current alternative or complementary medicine is based on enhancing the bioelectric fields of our bodies, which closely reflects the ancient beliefs; humans need to experience vortexes and leys. This special energy flow attracted people to sacred places for rituals and festivals during special times, and this created community.[9] *Living harmoniously with Earth was their religion; vital living was their prayer.* I use the word *prayer* because I will never forget the time when I was walking among the gigantic megalithic standing stones within Avebury Circle muttering, "Why did they build these?" My husband replied, "This is their cathedral." I opened this chapter with a quote about the Goddess because I have always felt that Avebury Circle and Silbury Hill are temples of the Earth Goddess. Michael Dames says this in *The Silbury Treasure: The Great Goddess Rediscovered.*[10] The latest new thoughts about Avebury come from new paradigm writer Ralph Ellis; he successfully argues that *Avebury Circle, seen from above, is a representation of Earth floating in space!*[11]

Sacred Sites, the Ether, and Time Discontinuities

Successive cultures built their sacred sites on older remains; thus, like the myths, sacred sites are layers of Time. For example, when the Roman Catholic Church dominated Europe during the Dark Ages after the fall of Rome, they located their churches right on top of megalithic power places, many of which were on top of Paleolithic sites.* Regarding the intentions of these early church builders, John Michell says, "The first missionaries founded their churches at those places where the celestial forces asserted their strongest and most beneficial influence, proving thereby to the local population their knowledge of these forces and their ability to maintain the fertility and prosperity of the district by their invocation."[12] Once the Church took control of these venerated sites, the local people were gradually blocked from creating their own ceremonies there and eventually were denigrated by being called pagans and witches if they did so. Once the Age of Science began, the Roman Catholic Church ended the ceremonies based on the natural cycles. The people could not feel the rejuvenating energy anymore, they lost the connection with the ancestors they venerated in these places, and the Church decreed that a priest was required as an intercessor. Cruelly evicted from their sacred sites, the indigenous people have been progressively disconnected from Earth, while large control systems, such as the Vatican, used the available energy of these sites as power plants for their own programs. As already described, the Aymara culture on the Altiplano of Peru and Bolivia may have retained prediluvial knowledge, and their last lineage fell during historical times. After the Spanish Conquistadors finished with them, they sent in the Jesuits with their training manual, *The Extirpation of Idolatry*. Upon entering a village, the Jesuits got the lineage *waka* and destroyed it, and they destroyed or defaced the *pacarina*. (The *waka* is the holder of the ancestral knowledge, and the *pacarina* is their place of emergence.[13]) There is more about this period in Peru in chapter 7. No matter what anybody does, the power of Earth energy still exists in these places; however, it is heightened when people go there and meditate.

Victorian scientists called this special Earth energy the *ether*, and John Michell says ether is "a manifestation of the relationship between space and time."[14] We are evolving by a *new Time factor since 9500 B.C.*, and sacred sites are refuge zones, just as they were in the past, especially during times of rapid change. In general, ancient sacred calendars, such as the Maya calendars, are based on planetary and star cycles, which often are the

---

* In a letter in A.D. 601, Pope Gregory I urged St. Augustine to seek out pagan temples, purify them, and convert them to Catholic churches.

same cycles that sacred sites are aligned to. The calendars were studied and stored within sacred sites, just as the Torah is studied and stored in Hebrew temples. The planetary and star cycles documented in the calendars indicate *when* these sites are "active" or have more ether, such as during equinoxes and solstices. I have taught students how to tune in to the ether at sacred sites in Egypt, Greece, England, Indonesia, Mexico, and the Americas. Together, during carefully selected times, we've felt the past, present, and future merge when the ether has come into ceremonies at these sites. Often, we were seized by spontaneous recall of past and future events as our ancestors came to us. Once at Malia, on Crete, the alternate reality that interfaces with Malia suddenly superimposed itself on the site, and I was able to watch the original teachers teaching children in the temple. It is interesting, regarding this book, that elders were using a form of psychoanalysis to purge fear of earth changes from the minds of very small children. The original builders of these sites constructed them so visitors would always experience these connections during active cycles.* Once a person visits on a pilgrimage, they are a living part of the temple for the rest of their lives. *Sacred sites are libraries of Time and dimensional breakthroughs.*

We exist in linear space and time, and it seems as though that is all there is until we find ourselves in a simultaneous-reality experience. This is the *vertical axis* of consciousness, where there are many dimensions, some solid, some not. This is not as esoteric as it may sound. For example, advanced mathematics is based on proofs of many other dimensions and time zones. People get Ph.D.s and awards for these proofs, yet how does the existence of these other dimensions affect us?[15] Shamans travel into the underworld or upperworld by journeying down or up the sacred tree, which is a *vertical axis*. Anthropology describes these kinds of journeys of indigenous people, and according to consciousness research, these dimensions can be *experienced* by anyone who develops the paranormal skills to *access* these other realities. Any one of us actually can be sensitized to the ether where the intersection with space and time exists. In my case, I have

---

* I experienced this vision at Malia, Crete, in March 1996 while teaching for Power Places Tours.

fun traveling around in these realms, and then I dedicate my research time locating credible sources for what I've already found. I write about these possibilities because Western society is dangerously out of touch with the vertical axis, the Tree of Life, the access to other worlds—which makes ordinary reality boring. I much prefer indigenous life, because in our expanded world, we live in normal space and time while totally in touch with other realms all the time. Judging by how indigenous people and their sacred sites have been treated for the past 2,000 years, the bored Western mind planned to end this opportunity, and then Felicitas Goodman discovered the ritual postures. Mathematicians and physicists concoct formulas and conduct experiments that *prove* other dimensions exist, and they often become mystics when they discover the vertical axis. Most of us can't understand their scientific equations, yet we can easily discover the vertical axis by going to sacred sites and just feeling it. The point is, tuning in multidimensionality is fun, very informative, and necessary for life. Why *not* just assume these nonphysical and nonlinear worlds are real and then contact them?

Sacred Sites as Energetic Safety Zones

Many people return to the great sacred sites at equinoxes and solstices, and energy is building in these places as we get closer to the Galactic Winter Solstice: 2012. The ancients created these places with Time-release art forms that are enlivened by human interaction during special times. Sacred sites and the areas near them are *energetic safety zones* during the most intense phases of the galactic alignments. Archeologists have rebuilt many crumbling sacred sites during the past hundred years, and many people who visit them experience spirits, time discontinuities, visions, spontaneous recall of past lives, and feelings of connection with the original builders. What is going on? I can personally report that the more people visit these places, the more the mysteries deepen for them, unless they travel like common tourists. Sacred-site quests are creating a new global mythology, because in these places *another world opens that is enfolded right in the middle of mundane existence.* From the indigenous point of view, Earth is the divine planet because so many realities coalesce on Earth and move through the Milky Way Galaxy to connect with the stars.

Without sacred places that focalize these subtle forces, we are stuck in linear space and time like butterflies on pins in glass cases while the Galaxy sparkles with the lights of billions of stars. The people who first constructed the temples knew or felt how Earth's energy works according to specific laws. Later, based on what the ancients had already discovered, church builders—Masons—constructed steeples, naves, high ceilings, symbols, windows, and altars to enhance these forces. Like modern archeologists, they participated in maintaining the geomantic system, yet the purpose of their directors was to control the world by drawing energy-starved people into the churches. When I was a very small girl, I used to steal into the Catholic cathedral next door to my house because there was so much energy in the sanctuary. As an adult, I discovered it was built right on top of a great Native American sacred site, which made me acutely sensitive to Earth energy.

According to geomancy, the vortexes form a global network of enhanced electromagnetic fields, and often major stone complexes mark these zones. Prediluvial cultures enhanced these places, but their work has been mostly destroyed. Megalithic standing stones often mark the sacred sites of lost cultures. For example, Roman roads were built on megalithic roadbeds that may overlay Paleolithic roads. John Michell says, "The Romans were not particularly surprised to find so many stretches of straight track in Britain, for they came across them in every country they invaded."[16] What did these original builders know? Most importantly, what if we *need* to enhance this global system again for our health, well-being, and planetary viability? As already discussed, the legends of various cultures are connected to their sacred sites. Many new paradigm researchers are building connections between the sites and related literature that universally tell of past catastrophes and the later reemergence of the people. It is awesome to visit the sacred places of mythic cultures that were destroyed by "monsters in the sky" who brought floods, hurricanes, volcanoes, and earthquakes. The similar myths of the *Enuma Elish* (Sumer), the *Popul Vuh* (Maya), the *Mahabharata* (India), and the Flood story in Genesis are the stories of these times. As a result of the catastrophic data convergence, we now know that these great records describe real events and when they occurred. This makes the great disasters intensely *real*. For example, the *Mahabharata* actually describes the destruction of Harappa and other sites on the Saraswati Plateau of India about 4,000 years ago.[17] *A new global myth is emerging, and, as always, the sacred will be the inspiration.*

Everything that has ever happened on Earth is available to us. All of us can open our memories over great spans of time just by following our passion. By going on the trail of your personal mythos, you enter the quest. When we reawaken archaic memory, dormant parts of the brain activate, and we become fascinated by the flood of ideas coming directly from our ancestors. We will go directly into the Egyptian initiatic library in this chapter, because so many people are finding the sacred realm by studying Egyptian mysteries. Our sense of self comes out of our conceptions of those who walked before us: Think of yourself as having evolved from apes and rushing madly on to computer man; then imagine your ancestors as members of a global maritime civilization that was using mysterious technologies that were in resonance with Earth; and then ask yourself which concept is more useful to us, now that we are becoming global and the newest technologies are based on frequency waves? We have arrived at a truly amazing moment: Secret temples can be visited, previously hidden sacred texts can be read, and we are hearing the real stories of our ancestors.

As archeologists dig up and reconstruct villages and temples that were described in mythology thousands of years ago, scholars are crafting a new time line. We are redefining ourselves as a species by this collective effort. Those who are blocked by unresolved trauma from cataclysmic memories find the past illusive; their curiosity is dulled. However, calendars and signs in the sky say that now is the time to create an entirely new future based on a correct reevaluation of the past. The events of the Pleistocene epoch are distorted by great emotional blocks, and scientists tend to push the date of the ultimate horror as far back in time as possible. Popular cataclysmic theory focuses on the extinction of the dinosaurs 65 millions years ago, because science has stressed the story of the asteroid that plunged into the Gulf of Mexico. Children were scared half to death by the film *Jurassic Park*, which was marketed to them through McDonald's. Astronomer Tom Van Flandern bases his "exploding planet theory" on the origins of comets 3.2 million years ago.[18] However, both these events are way too far back in time to be the Cataclysm that is recorded in global mythology.

Fig. 5.2. The Sedge and the Bee, adapted from Tomb 261, Thebes.

Axial Tilt Theory

The most significant change in human cultures at the beginning of the Holocene was the adoption of agriculture, which I believe was forced on cultures by the new seasons and the destroyed landscape. Before the Cataclysm, people were much freer as hunters and foragers. Suddenly everybody had to work all the time, and it is unlikely that they would have chosen this without necessity.[19] Seeds were sacred to these early farmers, and they would have always carried them with them. Consider the earliest pharaonic cartouche, the Sedge and the Bee, which has never been deciphered; to me this represents seed and pollination as the basis of pharaonic power. Pharaonic Egypt, by the yearly flow of the Nile, is a model of a theocratic system created around agriculture. The 9500 B.C. Cataclysm explains many of the truly bizarre elements in the wild creation stories in mythology that are consistent around the world. Egyptian mythology and mystery plays have many signs of a recent axial tilt and related disruptions in the sky. For example, the story of the dismemberment of Osiris by his brother, Seth; the search for his body parts by Isis; and the battle between Horus and Seth in which Horus loses his eye and Seth loses his testicles all read like an anatomy of the Cataclysm.

There is much evidence for earth changes in the Egyptian records, because the myths are very astronomical. These records have survived because of favorable climate and a powerful and long-lived temple tradition, and intuitive access to them has always been notably potent. There are multilayered human cultures throughout the past 15,000 years along the Nile, and the First Time represents a period *before* the Cataclysm. Dynastic Egypt based their temple technology *totally* on the mythical First Time, and they preserved that record in stone. The Elder teachings from before the Cataclysm are the foundational unifying source of pharaonic rule; therefore, *the Dynastic records propel us right back to before the disaster.* The Dynastic power, divine kingship, was derived from the elders or sages, the Shemsu Hor, yet also there were significant changes, because *the universe itself had changed.* The Dynastic Egyptians were adamant that Zep Tepi was eternal, timeless, and harmonious, but the systems they adopted are obsessed with duality, time, and seasonality! The very conception of the two kingdoms, Upper and Lower Egypt, is profoundly dualistic. Something really had changed, and I believe it was the division of the Earth (Geb) and the sky (Nut) caused by axial tilt. That is, the tilt split the woman from the man because Earth discovered a new relationship with the Sun.

Egyptologist Jeremy Naydler says, "Egypt is an image of heaven, or so to speak more exactly, in Egypt all the operations of the powers which rule and are active in heaven have been transferred to a lower place. Even more than that, if the whole truth be told, our land is the temple of the entire cosmos."[20] The Dynastic foundational ceremonies were devoted to reconciling the axial tilt so that the land by the Nile reflected the whole cosmos. They actually found a new way to bring heaven into Earth. Of course, ceremonies and sacred texts are always devoted to reconciling the sacred and the profane and connecting Earth and sky. However, the Cataclysm caused a schism; it introduced a more radical level of disorder that threatened to cut off access to the divine. This is a current crisis, and Egyptian sacred science offers profound meaning for modern life. The yearning for the Garden of Eden *still* persists today, but that timeless order does not exist anymore. As I've shown, Earth's geology, as well as its climate, was radically altered. The Dynastic Egyptians *took action to reestablish divine order in the world,* they maintained this Maat for thousands of years, and they recorded exactly how they did it. From now on, we will use the term *Maat* for their world in which earthly order was continually created by divine manifestation. The sacred was recognized and observed in ordinary reality by participating in multidimensional mystery plays, as the altered sky was constantly anchored in the mundane by marking the cardinal directions.

In modern times we find it very difficult to enter the Egyptian mind because we exist in complete disorder with no cosmology. Axial Tilt Theory sheds light on how the Egyptians maintained Maat by divine kingship, and they always included chaotic elements to keep things balanced. They adopted the goddess of chaos born in the cataclysm—Sekhmet—and the god of chaos—Seth—as representatives of the principles of cosmic order. In so doing, they helped their people live harmoniously with Earth, because disasters are part of human experience. They believed that personal alchemical transmutation causes heaven to exist on Earth, and they precipitated the divine into everyday life on the Nile by means of yearly ceremonies. The Egyptian records describe exactly how they did this year after year. Knowing that the Cataclysm caused the initial disharmony, they worked with these gods, or neters, to reweave the dimensions. Their records are the most complete and accurate ancient source on how seasonality altered life for all human societies 11,500 years ago. The Pharaoh or King is merely the exemplar of the cosmic principle; in fact, all Egyptians were encouraged to aspire to the same personal transmutation, and if many individuals achieved spiritual consciousness, the whole field of Egypt transfigured. The Pharaoh is the exemplar, simply because societies deteriorate when they are led by immoral, unethical leaders.

Allow me to speculate a bit, which is hard to avoid in such a broad reassessment of the past. Only a task force of astrophysicists could *prove* the Axial Tilt Theory. As for the database I will dive into next, current Egyptology is a compendium of guesswork by scholars who are the first to admit they cannot understand what the ancient Egyptians were talking about. Scholars have had to build upon an edifice of many incorrect initial conclusions by archeologists from more than 100 years ago, who were often little better than pirates instructed to fill museums with their loot. As soon as the hieroglyphs were deciphered and Egyptologists could read the ancient books and the inscriptions on the walls of the tombs and temples, their monotheistic prejudices made it nearly impossible for them to correctly interpret what they read. And they interpreted the sites by means of a faulty time line. The monotheistic bias and faulty time line are finally being corrected, and recently enough texts have been more correctly translated to make it possible to begin to enter the ancient Egyptian mind. The early Dynastic Egyptians insisted that their culture was totally derived from a much older First Time, and there is no reason not to believe them. The Dynastic Egyptians retained their records by means of ritual and mystery plays, and we will use them to explore key ceremonies because we have such detailed reliefs and documents explaining these ceremonies.

The Mystery Plays in the Temples

In the dramas in the temples, actors in many dimensions play out their relationships with the cosmos. The Pharaoh is always there in the center linking heaven and Earth in correspondance with the *Dynastic cosmogenesis:* the Unification of Upper and Lower Egypt by the divine kingship of the Pharaoh or Horus King. The Pharaoh or King was the mediator between the world of the people and the gods who lived in Time in the temples. Zep Tepi was alive in the temples, and events that happened on Earth also occurred in the spiritual world. This is the same as John Michell's argument that ether is a manifestation of space and time; that is, this precipitation of Time into the temple is totally multidimensional.[21] The priests and priestesses cared for the homes of the gods, but the King and the royal family were the mediators. The interiors of the temples where the mystery plays were portrayed in sacred art were never seen by the common people, and so it is amazing that we can look at what was going on. All Egyptians believed that what went on in the temple created their world on the Nile, and sometimes they observed some of the ceremonies. For example, at certain times of the year, the gods would come out of the temples and be carried in processions. *For the ancient Egyptians, the physical world emerged out of the spiritual landscape, and the divine landscape was continually painted during temple ceremonies and public festivals.* If these scenes were *not* painted in ceremonies, how were the gods to know how the humans chose to live? In other words, those who served in the temple talked to the gods to express their intentions for a good life. Although the people never entered the inner sanctums of the temples, they lived every day knowing that the god lived in the *naos,* or central heart of the temple.

Priests made daily offerings to the gods whose dramas and daily lives were portrayed on the walls, which showed the gods being blessed by the

Pharaoh. These scenes were eternal and active in other dimensions where the gods actually lived. If the King blessed a god or neter—divine energy form—the neter had a job to do for the King, such as make sure the people were fed by blessing the Sun and calling for rain. In the new Dynastic reality, the Sun was taking a new journey on the horizon, which was utterly fascinating and fearsome. What if the Sun didn't stop at the Tropic of Cancer or Capricorn one day and kept on going north or south? To deal with that problem, they located one of the most ancient temples, the temple of Khnum, at Aswan. There the Nile emerges from the heart of Africa through the First Cataract right on the Tropic of Cancer where the Sun stopped and turned at the summer solstice and the measurement of the Inundation began.[22] The Sun needed solar barques called boats-of-the-sky to carry it and sometimes humans had to persuade the Sun to maintain its journey by sacrifices and agreements.[23] People needed to become the Sun to know it, and then the plants would thrive.

The temples were constructed of stone, and the reliefs were cut in granite walls to make them eternal, just like the nonphysical worlds and the gods. Also, stone resonates to sound and vibration, and stone that had a high quartz content was often chosen. Meanwhile, all the people, including the royal family, lived in mud-brick homes because the gods had originally made them out of the Nile mud, like the first man who was made of clay in Genesis. We can see by their pictorial renditions that the Egyptians were profoundly grounded in the mundane life by the Nile. Remember, as you consider this exquisite relief, that they believed life would continue this way if they depicted it artistically. Because the people lived in the land of the gods called Khemet, minute pictures of their daily lives were depicted in stone on the walls of tombs and temples, even though nothing is left of their houses and villages. Life by the Nile would continue as long as it was continually drawn on the walls. If you ever go to Egypt, you will know this is true, even in spite of the Aswan Dam, which stopped the flow of the yearly inundation.

The theological reliefs are pictorial and highly symbolic, and they are captioned by fragments of the myths from sacred texts. Similar texts were used and reused for different scenes, and the texts invoke energy from other dimensions, bringing the sacred into this dimension. Now that many of

Fig. 5.3. Everyday Life by the Nile, adapted from Tomb 261, Thebes.

these sacred texts have been translated, whole scenes come alive; the intuitive mind comprehends symbols and mythological scenes. Like a painting being painted, a whole worldview becomes visible, and possibly even this changes the modern world. Assuming that the gods actually do exist in another reality, what happens to a person who goes to Egypt now and contemplates these sacred scenes? I have been staring at these walls and meditating with them in books since I was five years old, and I have taught in the temples many times with my Egyptian master teacher, Abdel Hakim. Like an ancient face lying on the bottom of a muddy stream that becomes visible when the silt clears, the new and emerging translations are giving me sight. But still most of my understanding is intuitive. Who were these people on the Nile who believed the divine lived in their world because they maintained a living relationship with it?

The Emergence of the Primeval
Mound and the Divine Cow

When the Nile receded at the end of the Neolithic subpluvial, a time of abundant rain, about 6,000 years ago and cut a new channel, vast lakes dried up and new shorelines formed. Long before this time, the creator Atum came out of the Primeval Mound and begat Shu (air) and Tefnut

Fig. 5.4. Geb and Nut, adapted from the Papyrus of Tameniu.

(water), who begat Geb and Nut. Geb lay on the ground and became the god of Earth, and Nut made her body into a canopy of stars over Geb and became the sky. When the mounds and shores emerged again, Geb and Nut begat Osiris, Isis, Seth, and Nepthtys. Before the birth of the four children, who symbolize among many things the four directions, the earlier divine parents ruled Earth during the First Time. After the Cataclysm, Osiris and Seth carried on a great battle over their sister Isis. Osiris was dismembered by his brother, his son Horus avenged his father by battling Seth, and Osiris became a transfigured green god of annual resurrection. As previously mentioned, this myth reflects the Cataclysm, and because Osiris arose again, when the seeds germinate, life will always return with the Sun.

Before the Aswan Dam was built, each year the Nile made layer after layer of mud. The people emerged on the Mound of Creation when the waters receded, and the struggles of the gods helped them understand their own lives. The elderly people in Egypt still remember the rising Nile before the Aswan Dam. Sometimes there were great inundations that forced them to move their mud houses, and the Nile relocated at times. They know that the records of their ancestors lie somewhere deep in the mud or out in the red desert, the home of the fire element. The key pharaonic gestures, ceremonies, festivals, mystery plays, and sacred texts come alive in Maat, the land where the Primeval Mound rises out of the waters and Isis searches for Osiris so she can birth Horus. The Sun, or Re, as viewed from the river, which lies north and south, mysteriously moved north and south on the eastern and western horizons. Yet during Zep Tepi, the Sun rose and set at the same place on the horizon all year as the stars rose and set nightly in the same location. Once Egyptian culture began again around 4,000 B.C., a potent new cosmology took form as Khemet reentered the universe and sent waves of intentions to the heavens. The sacred temples were built for the gods to live in, yet a new hologram was needed because the relationship with the gods had changed. The four children of Geb and Nut as the four cardinal directions created new sacred space.

Once the waters receded, nearly all of the temples from the First Time were buried deep in the mud and sand. Archaic elements carried forth in Dynastic ceremonies indicate that the sages possessed the records of Zep Tepi, and they venerated the few temples that miraculously survived the Cataclysm, such as the Osireion and the Valley Temple of the Sphinx. Seti I aligned the naos for Ammon with the naos of the Osircion, and he designed his temple with the records from the First Time, as you will see by *The Standard of Abydos*.[24] Just as we venerate old sites we find when we build something new today, Seti discovered and restored the Osireion from the First Time. The reliefs and geometry of Abydos Temple show that it was a re-creation of Zep Tepi, and it is one of the most potent geomantic places on Earth. This temple is fascinating, because Seti I is named after Seth, who dismembered Osiris. Life in Khemet resolved dualities in the past and current world, and the Dynastic Egyptians reanimated their Elders when it was Time. Sages appear when the homes of the gods are maintained, because they can communicate with the Elders in the sacred places. Like sowing a field with grain, all they had to do was link heaven and Earth with their minds and hearts by stating their intentions to the gods, and the sacred precipitated into the world 6,000 years ago.

The Dynastic Egyptians certainly remembered the Cataclysm, which is obvious by the dismemberment of Osiris. A less well-known and very archaic myth, "The Book of the Cow of Heaven," is inscribed in five New Kingdom temples.[25] This myth was very important to them around 1500 B.C., when the eruption of Thera devastated the Mediterranean and wreaked havoc in Egypt, especially in the Delta. This story was used for instruction to help people understand why another disaster had come about, and it explores whether human behavior causes earth changes. Before the New Kingdom, there are few signs of preoccupation with human guilt, which suggests a significant breakdown of the bicameral brain and can be seen in the story itself. *Long ago when the gods lived on Earth ...*

The Sun god Re called the gods together for advice. The human race was plotting against him and fleeing to the desert. The gods told Re to destroy the human race by sending out "the Eye of Re," as if Re could separate an aspect of himself to use as a weapon. Instead Re sent the Eye out as Hathor, the divine cow, to slay the people in the desert. Normally Hathor is the goddess of beauty who suckles the Pharaoh, so in this action Sekhmet, the goddess who rages against humans whenever they need a lesson, came into being as an aspect of Hathor to do the deed. She was ready to destroy the world again (the cataclysmic repeat), but Re relented. He got Sekhmet drunk to stop her raging and peace was restored, yet Sekhmet remained as the goddess who would destroy the people again if they did not respect the Sun god. In the last part of the myth, Re became weary of governing society, so he withdrew into the sky and charged the other gods with the rule of heaven and Earth. Before ascending to the sky, Re created cyclical time, and perhaps this withdrawal was when the Sun's path was altered in the sky.[26] Certainly the emergence of Sekhmet came during a very troubled time in Egypt, which is dramatically described in the *Papyrus of Ipuwer,* a lament of cataclysmic destruction, which sounds very much like the plagues of Egypt described in the Bible.* Of course, the problem was the destabilization caused by the eruption on Santorini and related earth changes, which I think profoundly shut down bicameralism.

The Battle of Horus and Seth

How to deal with chaos is an active part of Egyptian theology. Life on Earth is a continual struggle between the forces of chaos and order. Divine kingship was instituted by Menes around 3200 B.C., and thereafter the Pharaoh was the divine incarnated son, Horus, who held Egypt in Maat. However, every time the King died, the possibility of chaos returned. Therefore, in the ceremonies of succession, the dead Pharaoh became Osiris exactly when the successor becomes the Horus King. This was a passage of the power of the dead King into the new Pharaoh, who in turn

---

* Miriam Lichtheim, *Ancient Egyptian Literature,* vol. I (Berkeley, Calif.: University of California Press, 1980), 149–61. Hundreds of statues of Sekhmet were set up all over Egypt at the time, and many of them ended up in the Vatican Museum and the Louvre.

helped him become Osiris. Both of these vital passages required a great amount of energy, so the ceremonies were based on the most foundational myth of Egypt: the great battle between Horus and Seth. The formation of the political order came with Menes, the first Dynasty King, who is named after the ithyphallic god Min, who embodies the sexual powers of the Pharaoh. Menes assumes the Horus form as one who battles chaos and establishes divine kingship, which is the reintroduction of the divine plane into everyday Egyptian life. The politics and theology of Menes must be understood before we can see how these aspects of kingship by the Pharaoh were played out in various mystery plays.

Once a new unity of Upper and Lower Egypt was accomplished, in that pregnant moment, duality, chaos, and disorder were banished. *Order was held in place by continually repeating the original formula:* the institution of the *dual monarchy of Osiris and Horus.* In *Kingship and the Gods,* Egyptologist Henri Frankfort describes how Egyptian theological beliefs were the foundation of politics that were enacted in the mystery plays.[27] Frankfort describes kingship as a *living force* that did not exist before Menes, who put together an institution that acquired "transcendent significance for the Egyptians . . . He imparted to it a form harmonizing so perfectly with the Egyptian mentality as to appear both inevitable and perennial . . . This extraordinary conception expressed in political form the deeply rooted Egyptian tendency to understand the world in dualistic terms as a series of pairs of contrasts balanced in unchanging equilibrium."[28] This dualistic sense of the world was thought of as Horus and Seth, as north and south, or as the east and west banks of the Nile. The Egyptians believed that any totality was comprised of opposites, an idea that I think is better expressed these days as *polarity,* a condition that recognizes that things operate in a spectrum from dark to light, negative to positive, or black to white. I think the Egyptians actually thought more in terms of polarity; however, because Judeo-Christian theology is profoundly dualistic, most writers characterize Horus and Seth as primarily dualistic. This is because Judeo-Christian theology suppresses the dark side, the Sethian forces, whereas the ancient Egyptians always balanced the dark and light.

Frankfort says regarding the First Dynasty of Menes, "A state dualistically conceived must have appeared to the Egyptians the manifestation of the order of creation in human society," and he notes that "the dual monarchy had no historical foundation," and it was a "totality as an equilibrium of opposites."[29] This enabled them to create a new political order in a world continually ravaged by catastrophe, and the equilibrium of opposites brought in divine forces. This was carried out because they believed that right order and divine connection prevent chaos; Sekhmet would not rage again. Assessing the spiritual significance of Menes's achievement, Frankfort says, "A historical innovation of such importance could be only the unfolding of a preordained order, the manifestation of what had always been potentially present."[30] The Dynastic Egyptians exactly followed the ceremonial practices created by Menes for more than 3,000 years. (See appendix A.) Therefore, these practices contain many elements from archaic prehistory, and the mystery plays are a record of human adjustment to seasonality and agriculture. In them, we can look for activities that suggest that the axis tilted, such as in the Mystery Play of the Succession and the Heb Sed Ceremony. I will not constantly point out the obvious signs of adjustment to the tilted world because it is expressed by the ritual form itself.

The Mystery Play of the Succession

The Mystery Play of the Succession was carried out so that the new Phaorah could become the Horus King exactly when his predecessor became Osiris in the Underworld. The funeral of the old Pharaoh and a preliminary coronation of the new Pharaoh had already occurred, and the succession was performed during a time that had cosmic significance. It was performed up and down the Nile to bond the people to their new King and to assure them of the eternal life of the old King. During this ceremony, the Pharaoh assumed power over the annual flooding of the Nile and the harvest by assuming the seed potency of Osiris, and he restored harmony between the cosmos and society by becoming the new Horus. Each action in this play could not be altered without dire consequences, because it was a formula for the simultaneous assumption of power and the transfiguration of the mummified King.

After the initial opening scenes, the King becomes Horus by taking his Eye, which opens the mythological level. In the myth, Horus grows up and takes back his Eye after avenging the death of his father, Osiris. The

Eye of Horus has the power to revive Osiris, so the new King assists his predecessor to become Osiris.[31] The next scene is the threshing of the grain, because agriculture is the basis of the King's power; then the Djed Pillar is erected. You will recall from chapter 3 that the tilting Djed Pillar represents the time the axis tilted and the world fell into chaos. Whenever it is erected to a perpendicular position, cosmic imbalance is being corrected by human actions. By erecting the pillar during his succession ceremony, the King demonstrates that he will maintain the land in harmony, and the vertical axis to the sky is reinstated. Then the Djed Pillar tilts, and a mock battle is fought in which Geb, the Earth god, resolves the discord in the heavens.[32] Thus the essence of Kingship is revealed: *Kingship holds chaos in abeyance while order in the political realm brings Maat.* The products of Egypt—furniture, food, jewelry, and clothes—are brought and named "the Eye of Horus," and then the climax occurs. Standard-bearers come in carrying powerful fetishes of the Shemsu Hor, and mysterious Spirit Seekers go around them and make the King *both* Horus and Seth.[33] The King will embody chaos within order, and as Frankfort explains, "The duality of kingship represents conflicting powers in equilibrium."[34] The gold crown is brought in, sacrifices from the two regions are carried out, the crown is put on the King's head, and the King's first act is to distribute bounty to the people, showing that he will be beneficent. This ceremony demonstrates that the King has assumed power over the forces of chaos.

Finally it is time for the transfiguration of the previous King, now that Egypt is safe from chaos. The timing is very interesting. It shows that the people believed that their political order could prevent future chaos because Osiris is a potent figure of the Cataclysm itself. Cosmologically, Osiris probably represents the planet that orbited between Mars and Jupiter, Tiamat in the *Enuma Elish,* and the Greek Phaeton, which is now the asteroid belt. In our culture, we retain this memory as Humpty Dumpty, who fell off the wall and couldn't put himself back together again. Think how often that little rhyme has been repeated. Even the king's men couldn't put Humpty Dumpty back together again, yet the ancient Egyptians have more insight: They transfigured Osiris because he died in the Cataclysm, yet we survived. *This ceremony means that the dual monarchy Menes created resolves catastrophobia.* Now the previous King is

Osiris, but next in the play, Osiris is embraced by Horus as if the new King also can travel in the Underworld! This is accomplished by means of an archaic reed bib worn on the front and back of the King, the Qeni, which is imbued with the immortal essence of Osiris.[35] At this moment, the divine power of kingship is transferred to the new King as the previous King is supported in his transition to the hereafter by the vital force of his son. The pharaonic transfer is complete again, and Frankfort notes that the Qeni hearkens back to the times of the oldest shrines in Egypt when the Nile Valley was swampland before the end of the subpluvial.[36]

This power transfer is exceedingly archaic and imbued with cataclysmic memory: Osiris represents those who died on the Nile thousands of years before Menes. What was new with Menes was the full and long-lasting integration of all the shrines on the Nile into a unified system of controlled agriculture. The King is responsible for agriculture and water management, because the sudden arrival of seasons necessitated planting and storage. The emergence of the Primeval Mound called for management of the Inundation by means of canals and overflow lakes, with the dike system managed by nilometers that measured the flow of the water. Imagine how life changed then, and reflect on how the Aswan Dam traumatizes Egypt. Next we will look into the ceremony that *renewed* the powers of the King.

The Heb Sed Ceremony

There is a literal obsession with seasonal solar cycles in the Heb Sed Ceremony, which was held for the Pharaoh whenever he was losing his powers. When he was in his power, the Nile did not flood excessively or dry up catastrophically, and the grain fed the people and many refugees who came for food. No matter what, this ceremony, the Jubilee, was performed after the Pharaoh's first twenty-nine to thirty years, which is the exact cycle of Saturn around the Sun, and then every three years thereafter.[37] He requested it whenever he felt his personal or political power waning, and it renewed the faith of the people in their leader, although it was quite arduous. The oldest cycles observed in ceremonies were lunar, which were always a critical part of the Egyptian sense of time. The solar cycles, such as Saturn around the Sun, are obsessed with the journey of the Sun rising in the east and setting in the west and its journey on the hori-

Fig. 5.5. The Heb Sed Ceremony, adapted from reliefs at Abu Garob.

zon. At summer solstice, the Sun attained zenith position over Aswan, where the Temple of Isis was built on a mound above the cataracts. Isis is the mother goddess who generates all life, and her energy came from the Sun's zenith over the place where the Nile flowed in. Before the tilt, the Sun was always above the equator, and Khemet was in a perennial warm springtime, the First Time.

This festival is more specific about the pharaonic system controlling seasonality, whereas the Succession is more about the *transfer* of power. The Heb Sed reveals how *the King holds power within the four cardinal directions as the new cosmic field.* As we look into it, remember that most if not all indigenous cultures on Earth locate themselves by the four directions as centering sources of power. Everything changed when the Sun began to rise and set in changing locations. The ecstatically free, exceedingly psychic, and cosmic simple life of the Nile foragers had to be given up for agriculture.* A well-documented site on the Anatolia Plateau offers insight about this moment. The settlers of Abu Hureya on the Euphrates River adopted farming about 8000 B.C. after being foragers. Suddenly their previously well-formed skeletons "show clear signs of malformation resulting from

---

* Felicitas Goodman has said many times in class at the Cuyamungue Institute that visiting the alternate reality in preagricultural times often reveals that people were more shamanic and free before they adopted farming and settled down.

long hours spent on their knees grinding grain."[38] The Dynastic Egyptians *had* to farm, which necessitated a central power, the Pharaoh (and Saturn rules the principle of necessity). This renewal by one Saturn cycle causes the Pharaoh to *become* Saturn, or Father Time.

The Heb Sed began with the building of a special festival hall with a throne, a court, and a palace made of reeds to symbolize archaic times. Once complete, the structures were purified as barges with statues of gods arrived from the Nile. The King would meet with their officials, signifying the reception of the divine plane. Also present were "the Great Ones of Upper and Lower Egypt," who had been at the King's Succession. All divine and regional powers participated, including representatives of the people-from every social level of every section of Egypt. This connected the whole country. The festival opened with a procession of all the gods and people presided over by Sekhat-Hor, another form of the cow goddess who suckled the King. Then there were days of blessing and visiting shrines and more processions, and all the power fetishes from modern and ancient times were blessed. Frankfort's detailed text catalogues many wonderful archaic elements that prove that this ceremony is already very ancient.*

Finally it was time for the Pharaoh to do the "dedication of the field," a section of the courtyard made into a fourfold course set out to the cardinal directions, which represented Egypt as a whole. This ceremony empowers him as the one who *controls the directions*. He crosses the directions by a fast long-strided step as if he is flying, first as ruler of Lower Egypt with the Red Crown, then of Upper Egypt with the White Crown and carrying a shepherd's crook and flail. The flail held by the flying King caught my eye because the angle is *exactly* 23½ degrees, as we've already seen with the tilting Djed Pillar. He leaves the crook and flail in the palace and picks up a house document called the "will," the "Secret of the Two Partners"—that is, Horus and Seth, again reconciling the two. The Edfu texts say about the King: "He runs crossing the ocean and the four sides of Heaven, going as far as the rays of the sun disk, passing over the earth, giving the field to its

---

* Henri Frankfort, *Kingship and the Gods: A Study of Ancient Near Eastern Religion and the Integration of Society and Nature* (London: University of Chicago Press, 1948). See especially pages 83–85; this whole description is drawn from pages 79–87.

mistress."[39] This action is cosmic and obsessed with the four directions. As King of Lower Egypt, the King is carried in a boxlike litter by "the Great Ones of Upper and Lower Egypt" as two officials from ancestral cities stand on either side of the King and sing an antiphonal hymn. Then they change places and sing from before and behind the King, so that each has spoken to the directions. This is repeated until each man has sung to each direction, and then it is time to do the same action, but for Lower Egypt. Ultimately, the King is carried in a basket to the chapel of Horus of Edfu. There a priest gives him a bow and arrows, which he shoots to each of the four directions, after which he goes to the chapel of Seth of Kom Ombo and shoots four times again. Clearly this ceremony even reaches back to Zep Tepi, before seasonality, when the King's greatest power was as a hunter! Finally, he is enthroned four times, once to each of the directions upon a throne ornamented with twelve lion heads (the constellations on the Ecliptic), and he pays homage to the royal Ancestors, the Shemsu Hor.

The Standard of Abydos

We return to Seti I's temple at Abydos to place the two great mystery plays into context. The Standard of Abydos is illustrated because it is an important model of the four cardinal directions and the vertical axis. It was carried in the Procession of Osiris, which was a yearly festival at Abydos, a favorite procession for all the people of Khemet. Osiris was the most popular god because he emerged out of the primeval waters when time began, yet was dismembered by his brother, Seth, and fathered Horus, the King. Osiris is a powerful symbol for sexual potency, death, continuity after death, rebirth, and dismemberment. Therefore, Osiris kept the hearts of the people alive in life, and when they contemplated their inevitable demise, they believed Osiris would lead them beyond death into heaven.[40] The Standard of Abydos is an *ideal model for the vertical axis of consciousness,* and it shows that Abydos was the funereal and ascension center of Khemet. With Abydos as the vertical axis ascension center on the Nile, then it becomes easier to see that the main pyramids, especially at Giza, are scientific, whereas Abydos is theological. Now that we have seen how the Pharaoh took and held his power by the mystery plays, we must understand more about Abydos, the central location of the journey to the sky.

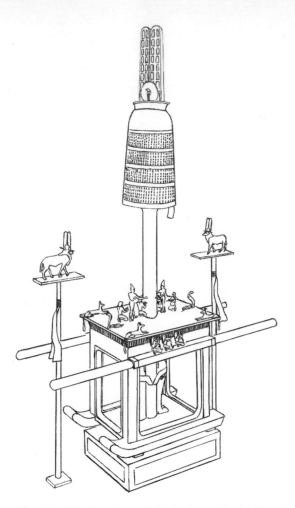

*Fig. 5.6. The Standard of Abydos from Abydos Temple
in the Cult Chapel of Osiris.*

Let us consider this mysterious Standard, which is depicted in the Cult Chamber of Osiris at Abydos Temple.

Ta Wer is the original name for Abydos, which means "Mound of Creation," on which Osiris emerged after the Cataclysm. This fetish represents the rebirth of Osiris because the round object on the top, divided by four levels (like the Djed Pillar), represents the head of Osiris, whose head was buried at Abydos.[41] The long pole represents the vertical axis that connects Earth and sky, and it emerges through a platform at mid-level (Earth), which has figures aligned to the four directions with two Anubi and two cobras on the cross directions. The whole device is locked in place by standards supported by Ankhs (life) holding up lions on higher platforms that wear the headdress of the invisible god, Amun. The lions are the double lions of the Ecliptic, Aker. The pole itself seems to be actively birthing the head of Osiris out of the Earth dimension, which is the platform with the figures supporting it by the directions. Researcher Alan Alford says about Utterance 356 of the Pyramid Texts, "This passage explicitly states that Seth was buried *beneath* Osiris at Abydos." Alford suggests that Seth is the pillar itself.* Noting that some texts say Osiris passed through Abydos during his transfiguration, Alford sees this passage as from the interior of Earth, passing vertically up through Abydos (probably the Osireion) and to the sky.[42] The idea that the vertical axis is the Sethian force itself is profoundly transformative, because it explains why spiritual seekers usually have an encounter with the dark forces every time they move deeper into the initiatic quest. This Standard was carried yearly at Abydos among the people, and it helped them understand their life on Earth by the four directions, and then their ascent on the vertical axis of consciousness. This Standard is an exquisite rendition of birth, mortality, and transfiguration for every human being. It explains why anybody, including Osiris, would want to incarnate. Jeremy Naydler says about the current loss of this sense of the vertical axis, "The decline of this mode of experiencing the world, which led to objects becoming increasingly opaque and incapable of transmitting any transcendent value, lies behind the development of the secular, materialistic worldview of modern times."[43]

We leave the mysterious land of Khemet for now because it is time to explore some of the cultures that formed from 9000 to 4000 B.C., when there is an absence of available sites in Egypt—that is, during the Blank. Of course, we will be watching for any signs of wandering Egyptian sailors around the world, as the basic premise of this chapter is that *the Dynastic revival was based on the culture of the First Time that existed before the Cataclysm,* which must have been extremely advanced given the

---

* Alan F. Alford, *The Phoenix Solution: Secrets of a Lost Civilisation* (London: Hodder and Stoughton, 1998), 326–27. See R. O. Faulkner, *The Ancient Egyptian Pyramid Texts* (Oxford: Oxford University Press, 1969), 113–14, for "Utterance 356." This describes an aspect of Seth—his *iru* that manifests out of his *kheperu*—his divine form, as discussed in Dmitri Meeks and Christine Favard-Meeks, *Daily Life of the Egyptian Gods* (Ithaca, N.Y.: Cornell University Press, 1993), 56–63.

complexity of the Dynastic model. As we can see by looking into two mystery plays and the Standard of Abydos, once Dynastic Egypt was conceived it was obsessed with the cycles of the Sun by the four directions and with agriculture. Osiris brought agriculture to Egypt as a green god fecundating Khemet from the Underworld. Every Pharaoh became Osiris after death, yet while alive, the Pharaoh was the Horus King. He was the most popular god of the common people. Abydos contains the richest early predynastic sites as well as the precataclysmic Osireion. It is no accident that Seti I is named after Seth—he had the artistic and theological brilliance to restore the Osireion and to build a temple that depicts the mystery plays and various devices describing the vertical axis. Abydos Temple is one of the most multidimensional places on Earth, and Ta Wer is a powerful way to depict the vertical axis of consciousness.

6

Çatal Hüyük
& Noah's Flood

... Whatever other hand than mine
Gave these young Gods fulness all their gifts?
              ... Like forms
Of phantom-dreams, throughout their life's whole length
They muddled all at random, did not know
Houses of brick that catch the sunlight's warmth,
Nor yet the works of carpentry. They dwelt
In hollowed holes, like swarms of tiny ants,
In sunless depths of caverns; and they had
No certain signs of winter, nor of spring
Flower-laden, nor of summer with her fruits ...
Until I showed the rising of the stars,
And settings hard to recognize. And I
Found Number for them, chief devise of all,
Groupings of letter, Memory's handmaid that,
And mother of the Muses. And I first
Bound in the yoke wild steeds, submissive made
To the collar or men's limbs, that so
They might in man's place bear his greatest toils ...
                 —Aeschylus, (460 B.C.)[1]

The Wanderers after the Cataclysm

To discover where the advanced cultures on Earth went after the Cataclysm, we need to identify their basic characteristics. The survivors were great seafarers and astronomers, and they sailed away to find new homes. They were great temple builders as well as magicians—this was required to build the cyclopean monuments. They believed in various forms of divine kingship, priestly orders, and Goddess worship, based on what the Dynastic Egyptians said about them, and once they found a home, they would have attempted, at all costs, to re-create their civilizations. Logically, unusually advanced cities and villages from 9000 to 6000 B.C. are the new homes of survivors who landed in boats or of people who crawled out of caves. This happened all over the planet. Appendix C shows how earth changes correlate with the emergence of Holocene cultures. For example, the dispersal in the Middle East is thoroughly described in *The Gods of Eden* by Andrew Collins, and the Altiplano in Bolivia has precataclysmic cyclopean structures that are as compelling as the Valley Temple on the Giza Plateau. I will focus on the Mediterranean region, because it is the location of the greatest number of advanced archeological sites. This makes it possible to seek a progressive series of cultures there from 9400 to 3000 B.C. because much is known about the climate and earth changes during that time. This region has great memory resonance for Western civilization because its mythology and sacred texts come out of this period.

After the Cataclysm, culture flowered again in the Middle East during the Early Holocene—9500 to 4000 B.C.—a time when the rising seas and crustal movement totally erased the activities of many early people in many parts of the planet. Plato catalogued the main cultural prototypes in the Mediterranean region—the Atlanteans, Magdalenians, Athenians, and Egyptians—and we will begin by looking for what happened to them. The Atlanteans are mentioned in the early records of many world civilizations, yet they did not establish another homeland that came down through history.* They are essentially precataclysmic, and their cultural imprint is potent in many places. Many archaic myths refer to them, and the Aymara language may be their language, and in that sense, one could say Peru and Bolivia are their homeland. The Magdalenians and other artistic cave cultures disappeared as distinct cultures, but they are probably the precursors of the Azilian and Vinca cultures.[2] Recalling the ritual cave of Lascaux,

---

*The Atlanteans may have had colonies in the Americas, because the Maya claim descent from them. The Atlanteans may have gone to what is now known as Tibet, archaic India, even China, but this is beyond the scope of this book. See appendix C for cross-cultural information on Holocene diffusion.

Magdalenian mythology seems to have carried into Indo-European mythology, which helps trace the wandering people. The Athenians were the precursors of the Minoans, who are the ancestors of the Greeks. The Egyptians reemerged on the Nile, first as the Gerzean and Nagada cultures, who by predynastic times show signs of descent from the Shemsu Hor. Both the Minoans and early Egyptians established civilizations after 9500 B.C., and both were early seafarers, so we will look for their original ancestors right after the Cataclysm. The Fertile Crescent, Anatolia, and Iran must have been quite hospitable, because many advanced sites from circa 9000 B.C. are there.

Evidence for a close relationship between the Minoans and Egyptians is on the walls of the Fifth Dynasty Pyramid of Unas at Saqqara in Egypt. Minoan geometrical designs and the double axe (labrys) are incised and painted with red ochre and blue lapis lazuli on the walls behind the sarcophagus in the chamber where the Pyramid Texts were inscribed circa 2500 B.C. One might assume that this means that Unas married a Minoan queen, but everything on the walls of the Pyramid of Unas is an archaic record of a time Unas wished to commemorate. As you will see later, the double axe is a symbol for the Age of Gemini—6640 to 4480 B.C.—which may mean Unas was indicating that the Pyramid Texts from the First Time were catalogued in the Age of Gemini, but they contain many precataclysmic elements. Many researchers think that Çatal Hüyük precurses the Minoans, which makes Çatal Hüyük an ideal place to look for a Minoan/Egyptian connection. The Egyptian connection to Çatal Hüyük is evident in predynastic 6,000-year-old tombs at Saqqara. For example, the Tomb of Uadji has raised bull reliefs that are *exactly* the same artistic style as the bulls' heads of Çatal Hüyük, as in figure 6.1.[3] The boats buried near the pyramids at Abydos and Giza are very similar to the great Minoan flotilla depicted on the walls of Akrotiri on Thera, which was well preserved by volcanic ash during Thera's eruption. Akrotiri is a time capsule of the seafaring Mediterranean world that was derived from the Holocene global maritime civilization. Furthermore, during the Fifth and Sixth Dynasties in Egypt, Minoan culture was at its peak. Pyramids were built in the Peloponnese that have recently been dated to this time, when there was major pyramid building in Egypt.[4] *The Minoans and the Dynastic*

Fig. 6.1. Bulls' Heads of the Tomb of Uadji at Saqqara.

Egyptians are the direct descendants of Holocene seafaring cultures, who derived from wandering Cataclysm survivors. Remember, Plato said that the Athenians led the Egyptians in the war against the Atlanteans. However, later history reveals that the Egyptians were able to retain their cultural hegemony more successfully than the Athenians/Greeks, who were constantly challenged by greater earth changes. The Egyptians often assisted the Greeks in their travails.

Andrew Collins, in his brilliant examination of the Edfu Building Texts, has successfully argued that after leaving Egypt circa 9500 B.C., remnants of the Egyptian Elder Culture sailed to the Levant and built Nevali Çori in southeastern Turkey as an astronomical temple during the Age of Cancer.* Collins puts early Anatolian sites in context with Çatal Hüyük, and it can be seen that there were many advanced cultures in this region. Their sites may never be found because of flooding and migrations, but Çatal Hüyük sets a standard for the levels of many other people who must have existed in this region. There has to be a reason for such advanced early development at this site, which I will describe in detail later in this chapter. Çatal Hüyük also is the basis for the deep linkages between the Egyptians and the Minoans. The builders of Nevali Çori probably went to

---

* Andrew Collins, *Gods of Eden: Egypt's Lost Legacy and the Genesis of Civilization* (London: Headline, 1998), 327–66. Collins notes that the site has been carbon dated to 8000 B.C.; his date of 9000 B.C. is by star alignment to Cetus and Eridanus.

Çatal Hüyük and other sites such as Çanyönü. Collins points out that in the Edfu texts, the Egyptian Elders themselves say that they sailed away and lived in exile for thousands of years. This Elder Culture, using Andrew Collins's excellent term, is the nexus point in the genesis of the neolithic world. He also argues that they may be the ones who inspired the later Mesopotamian pantheon.[5] We are suggesting that the Elder Culture settled in many places in Anatolia and the Levant after the Cataclysm, and once the Nile was habitable again, they returned to Khemet. They retained their records about the time of blackness and chaos before their ancestors crossed the sea to repopulate the Nile at *"the beginning of time."*[6] As was discussed and illustrated in chapter 3, there are many Egyptian elements in early cultures west of the Nile in the Libyan desert, such as the Tassili n'Ajjer after 9000 B.C., which suggests that other Egyptians fled out to the desert.[7] Possibly, the people who fled to the desert are represented by the pharaonic Red Crown and the seafarers by the White Crown, and they were reunited as the Double Crown for the Unification.

Let me summarize the cataclysmic dispersals before going into more detail. A few thousand years before the Cataclysm, the Atlanteans moved out of Antarctica and resettled on a large island outside the Straits of

Fig. 6.2. Nevali Çori Courtyard, illustrated from the photograph in Gods of Eden.

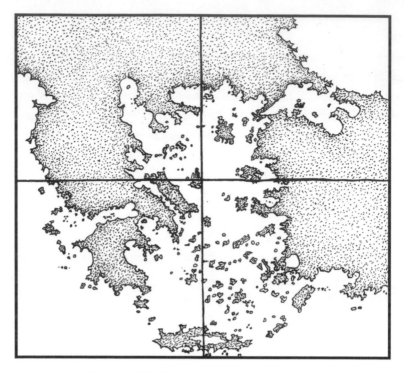

Fig. 6.3. The Ibn ben Zara Map (above), and
The Modern Aegean Map (below).

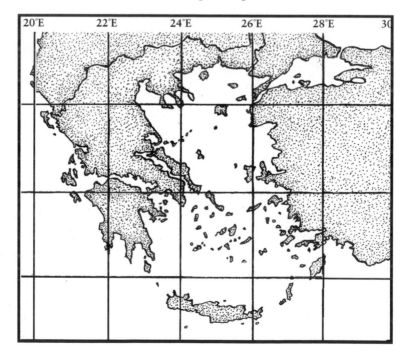

Gibraltar; from there they exerted pressure on the Mediterranean cultures. Circa 9600 B.C. the Atlanteans attacked the Athenians; the Athenians led other cultures into battle against them, including the Egyptians; the Athenians won; and the global maritime world was engulfed in the great disaster. Coming off mountains and out of caves and deporting boats, the seeds of the cyclopean Elder Cultures birthed new cultures circa 9000 B.C., just before the Age of Cancer began. Because this was a time of constant global climatic upheaval, any sites that survived in the more stable Mediterranean arc the most informative.

Archaic Mediterranean Archeological Sites

Climatologists have profiled global climate during the past 20,000 years, which is totally revising prehistory. Archeologists are incorporating *settlement archeology*—the study of entire regions—which puts sites into context.[8] Ecologists and geologists are teaming up with archeologists and anthropologists and inventing new fields, such as geoarcheology.[9] Climate and earth changes in a given region indicate that there must be archaic sites that are underwater or buried in ash or mud. These would be *the sites of the precursor cultures of the great civilizations that "just appeared."* The Aegean Sea rose 300 feet from 16,000 to 7000 B.C. (or land sank), and the coastlines were inundated so that seacoast cities that did exist are deep underwater. *Any* remains in the region from before 12,000 years ago would prove that people once lived there but had to leave. The discovery of an inhabited cave in the 1960s—the Franchthi Cave in the Peloponnese—provides the first evidence of seafarers in the Aegean before the Cataclysm.[10] Until this site was found, it was assumed that *nobody ever lived in the whole region before 6000 B.C.*[11] Just like the Magdalenian caves, the Franchthi Cave site offers little information about the true level of attainment of the Greeks 12,000 years ago. It is a peripheral or marginal site and does not reflect the true level of Late Paleolithic Greek culture. Then there are no sites from 9000 to 6000 B.C., very much like the Blank in Egypt, which establishes the magnitude of the earth changes.[12] Confirming the long relationship between the Minoans and the Egyptians, the Egyptians said to the Greeks in Plato's day, "You are left, as with little islands, with something rather like the skeleton of a body wasted by disease; the rich, soft soil has all run away leaving the land nothing but skin and bone."[13] Compare the Ibn ben Zara map of the Aegean, which is thousands of years old according to Hapgood, with the modern map of the Aegean, and it is obvious why the advanced sites are a few hundred feet underwater.

In nearby Palestine, Syria, and Anatolia, there *are* advanced sites from 11,000 to 7000 B.C. They reflect the movement and settlement of cultures, and this is where the similarities and connections of the prediluvial cultures are found. The richness of these sites indicate that this area did not succumb to the rising seas, and they are probably representative of what is underwater in the Aegean. The Natufian culture was extensive throughout the eastern end of the Mediterranean, where there was a "virtual explosion of arts, crafts, and technologies."[14] Suddenly there was advanced ancestor worship and wonderful art, as well as elements that are very Atlantean, such as veneration of the bull.[15] Regarding these sites, archeologists have said, "The Natufian impulse was already old at the moment of its appearance in this land which formerly knew no art, or at least no imperishable art, of any kind."* These "already old" cultures sound like groups of refugees from destroyed cities who began again. Global maritime seafarers *must* have gone there after the crust shifted and mixed with indigenous people, and Mary Settegast even suggests that Çanyönü, a very early East Anatolian site, was probably founded by the refugees of the *Timaeus*.[16] The story of the Black Sea Flood is a graphic example of cataclysmic cultural dispersal that puts sites in the whole region into context. The following is my summary of senior scientists William Ryan and Walter Pitman's powerful case in *Noah's Flood* that the Aegean Sea flooded into the Black Sea 7,600 years ago.[17]

Noah's Flood and the Rising Seas

The story begins 20,000 years ago, when the seas were 400 feet lower than they are today. Northern Europe was melting, and water raced into the Black Sea, which was an ice lake. The glaciers melted while the earth sprang up once the

---

* Mary Settegast, *Plato Prehistorian: 10,000 to 5000 B.C.—Myth, Religion, Archaeology* (Hudson, N.Y.: Lindisfarne Press, 1990), 51. This is Settegast's notation of the archeologists.

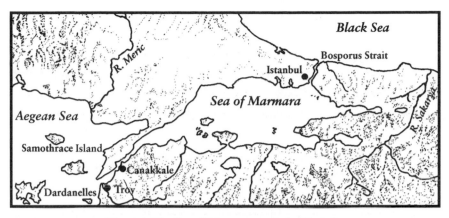

Fig. 6.4. The Sea of Marmara and the Black Sea.

heavy weight lifted. The burgeoning lake found an outlet through the Sea of Marmara through the North Anatolian Fault and into the Mediterranean Sea. Cold returned 12,500 years ago during the "Younger Dryas," and the glaciers sucked up the water in the Black Sea, which became an isolated lake. The old outlet, the Salkarya Channel, filled up with debris and formed a huge earthen dam. New river valleys cut down to the edge of the retreating lake, and people came there in retreat from the desiccation in their own regions. They began early farming in the rich deltas of fecund silt. The Black Sea was an oasis in a desiccated world for 1,000 years. There is much evidence of struggle and near-starvation all over the region. Then 11,400 years ago, the people who were left moved away and settled elsewhere to farm.

From 11,400 to 8,200 years ago, people lived in villages and farmed all over the Near East, such as Çatal Hüyük, Çanyönü, and the Natufian sites. The Mediterranean rose a few hundred feet, but the Black Sea was cut off by the dam in the Salkarya Channel. In 6200 B.C., cold and dryness returned again, and people abandoned their villages, including Çatal Hüyük. Some returned to the shores of the Black Sea to farm in the river valleys and deltas. The climate warmed again in 5800 B.C., and many of the abandoned villages on the Anatolian Plateau were reoccupied. By 5600 B.C., the Aegean Sea had risen so high it was poised to breach the dam that kept the seawater from the Black Sea. The winds and tides caused periodic incursions, until finally the water began to cut a river across the slope and down to the old channel toward the lake. Within days the small river became a torrent carrying tons of debris and mud. It cut into the bedrock, gouged a 475-foot-deep flume, and 200 times the amount of water that flows over Niagara Falls rushed in. The rising water swallowed the shores, and *the flood continued long after the people had fled. After two years the Black Sea had risen 330 feet. The freshwater lake became a salt sea. Dense Aegean salt water still flows through the bottom of the Bosporus into the Black Sea, where-as fresh water flows on top in the opposite direction.*

Ryan and Pitman argue that the Vinca farmers on the shores of the Black Sea took their culture with them and seeded many cultures: west to the Balkans and all the way to Paris; north to the Dnieper River in Russia; by water into the Aegean and Ionian Seas; east to the Caspian Sea; and south to the Fertile Crescent, where they seeded the 'Ubaid culture, the precursors of the Sumerians.[18] The Sumerian legends are the basis of the Flood stories and Noah's Ark in Judeo-Christian traditions, which is why Ryan and Pitman titled their book *Noah's Flood*. The true Noah's Flood is, of course, the 9500 B.C. Cataclysm. However, the Black Sea Flood is a great example of how later cataclysms got mixed up with the main one and then triggered more collective fear. Many new theories are coming forth regarding the ancestors of the Sumerians, the 'Ubaids, which of course raise new questions about the Flood legends in the Bible. Stephen Oppenheimer's *Eden in the East* posits that the sailors from Sundaland seeded the 'Ubaid culture, whereas *Gods of Eden* by Collins presents evidence that the 'Ubaids are from the neolithic village of Jarmo in Iraqi Kurdistan.[19] These are great examples of the major revisions that are coming in ancient history, which I will discuss more in subsequent chapters. Here we need more information about climate and earth changes in the region.

Crustal Shifting in the Cradle of Civilization

Çatal Hüyük in present-day Turkey is a precursor site to the Minoan sites that were destroyed during the period of crustal shifting in India and throughout the Mediterranean region less than 4,000 years ago, such as Knossos and Akrotiri.[20] Terror from these cataclysms in the Aegean is deeply hidden in the Western psyche, because the cataclysms occurred within historical times in the "Cradle of Civilization." The courtyard of Knossos was exquisitely decorated with hundreds of raised bull horns, and the central ritual carried on there was bull dancing. Palace life and the mystery plays, such as bull dancing, continued right up to when Thera erupted. The seafaring

Fig. 6.5. Knossos Palace on Crete during Minoan times.

Minoans were caught in the middle of the crustal adjustment, and then they were overwhelmed by the warlike Mycenaeans, who overwhelmed the Minoan Goddess culture. For them, this collapse was a repeat of two previous cataclysms: the 9500 B.C. Cataclysm and the Black Sea Flood.*

Earth changes in the Mediterranean approximately 3,600 years ago caused the final breakdown of the bicameral brain, which is why I stress what we've lost in these cataclysms. The Minoans loved art, theater, Nature, human beauty, and architecture. Because their palaces and cities were buried in volcanic ash, we know a lot about them, and they were one of the last intact Goddess cultures. The problem was that *the Goddess was responsible for the pacification of the Earth*. As the Earth quaked and fumed, she lost her power, and a culture of great art and beauty was destroyed. In Egypt, Sekhmet as the raging Goddess of earth changes prevailed over Hathor, the goddess of beauty and love, and the Egyptians became warlike for the first time. Before then, they were mostly a defensive country. Hapgood says, "A

---

* Memories of Thera's eruption often come up when people are regressed, and if the therapist goes deeper, the client encounters a gaping black hole of fear. See Barbara Hand Clow's *Eye of the Centaur* (St. Paul, Minn.: Llewellyn, 1986) and *Heart of the Christos* (Santa Fe: Bear & Company, 1989). The past-life therapist Gregory Paxson told me that people often recover memories of lifetimes when they died during Thera's eruption. The eruption of Thera and the destruction of Santorini are frequently thought to be the same event as the sinking of Atlantis. I believe this is because of the memory resonance.

Fig. 6.6. Three Ladies of Knossos Palace.

world-wide geological upheaval took place around 1400 B.C., and there was the *final* readjustment of the Earth's outer shell to its new position after its last displacement."* The Aegean basin subsided when Thera erupted: Crete was devastated, and the Minoan palaces were buried in ash. There were massive earthquakes in Egypt, when many of the temples, including Karnak, were severely damaged. Whole islands in the western Mediterranean sank, and the Caspian Sea, where the Russians have since found a sunken city, subsided. Nearby in India, the Saraswati River region uplifted, destroying the Vedic culture, which is described in the *Mahabharata*.[21]

According to seismologist A. G. Galanopoulos, Santorini's volcanic core collapsed and formed a deep caldera, which sucked in billions of gallons of sea-water and generated a tsunami that was *300 to 600 feet high*. The great wave moved out from Thera into the Aegean to the distant Mediterranean shores, where it crashed over the Cycladic Islands and Crete.[22] Oceanographic engineer James Mavor says, "The eruption and collapse of Thera (Santorini) is the greatest natural catastrophe that has occurred in historical times."[23] The Aegean region and the entire Near East were thrown back into a regression as the war god of the Age of Aries ravaged the land and people. Western civilization emerged eight centuries later in Athens with little memory of the recent cataclysmic activity. Just as the people in the late Roman Empire did not know about Pompei, the early Greeks did not know about the Minoan

---

* Charles Hapgood, *Maps of the Ancient Sea Kings: Evidence of Advanced Civilization in the Ice Age* (London: Turnstone Books, 1960), 187. Most scholars now date Santorini's eruption to 1626 B.C.

palaces on Crete or the cities on Thera. Until a hundred years ago, people believed Greek was the first language in the region. The Minoan culture was so totally devastated that their scripts are still only partially deciphered.*

The Classical Greeks "just appeared" in Athens 2,800 years ago. Alexander the Great eventually spread the Greek ideal all over the Cradle of Civilization; it became the credo of the Roman Empire, and the Greco-Roman ideal is still the basis of Western education. However, our real past is so much older, richer, evocative, and feminine. Our memories of thousands of years of life, art, and rituals in happy cultures were buried under volcanic ash until recently. The day Thera exploded, our forebears who sailed the Aegean from 9000 to 1600 B.C. were forgotten. As the Egyptians said to the Greeks, "You are all young in mind, you have no belief rooted in old tradition and no knowledge hoary with age . . . Writing and the other necessities of civilization have only just been developed when the periodic scourge of the deluge descends, and spares none but the unlettered and uncultured, so that you have to begin again like children." [24]

J. B. Delair says that *most of the Holocene terrestial disturbances were aftermaths of the crustal disturbances generated 11,500 years ago.* [25] Appendix B covers this aspect of Delair's work in detail. As difficult as it is to even imagine the Goddess in the midst of the war-ravaged twentieth century, *earth changes have been steadily diminishing, and now we must heal the emotional response patterns caused by them, such as constant warfare.* The Age of Aries was the age of war and aggression, and we are still dealing with this today. Now we will go deeply into the lost culture of the Goddess, because it awakens our latent creativity, which can terminate violence and warfare.

Çatal Hüyük and the Precession of the Equinoxes

Mary Settegast says, "The range and beauty of these Neolithic settlers will not be fully appreciated until we come to the well-preserved site of Çatal Hüyük in the late seventh millennium." [†] Its discoverer, James Mellaart of

---

* Sir Arthur Evans discovered Knossos and the written languages of the Minoans, Linear A and B. See also Stephen Roger Fischer, *Glyph-Breaker* (New York: Copernicus, 1997).

† Settegast, *Plato Prehistorian*, 128. This should be eighth millennium, but Settegast did not tree-ring calibrate all of her dates. See page 9 for how she handled dating. I tree-ring calibrated the dates that seem to be uncalibrated in her text, and I checked those against other sources.

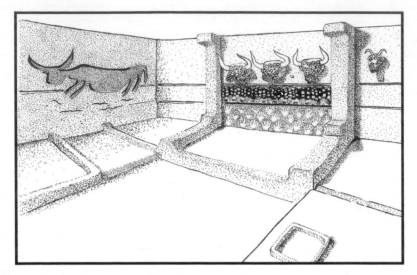

Fig. 6.7. Çatal Hükük Bull Shrine VI.8, adapted from figure 35 of Çatal Hüyük.

the Institute of Archaeology at the University of London, was amazed by its similarity to Minoan sites, as are most people who compare them.[26] His discovery shocked archeology, because it was believed that the first urban communities arose circa 3500 B.C. Çatal Hüyük was an advanced urban farming culture that existed *thousands of years earlier than was thought possible;* this decimated the prevailing time line of Mediterranean and Near Eastern archeology. Mellaart was only able to excavate 4 percent of Çatal Hüyük before his funds were cut off, and excavations have only been recently resumed. Çatal Hüyük is replete with complex plaster shrines of bulls' heads and leopard sculptures; wall paintings; iron and copper beads;

clay stamp seals; greenstone axes; obsidian spearpoints; white marble sculptures (which resemble Bronze Age Cycladic sculpture); and extraordinary murals that seem to be calendars, as well as murals depicting battle scenes, figures, and landscapes.[27] To emphasize the sophistication of this site, which is more than 9,000 years old, many illustrations are given here. Unexcavated levels still lie below.

Fig. 6.8. Goddess Giving Birth on the Double Leopard Throne, figurine found in Level II.

Mellaart says Çatal Hüyük descended from an "upper Paleolithic culture, probably Anatolian, of which hardly anything is known."[28] The main mound goes back thousands of years before the culture of its top layer, which mysteriously was deserted in 6200 B.C. Then there is a gap from 6200 to 5800 B.C., when the people may have gone back to the shores of the Black Sea because there was a severe cold period during that time.[29] The top layers are time capsules from 6200 B.C., the early stages in the Age of Gemini. The bull cult was very prominent, suggesting Atlantean influence, and veneration of the birthing Goddess is also very evident, which suggests that the people retained symbols from the Age of Cancer. An exquisite clay figurine of a mother giving birth while sitting on a *double leopard throne* was found in a grain bin, as if she was there to enhance the harvest. This may suggest the end of the Age of Leo moving into Cancer. Until the lower levels are researched, there is no reason not to think that this site goes back to 9000 B.C. Çatal Hüyük was a key ritual center during the Age of Cancer—8800 to 6640 B.C.—when agriculture began. Collins argues they were practicing *vulture shamanism*. This resonates with the Age of Cancer, which was deeply involved with the Underworld.[30] The rooms were filled with numerous ritual heirlooms of families, birthing women, and embracing couples, and even a goddess giving birth to a ram above three bulls' heads. The lower layers of Çatal Hüyük take us deeply into the Age of Cancer, the deep core that reunites us with the Goddess.

Some murals exhibit very primal geometrical symbolism, exquisite

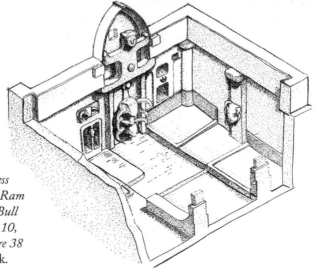

Fig. 6.9. Goddess Giving Birth to a Ram above the Three Bull Heads Shrine VI.10, adapted from figure 38 of Çatal Hüyük.

Fig. 6.10. Wheeled Cross Mural from
Shrine VI.A.66, adapted from figure 112 of Plato Prehistorian.

metamorphic paintings, and animal, human, and landscape art. There are some strange murals with netlike patterns that are astronomical. Two murals to be discussed here describe time and cycles, as other researchers have also suggested. In figure 6.10, note the double axe on the left of the mural, which was later a symbol of Knossos. Hertha Von Dechend "proposed that the double-axe was actually associated with the Precession of the Equinoxes."[31] *This is the oldest known representation of the double axe on Earth.* Along with sacred twinship, the double axe is a key symbol for the Age of Gemini because it expresses duality. The fact that this mural was painted during early Gemini suggests that tracking precession may have become an important activity during this age, especially because Gemini is ruled by Mercury, the planet that influences mental comprehension. Once precession was noticed, marking the shifts between the ages would have become a big deal, and it makes sense that a key ritual center such as Çatal Hüyük would have memorialized this great change in the sky. I am proposing that *Çatal Hüyük actually has precessional information from the Age of Gemini.* This is extremely important because it suggests that this site was active when the new religion of this period—Zervanism or Magism—was founded, a religion obsessed with cosmic time cycles.[32]

In the mural, the double axe on the left signals that the Age of Gemini has arrived. In the center of the mural, note the distinctive "wheeled cross," which is the wheel of Time spinning as a four-directional, nearly equal-armed cross with arms ending as Poseidon's trident.* Poseidon was the legendary founder of Atlantis, and his trident ending the arms of the wheel says

---

* Settegast, *Plato Prehistorian*, 189. J. B. Delair commented in his note on this part of the manuscript in January 2000 that the trident was "specially made for Marduk by Ea (for Indra by Vishnu/Tavashtri), who was none other than the Phoenician/Greek Sidon/Poseidon (Roman Neptune). The trident was a terrible weapon involving electricity and missile fights, and was used to dismantle/divert Phaeton or Marduk."

that he is in control of Time! As with Hamlet's mill, this wheeled cross—which Marija Gimbutas finds in later Greco-Balkan pottery to be "symbolic of the perpetual renewal of the cosmic cycle"—is the central image of Time here. It looks as if Poseidon's trident is "clicking" Time into place on the next wheel, which is divided into eight sections by the central cross, a very simple and graphic portrayal of cyclical time. There are also four divided wedges representing the two ages between the fixed cross, making the total twelve Great Ages. *The second wheel is the circle of the twelve Great Ages showing the Age of Gemini clicking in.* Next, to the right, there is a bull's head with wavy lines, which suggest energy flow, or maybe water for the demise of Atlantis. Possibly they wanted to point out that the Age of Taurus follows the Age of Gemini and will be very energized because it is a fixed age.

The symbols in this mural are very specific, and it shouts, "This is where we are now!" The most intriguing element is right above the place where Poseidon's wheeled cross is clicking in the Age of Gemini by the wedge that represents both Gemini and Cancer. Notice the *little human figures flying into the wheel, as though depicting the ancestors of Çatal Hüyük coming into Time or returning from the shores of the Black Sea.* Maybe these are ritual postures. These ideas may seem far-fetched, but archaic people were very deliberate in their art; they only included elements that meant something to them. Incorrect symbolism misrepresented the cosmos and the gods; it could bring evil or chaos into the world. This mural is very intentional. Furthermore, anthropologists have already suggested what some of the basic elements mean. This wheeled cross of Poseidon's trident is one of the oldest ones in existence, and it is a very potent symbol for a god and Time.

The next mural is much harder to interpret than the wheeled cross, so we need more background on these murals. First of all, they were painted and then quickly erased by a layer of white paint after they were used.[33] Today, Tibetan monks and the Déné (Navaho) make very complex sand paintings that depict patterns of cosmic harmony. They pray with the harmony created in the moment, and then they destroy the design by remixing all the grains. These are intensely sacred rituals because they create intentional realities. Once the designs are brought into the world, it would be destructive to fix them in time, because they access the ephemeral vertical axis uniting Earth and sky to influence events on Earth. This probably was

*"All welfare and adversity that come to man
and the other creatures come through the Seven and the Twelve . . .
for the twelve signs of the Zodiac and the seven planets rule
the fate of the world and direct it."*

—Bundahishn

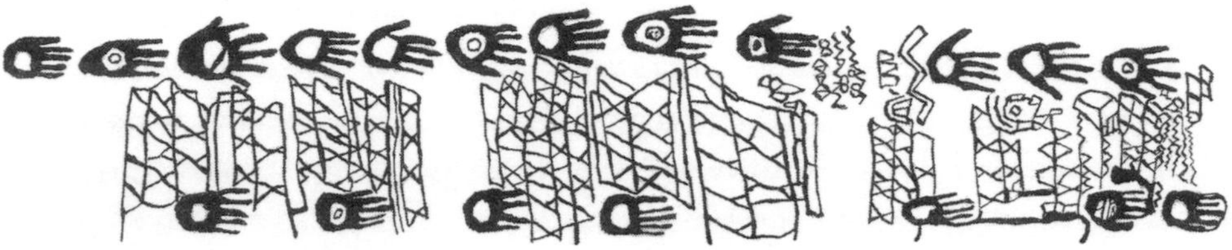

*Fig. 6.11. Twelve Hands Above and Seven Below
from Shrine VII.8, adapted from figuare 119 of* Plato Prehistorian,
which theorizes that the above quote is related to this mural.

much the same sacred technology as the Çatal Hüyük murals—they painted them and then painted over them until it was time to create another one. Because the Tibetan and Déné cosmograms depict cosmic cycles, then it is likely these murals also depict cosmic Time cycles. Anthropologist Brian Fagan says, "Clearly, these wall paintings had a profound transitory significance, perhaps as an element in powerful ritual performances that unfolded in the shrine."[34] It was never imagined that archeologists would remove the paint and reveal them in our times. In my opinion, *these are rituals that focus the human mind to time travel.*

The second mural is also precessional, and what it may represent is incredible. One's first impression is that this mural is *very* deliberate. Settegast argues that this mural suggests that Zervanism was practiced at Çatal Hüyük.[35] Zervanism is the religion of the Magi that conceived of Time as infinite, as eternity. When we factor in the wider context for the region in light of Ryan and Pitman's *Noah's Flood*, the Magi may have been the astronomer-priests of cosmological science for the whole region at this time. Just as the people who lived on the shores of the Black Sea before 9500 B.C. may have developed agriculture, they also could have experienced a cosmological breakthrough. Von Dechend and de Santillana's *Hamlet's Mill* posits the Age of Gemini was "Time Zero" because it was when the constellations Gemini and Sagittarius rose during the equinoxes.[36] As for the age and nature of religions in this area, the Indian-Iranian prophet Zarathustra (also known as Zoroaster) was a *reformer* of Zervanism. This makes his time later, and he already goes back thousands of years— Aristotle said the time of Zarathustra was 6350 B.C. Zarathustra *abolished* the worship of Time or Fate, which was the basis of Zervanism, and so Zervanism is much older. Çatal Hüyük may be a Magian or Zervanian site.[37] For the Magi, time was "zodiacally conceived," and Settegast believes that the text printed above figure 6.11 represents the Zervanite or Iranian Magite view of celestial influence on earthly events.[38] This mural is approximately *8,700 years old*. The text above the mural was written 1,000 years ago and dated to that time, yet if this text is expressed on this mural, the *Bundahishn* from which it comes has elements that are 8,700 years old or more. As we view the exactly dated mural in light of this text (assuming time was zodiacally conceived), the twelve hands above are the twelve signs and the seven hands below are the seven planets, which are connected by netlike patterns. "The netlike pattern of weaving between these rows of seven and twelve hands at Çatal Hüyük is itself a traditional symbol for the connections between the heavenly bodies."[39] These murals taken together strongly suggest that Çatal Hüyük was a major astronomical temple during the Age of Gemini that was devoted to studying planetary and precessional star cycles.

I think this mural traces the planetary influences during the Great Ages. The netlike lines probably represent planetary orbits. As we interpret it going right to left—as the Great Ages move in reverse order—the Age of Gemini is the black hand above, and the muralist seems to have put in some anticipated planetary movements that would occur as Gemini progressed. Next is Cancer, where new patterns are indicated, and the circular design may represent a simple hearth or early round house when the first people settled there. Next, back to Leo with a zigzag lightning bolt, odd hut, or cavelike dwellings; and then right in mid-Leo, a huge dichotomy that may represent a discontinuity in 9500 B.C. with isolated squiggles between two upper hands. As we move further back in time, the mural depicts earlier ages—such as Virgo, Libra, and Scorpio—because the people at this time would have thought of the zodiacal ages going back forever in time.

However, their portrayal of these ages before the dichotomy is radically different than the ages of Leo through Gemini, and the patterns are significantly more orderly, which may reflect the time of Paradise. Going back to the Age of Gemini, we see that there is much activity, and there is a rendering of a bull's thigh, which represented the stars around the North Pole in early cultures, such as Egypt. The netting going further back is more geometrical and orderly, *perhaps portraying a time before the axis tilted.*

The mural makers may have retained records of the patterns in the sky before the seasons began, and the order and clarity of the patterns before the dichotomy may depict the Golden Age. I am suggesting that this mural attempts to show 26,000 years of Time based on the mural maker's current knowledge of the Great Ages, and it shows radical astronomical differences in the planetary orbits before and after the axis tilted. *The change in the night sky would have been their central story,* and they would have painted murals to depict these patterns. We are so lucky to be able to consider these ideas, even though it is difficult to understand the archaic mind. The more we realize how the Great Ages have literally been mutating the human brain, the more it is logical that the people would have created paintings such as this one to depict the long cycles of time. It is *we* who have forgotten until very recently how important this information is. This mural may map planetary patterns and the Great Ages as the astronomers of Çatal Hüyük understood them. If they were observing precession and adjusting to seasonality, then they *would* have tried to make symbols and paint diagrams such as these. *We* are the ones finding it hard to imagine this because our culture is so short lived by comparison.*

The only way to break into archaic memory banks is to free our imaginations. No one will be able to prove what the ritual cave of Lascaux or the murals at Çatal Hüyük mean for sure; however, we can hope that we will be able to read more and more things into these ancient records as we

---

* J. B. Delair, personal letter, 22 November 2000. The Panamanian Cuna Indians after the flood remembered sages who "imparted details of the then-*new calendar*. Any then-new calendar would *have* to have incorporated the precessional *factor* (then itself very new) for the calendar to have had any lasting value. The factor is *allowed for* in the zodiac, and that too was traditionally invented by the early post-Deluge folk. So, if any credence can be given to these old beliefs and assertions, the precessional factor was discussed *very* early after the flood." (Delair's italics.)

learn more about the people who lived there. As we have better information on specific sites, then it is possible to connect ancient cultures to each other and understand their progressive patterns. I have used Plato as a guide for what the world was like 11,000 years ago, and I will complete this chapter by exploring another mystery that comes to us from Plato. The *Timaeus* opens with the Atlantis Myth as a society that existed in the days of ancient Athens, and this section is only six paragraphs long. Then the *Timaeus* goes on with *sixty more* paragraphs that describe the manifestation of the physical world after the mythical time. That is, *the main body of the* Timaeus *can be equated with Dynastic Egypt, and the Atlantean part can be equated with the earlier First Time.* Few people have paid any attention to Plato's odd and arcane description of the manifestation of the material world; however, because it follows his description of Atlantis (which is later completed in the *Critias*), I think it is worth considering. As you will see, it actually says a lot about human consciousness during the Age of Cancer—8800 to 6640 B.C.

The Earliest Writing and the Platonic Solids

The most peculiar part of my education with my grandfather was his insistence that I study the *Timaeus* and report back to him on my understanding of it. I was fascinated by the story of Atlantis, but Plato's writing about the physical world coming from the world of forms frankly gave me an eight-year-old's headache. Plato's ideas did make geometrical sense to me, especially that the physical world comes out of geometry. While writing this book, I finally began to realize something more was going on when I read that a group of research chemists have just succeeded at creating molecules based on the platonic solids. The chemists have made new molecules—such as octanitrocubane or ONC, which may end up being the basis of a cancer cure—that are the most powerful nonnuclear explosive ever found and are expanding the horizons of organic chemistry. Regarding the platonic solids, Plato says that the four elementary constituents are earth (cube), air (octahedron), fire (tetrahedron), and water (icosahedron), and the dodecahedron symbolizes the universe.[40] *The chemists discovered a new chemistry by studying Plato and following his forms!*

The next connection is by Near Eastern clay tokens that are found in

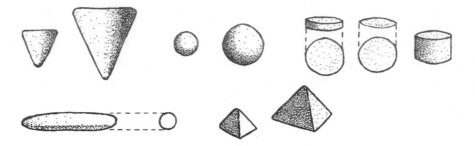

Fig. 6.12. Near Eastern Clay Tokens, adapted from figure 11 of The Lost Civilization of the Stone Age, *which is derived from the research of Denise Schmandt-Besserat.*

almost all sites in Iraq, Iran, Syria, Turkey, and Israel from 8000 to 6000 B.C. They are the first clay objects hardened by fire, and they are well-made miniature cones, spheres, disks, tetradedrons, cylinders, and other geometrical shapes—some of the platonic solids.[41] They were a system of counting or early writing that enabled people to bridge different languages, and, being so portable, they are universal and were well developed by 8000 B.C. If they had existed before the Cataclysm, I believe they would have been found in the caves and other sites, where prediluvial bones with notations have been found. I've already noted in chapter 4 that there is much evidence for writing systems from before the Cataclysm, and I think these tokens are evidence for an entirely new level of abstract thought.

Plato's essential doctrine—the material realm precipitates out of abstract forms—goes even further back in time. Anthropologist Richard Rudgely has a fantastic chapter in *The Lost Civilizations of the Stone Age* titled "Paleo-science."[42] Among many amazing finds, more than a million years ago, our Acheulian ancestors in Europe, Asia, and Africa exhibited a remarkable degree of uniformity in crafting their hand axes. It is always possible to recognize their hand axes because the chipping and cutting are so much the same that one craftsman could have made them all! Of course, that is impossible, and the conclusion is that this uniformity cannot be due to chance. It has to be some form of social knowledge—they had to have had an *image of the tool* in their minds. Rudgely says that the "origins of aspects of mathematical knowledge may be traced back to the time of the hand-axes."[43] He believes we can't understand the human story without taking into account the innovations and developments that occurred in the Stone Age. See archeologist Alexander Marschak in appendix D, who also discovered much about Stone Age innovation.

I agree with Richard Rudgely, but from a different perspective. Along with Allan and Delair, I think the Cataclysm ended 29 million years of human development. All that remains are stone remnants because of the destruction. I will present evidence in stone in the next chapter that supports this long evolution. Regarding the mysterious neolithic tokens, I think they are a brain tool that kept alive the most critical human knowledge—*matter precipitates out of abstract form*—which is obviously what mattered to Plato. Of all the things my grandfather stressed, he said that this is the most important, and now I see why. Once we realize that *our thoughts create our tools*, such as the Acheulian axe makers and the neolithic makers of platonic solids, we will understand how our ancestors could create the Great Pyramid.

7

The Fallen Angels
& the Stones of Ica

*. . . there exists a little-known society of devotees
of the zodiac. They recognize each other with the password,
"twenty-three and a half," the number of degrees of
the angle of the earth's axis; it is the inclination
of the zodiac over the equator.*

—Elémire Zolla[1]

Draco and the Great Bear

The constellations that travel around the North Celestial Axis—the *circumpolar constellations*—are a great clock that ancient traditions say reads the time of the rise and fall of humanity. Macrobiologist Michio Kushi says, "The circle of the circumpolar stars, as a whole tell a story, the voyage of human civilizations through the stages of the 26,000-year cycle. The ancients used the patterns of the stars in the night sky as we use printed books, movies, or television—as a medium for preserving and conveying information."[2] According to Kushi, we are ending a time of war and struggle and beginning the time of paradise. He describes the period we've been in since the Cataclysm as a time of wilderness coming to Earth, when we were heavily influenced by the constellation Draco, the Dragon or Serpent of the Biblical tradition, when we were expelled from the Garden of Eden.[3] During this time we've been devoured by negative vibrations, and we've almost lost our way as our thinking has become more and more deluded. Now, as we come to the end of this time, we see the fruits of our destruction. The orientation on the circumpolar circle is shifting to the influence of the Great Bear constellation, the heralded beginning of the time of paradise when we will find our way back into the Garden of Eden.

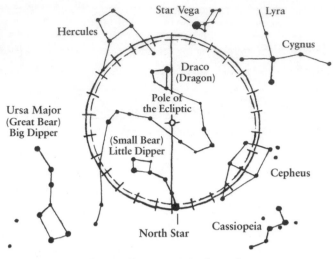

Fig. 7.1. Draco and the Great Bear.

During this time of darkness, we consolidated our efforts through institutions just to survive, and we became very solid and material. Now we must break down that pattern to become less dense, which would enable us *to use the full vibrational powers of thought in the material world.*

The previous chapter ends with a bald concept: Matter precipitates out of abstract form by our thoughts—or, more easily put, our ideas create the things that emerge in our material world. Of course, there are many other orders of creation, such as minerals, plants, and animals. As we've seen by the theories of Julian Jaynes and Immanuel Velikovsky, earth changes have functionally altered the human brain and cultures. We are becoming creatures who e-mail each other and interact less and less in person—yet who wants this? Are the ones who manifest such a system the devotees of the zodiac with the password, "twenty-three and a half"? As many religions seek an ultimate solution, time speeds up, and old ways of life just disappear. Amid this high emotional velocity, deep archetypal forces activate within individuals, which could form into a whirlwind that feeds on negative thoughtforms. This can be avoided if individuals process their own shadows or dark sides and avoid being the pawns of larger forces. The most important theme of this book is that many people believe the world is soon coming to an end; they pray for an apocalypse just to have things over with, which means they are perpetuating the idea of being victims.

Most people are not aware that the Plutonic shadows they struggle with are the direct result of the false story of the past. The real story was sanitized thousands of years ago, and people are encouraged to feel guilty about something they can't even describe. *These painful shadows were born during the horrific survival times, the long years following the chaotic earth changes.* These difficult periods need to be examined, because cataclysmic myths are always paired with stories that say that the earth changes were caused by humans who sinned against God. For example, in Genesis 6:1–12, the sons of God came down and seduced the daughters of men, giants were born from them, and evil came into the world. This caused God to send a great flood, Noah's Flood, but Noah, his family, and the species *survived.* After the Flood, the earlier sources of the story in the Bible say that in those days humans wandered around Earth in a daze among serpentine giants and great bird-gods, who taught humanity the arts of civilization. From this time, we saw ourselves as mixed beings of heaven and Earth; *we saw ourselves as the children of Fallen Angels as well as the indigenous people.* The time has come to investigate these stories, because they are the source of intensely shadowed and separated parts of our psyches that are all mixed up with cataclysmic memories. Otherwise, we are all just fallen sinners who can never recover from trauma that occurred long ago; we will all be forever in the grip of catastrophobia.

During the time of paradise, as it was before the Cataclysm, Kushi describes "the whole planet united in a time of peace, creativity, and harmony by the descending (centripetal) energy which formed the galaxy, the solar system, and this earth."[4] Kushi also agrees with my understanding about the Galactic Winter Solstice as being the time of the solstice alignments when Earth's axis points directly through the Milky Way, and we receive an "enormous flow of galactic current."[5] The mass of stars in that plane "shed their influence directly down through the central, vertical (north-south) energy channel both of the planet and also of humanity as well as all other life forms on earth. Not only is the human brain more active during that period, but all botanical sources of our food are much more vigorous, requiring hardly any cultivation."[6] Regarding Axial Tilt Theory, the time of paradise Kushi describes lasted at least 30 million years, and the last 11,500 years have been the time of struggle when the serpent Draco began to writhe in the sky by precession. That is, 21 December 2012 may be the first Galactic Winter Solstice, as suggested in chapter 1.

Kushi is describing the *vibrational world*. The creation of realities by thought requires the reception of energy throughout the whole body, not just thinking in the head. I have begun with our exciting future because the material in this chapter will be horrific and shocking for many readers. It has been deeply suppressed. We have been conditioned to avoid facing the darkness within; yet as paradise comes again to Earth, our bodies need fine-tuning so that we can receive these vibrational forces. Subtle glands that access very high frequencies, such as the hypothalamus and thymus, awaken, and if we have massive emotional blocks, our physical bodies cannot handle the secretions from these glands.[7] Even now, the recovery of archaic memories is causing a mind-bending spiritual crisis. As many people look deep within and face their own hidden violence and heartlessness, personal boundaries are dissolved and feelings intensify exponentially. People sense that their own inner anger and fear is related to the pain in the world; they *feel* Rwanda, Bosnia, Iraq, Israel, Egypt, and Washington. We are involved in a species-level awakening. Remarkably, each time a person lets go of his or her need to be separate from the whole, such deeply honest encounters with the self cause miracles: suddenly disasters in Nature or politics that seemed inevitable just don't happen. This is because *Nature reformulates her fields in resonance with the human heart that knows itself by clear intentional thought.* Nature devolves into chaos when lies and hatred are projected out into the collective by evil men. The divine is enfolded in the mundane world and it responds to love, and personal quests cause waves of grace in the material world. It is time to recognize the unrecognized dreams, loves, and magical powers of people lost in the Cataclysm when our cosmic dream was shattered. The songs of the ancient ones must be sung again.

The Collective Nightmare of the Global Elite

Moving out of our personal realms, which we so carefully construct around ourselves to feel safe, we can now explore the current group mentality, where there is a building collective madness caused by a net of invisible archetypal thoughtforms. The truth is that we live in a world that is controlled by covert Global Elite groups. These Global Elite members come out of old wealthy families who supply individuals to hold the important positions in politics, religion, medicine, banking, and business. This is not news; however, *how* they use the power is not well understood. They use the forbidden arts of the Fallen Angels—creation by thought, astrology, natural healing, and alchemy—while simultaneously debunking these arts so no one will see what they are actually doing. People outside the Elite cannot believe that this is what the Elite does, because they wear suits and red ties and smile benignly on television. For the public, any contact with these arts is a total embarrassment, like hanging out a shingle advertising that one is a palm reader, thus people are robbed of the use of these skills. Meanwhile, the Elite continually uses all the magical forces in their secret cabals.

The only way this program can be exposed is to watch the behavior of the Elite over great spans of time. As we've seen, the Elite have stolen the knowledge of sacred cultures and either destroyed it on the spot or stored it for reference in places such as the Vatican Library, archeological museums, the Smithsonian, and private collections. Using these powerful tools—calendars, totemic artifacts, bones, and divination systems—they've worked together in secret to control the world for thousands of years.[8] See the footnotes and endnotes for good books about Global Elite. To control the world, the Elite needs to control these forces, but *why?* Because people who live in small ecosystems can use these forces to live in harmony with the land and maintain freedom, and they can't be controlled. By taking the land and magical powers from the indigenous people, the Elite multiplies these forces within their own interlocked systems. Now we live in the era when they plan to call in their chips, because they know the time of paradise is coming. As Andrew Collins says, "Initiates and secret societies preserved, revered, even celebrated the forbidden knowledge that our most distant ancestors had gained their inspiration and wisdom, not from God or from the experiences of life, but from a forgotten race remembered by us today only as fallen angels, demons, devils, giants and evil spirits."[9]

Andrew Collins traces how the Angels of the Christian, Hebrew, Iranian, and various Middle Eastern scriptures interbred with the women of Earth thousands of years ago. He also describes how, during the crucial survival times, the Angels taught the forbidden arts and sciences to humanity; they were *physical beings who walked among us.*[10] Christianity conspired with the aristocracy to eliminate the evidence for the corporeal nature of the Angels, and this continues today. When the Europeans colonized the Americas, the Inquisition had already taken the forbidden arts from the common people of Europe. The conquerors of the Americas were trained to search out all traces of the knowledge, and the priests swept in right behind the legions and destroyed information outright or gathered it, and then they built churches on the indigenous sacred sites. They numbed the minds of those who survived the genocide, and people forgot the real story of the ancient times.

In the eighteenth century, people were digging up mammoth bones and dinosaurs, and the public was consumed with curiosity about these amazing finds. Often the discoveries contradicted the current science, which was dictated by theologians. The Elite set up university and museum systems to control and manage the finds run by well-paid archeologists, curators, and professors, who were instructed to select only certain parts of the data. The data was used to construct a mythology that supports the Elite—Social Darwinism—based on the premise that humanity is always evolving from primitive to more advanced, thus eliminating the possibility of prediluvial civilizations. This lie has severely retarded human development ever since, and it unbalances the entire culture, which is why the new paradigm movement is attacking it. No wonder the stories of the Fallen Angels were covered up. *The Elite assumed the power of the Angels themselves, a Faustian pact of major proportion and consequence.* But finally and unavoidably, the evidence for previously advanced cultures is flooding in, and our deepest memories are beginning to awaken.

Underground Cities and the Survival Times

The revised construction dates for the Sphinx, Valley Temple, and the Osireion; evidence of advanced machine tooling in Egypt; and the written records of Egypt all suggest the existence of a highly advanced Elder Culture in Egypt before 10,500 B.C. Heavy rain and flooding forced the Elders to sail away in great boats to seek safety, whereas others migrated west into Libya.* The Edfu Building Texts that were catalogued during

---

* D. S. Allan and J. B. Delair, *Cataclysm! Compelling Evidence of a Cosmic Catastrophe in 9500 B.C.* (Santa Fe: Bear & Company, 1997), 183–90. There was a global magnetic reversal called the Gothenburg Flip that apparently occurred between 13,750 to 12,350 years ago, which most likely triggered the Younger Dryas, a short ice age from approximately 12,500 to 11,500 years ago.

Dynastic Egyptian times record this primary exodus, and evidence has been discovered for where they went.[11] Around this same time, somebody built thirty-six underground cities in the center of the old Turkish kingdom, Cappadocia, that a total of *200,000 people* could have inhabited comfortably. The largest one, Derinkuyu, covers 2½ squares miles; only eight levels have been thoroughly explored out of twenty known to exist; and just this one complex could have adequately housed around 20,000 people. It has complex ventilation shafts of 4-inch diameters that go down more than 200 feet into the various levels, which would have required metal-tipped drills. Tunnels linking one city to another have been found.[12] Nearby surface caves in tufa towers have red ochre meander patterns and geometrical designs that match the 8,500-year-old level of Çatal Hüyük and paintings on the walls of predynastic tombs in Egypt. These troglodytic people "were hiding not from people, but from the forces of nature."[13] It would have been dark and damp, they would have longed for light, yet at least they could survive. The lowest and oldest levels have higher ceilings than upper levels, and they were carved out by stone tools found nearby that are dated to the end of the Paleolithic. This suggests the lowest levels were "designed to suit a tall race of people."*

Myths describe Ishtar, Inanna, and Persephone descending into the house of darkness—which I once thought was Çatal Hüyük, and there are countless ancient stories about people going underground during earth changes. Çatal Hüyük excavator James Mellaart notes that murals in levels above the unexcavated lower levels have paintings of archaic reed structures, the regional ancestral houses of 11,000 years ago.[14] These are very much like the structures that were built for the Pharaoh's Heb Sed ceremony, to honor the ways of life of the ancestors, the Shemsu Hor (see figure 5.6). As Andrew Collins reports, "The epoch surrounding the climatic and geological upheavals that accompanied the last Ice Age is the only time when humanity has spent long periods of time hiding away from the outside world."[15] Further, he surmises that the Elder Culture went to Derinkuyu in

---

* Andrew Collins, *From the Ashes of Angels: The Forbidden Legacy of a Fallen Race* (London, Signet, 1997) 286–87. As an example of what younger people understand, when I told my twenty-two-year-old daughter about Derinkuyu, we both tried to figure out how they fed themselves. She said, "This must be where the technology of sprouting seeds came from." As this region was a cradle of early agriculture, she may be right.

9500 to 9000 B.C. during the climatic upheavals.[16] I suggest that the Nile was afflicted by heavy rains during a period called the Younger Dryas—10,500 to 9500 B.C.—which occurred because of the Gothenburg Flip, when there was a drop in Earth's magnetic field and increased tectonic activity and climatic variation.[17] Also, according to Allan and Delair, before the Cataclysm, the Anatolian Plateau was on the northern edge of a vast continent from northwest Africa to Asia Minor (the Aegean continent or Tyrrhenia), and north of it was a vast lake, which can be seen in figure 2.4, the tentative map of the Prediluvial World.[18] With no Mediterranean Sea in the way of getting to the Anatolian Plateau, and with the Nile Basin flooding, the Nilotic people would have moved north to this high plateau. The Egyptian Elders may have built the lower levels of these cities during this phase to have a place to move their people, especially because the Younger Dryas was a mini Ice Age. People could have survived the cold underground for a considerable time at Derinkuyu. One of the most haunting Egyptian theologies is the twelve-hour journey through the Duat, a dark and weird underground place, which may be a distant memory of this terrible time. Possibly they chose this site because it is a huge geological basin of soft tufa stone between two great volcanoes. *The more that prediluvial geography and earth changes are taken into account, the more mythology makes sense.*

Middle Eastern mythology reflects two cataclysms: the end of the Pleistocene epoch in 9500 B.C. and the Black Sea Flood in 5600 B.C. In the Bible, Noah was instructed to build the Ark because a Flood was coming, which probably refers to the 5600 B.C. flood. The sacred Iranian text, the *Zend Avesta*, contains stories that go back more than 12,000 years. For example, the flood hero Yima was instructed by Ahura Mazda to build a var—a "subterranean fortress or city."[19] Yima was told to build the var to survive amid horrible cold, which in fact prevailed in this region just before the Cataclysm. It is common knowledge that there are great tunnels and caverns under the Giza Plateau, and my teacher, Abdel Hakim, told me that he walked in them when he was a child.* Many people report

---

* Lynn Picknett and Clive Prince, *The Stargate Conspiracy* (London: Little Brown, 2000) 89–94. The authors describe extensive covert testing and explorations seeking the locations of these tunnels under the Giza Plateau.

exploring huge caves in the mountains in Peru, and there are huge underground caverns under Jerusalem. Others surmise that modern Jews and Arabs battle over the entrances to the caves because they believe the End Times are coming soon and the caves are a refuge.[20] It is no secret that huge complexes have been built underground in Colorado for the Elite awaiting an apocalypse.

The underground cities probably saved people from 10,500 to 9000 B.C., and the story of Noah's Ark probably refers to boats that were used to survive the Black Sea Flood. The legends that describe building boats also suggest that the people had some time to prepare; research shows that the Black Sea actually rose gradually over two years. Archaic legends are later compilations of stories from many different times that got jumbled together in the oral tradition, and the scribes who wrote them down often could not figure out what they referred to. However, in today's age of science, with detailed knowledge about climate and earth changes, it is possible to determine which event the mythology is describing. To summarize, the Egyptian Elders built underground cities for survival during the Younger Dryas and occupied them. Once the Cataclysm spent its fury, the rivers drained, fertile soil was again deposited, and Earth could be settled again. They moved out of the underground cities and first settled in nearby Asia Minor in Kurdistan and founded many sites, such as Nevali Çori and Çatal Hüyük.

Archaic Sacred Texts and Zarathustra

The Fallen Angels of Christianity and "the Watchers" of the Judaic traditions exist in much earlier Iranian and Indian sources. Names for the archangels confirm "the powerful relationship between Judaism and the Indo-Iranian myths found in both the *Zend Avesta* and the *Rig Veda*."[21] Andrew Collins posits that "the source material for the fall of the Watchers really had come from the rich mythology of Iran."[22] According to orthodoxy, the Iranian hero Zarathustra lived circa 600 B.C.; however, this line of prophets goes back much earlier, as I discussed in chapter 6.[23] The Magi worshiped the oldest Indo-Iranian deities, the ahuras—shining gods basking in heavenly realms—and the daevas—ahuras who fell and became earth-bound devils, or Fallen Angels.[24] This fall occurred *before* Zarathustra, who reportedly slayed the daevas because they were sexually involved with Earth women, which is classic behavior by the Fallen Angels.[25]

The Persian *Bundahishn* tells the story of a pure couple who were seduced by Angra Mainyu (by the daevas in another source), a serpent with two feet, and the couple ended up worshiping their seducer. From then on their descendants are tainted and could only be forgiven by Mithra, a Persian god we will hear much about in the next chapter. This legend of the fall and the need for salvation is obviously similar to the story of Adam and Eve in Genesis.[26] Zarathustra preached against the daevas, whereas the Magian priests followed the dualistic doctrine of both kinds of deities. Zarathustra preached that only Ahura Mazda should be worshiped, so he accused the Magi of worshiping "the Lie."[27] That is, *Zarathustra stifled further discussions about angels being involved with humans,* but these juicy stories persisted in folktales and literature. For example, the Iranian Book of Kings, the *Shahnameh*, has many wild tales of daevas who could take physical form and "lie with mortal women to produce offspring with physical characteristics that matched, almost exactly, the progeny of the Watchers in the Hebraic tradition."[28] These angels are the same as the Watchers in the Book of Enoch, a major Judeo-Christian source that was not included in the Bible but suppressed by the early Church. One of the main characters in the *Shahnameh* is Kiyumars, who is Gayomar in the *Zend Avesta*, the same "First Man" in chapter 4. These stories all interlock, and if Settegast is correct that this myth is depicted in Lascaux Cave, then these are fragments of the prediluvial creation myths that reemerged after the Cataclysm. The only way to determine which source is the earliest is to examine them by the known characteristics of different time periods, which offers much information about the qualities of each Great Age.

The Watchers, the Nephilim, and the Fallen Angels

Who were these Watchers, and what were their physical characteristics? The angels in the Book of Enoch, the Elohim (who are also in the Bible), were tall with fair skin and thick hair like white wool. They were shining like the Sun, and their eyes burned into one's soul. People were afraid to look at them because their faces were like snakes or vipers.[29] The Book of Enoch, which is extremely ancient, was not available to Christians in the West until it was translated into English in the early nineteenth century. The Nag Hamadi and the Essene Scrolls, which contain much information about the Watchers and greatly predate the Bible, were found in the midtwentieth century. The Essene Scrolls are still only partially translated because orthodox Jewish and Christian theologians conspire to keep them hidden. The Nag Hamadi Bible has been translated, and all that theologians can do is debunk it. This is not difficult, because it contains so much weird and archaic material.[30] Both texts are loaded with graphic and odd stories about the same Angels and Watchers in the Book of Enoch and in Persian and Indian literature, and so it is not possible keep hiding these strange beings. The Essene Scrolls were hidden in desert caves near Jerusalem; the Nag Hamadi scrolls were hidden in Egypt; and then, a few hundred years later, the early church fathers banned the Book of Enoch as well as other apochryphal books that include the Fallen Angels. No wonder: These books report that the source of evil in the world is these Angels, not the sins of Adam and Eve—the dogma that supports Roman Catholicism.

The Book of Enoch was left out of the Bible, and other books that contained Fallen Angel stories were severely edited. The fact is that these recently discovered early sources *are more genuine sources for early Christian beliefs than the Bible.* These finds expose the fourth-century Biblical "doctoring," which is gradually becoming self-evident no matter what the Church does. For example, the Genesis story of Eve being tempted by the Serpent is actually a garbled account of viperlike Watchers luring human females reported in the Book of Enoch and other Jewish legends. In the Book of Enoch, two hundred Watchers led by Shemyaza descended from the mountains of Northern Palestine to mingle with humanity and sample the delights of women.[31] The women gave birth to babies called Nephilim—fallen ones—giants who sinned against animals, devoured the locals and each other, and drank blood.[32] Before they became hungry, they taught the secrets of heaven, such as metalsmithing, geography, healing, astronomy, and architecture.[33] The Bible is very confusing and contradictory about God bringing on cataclysms to rid Earth of these fallen creatures. However, the Book of Enoch describes angels begging God to not destroy them, and "there is much evidence to suggest that some members of the fallen race actually survived these troubled times."[34] The most clear evidence in the Bible for the existence of these Watchers is in their

Nephilim children—the Anakim, Emim, Rephaim, and Zuzim—who were giants wandering around Canaan when Abraham and the Jews arrived circa 1800 B.C. There are reports of battles with giants in the Bible, such as David and Goliath, and Joshua sending out a spy, Caleb, to murder the giants in their chief city, Hebron.[35]

According to Roman Catholic doctrine, Eve's sin was that she ate fruit offered to her by the serpent, and thereby got the "forbidden knowledge." Because she disobeyed God, her progeny is doomed to misery, suffering, and an evil nature; just by being born, they are sinners. The Church must cleanse this sin soon after birth by baptism, and if you obey the will of God, as interpreted by the Church, you will be saved. As for Eve, St. Augustine put the blame on her—Original Sin—which makes her a temptress of the Serpent. *The stories of the Fallen Angels suggest that Eve's progeny are the children of the Watchers.*[36] The name Eve in Hebrew means "snake," and in some Jewish accounts, Eve is the "ancestral mother of the Nephilim."[37] When the early Church formulated the canon in the early fourth century, the common people knew these legends. The problem was that people who followed the Book of Enoch often became Manicheans or Gnostics. The early church fathers knew that these old tales were directly in the way of their plans to control the human path to salvation, so they developed campaigns against *heresy*, which simply means "to think differently." The Alexandrian Library was burned, many early Christians were persecuted by both Rome and the Church, and Satan was selected to be the root of all evil in the world. The Church's core creation doctrine is based on a sinful primordial mother, Eve; therefore, attention was shifted to the mother of Jesus, Mary. Meanwhile, Mary Magdalen, a priestess who was the probable wife or consort of Jesus and was at the very least one of the early disciples, became the whore.[38] Christianity is founded on the hatred of women: misogyny.[39] Once the Bible canon and the priests were organized, the Roman Catholic Church moved out with the army of Christ and claimed territory by building their churches on the ancient sacred sites. The Vatican Library and inner Church cabals are a power repository of the stolen records of conquered cultures.

Some writers argue that the Watchers and the Nephilim were extraterrestrials who came down to Earth to control and assist humanity after the

Flood—the Ancient Astronaut Theory. Collins supports a much more reasonable explanation, one that naturally emerges by staying in the context of the terrible conditions humanity had to bear during this time. The Watchers sound very much like stronger humans, masters of great shamanic skills who intervened to help totally destitute survivors.[40] The archaic sacred texts and the Bible contain stories of daughters bearing children by their fathers, sisters bearing children by brothers, and fathers being asked by Yahweh to sacrifice their sons. This reflects a terrible time when people were unable to produce enough children to keep themselves from dying out, and there was massive starvation. The stories of sacrificing children may be about Nephilim children born to distraught mothers and fathers, such as Noah, or as you will see next, Zal. Stories of giants devouring people and themselves must be from times of mind-boggling chaos, when races of people who were larger or somehow more powerful mixed with desperate survivors. Can any one of us judge people who live in times when people have to survive at all costs? So, why is the Elite—the potent brew of priests and kings—so determined to cover up these stories?

Vulture Shamanism and the Birth of Zal

Where did the angels, Watchers, and giants come from? As we've seen, Kiyumars, the hero of the *Shahnameh,* which goes back to the earliest times in Iran, is the same as Gayomar, the hero of the *Zend Avesta.* A text in the *Shahnameh,* the Birth of Zal, is an archaic story of how a line of Iranian kings was founded.[41] The legendary Kiyumars worked metal tools and weapons, irrigated the land, and founded agriculture—always the skills of the advanced people who appeared after the Cataclysm, during the Age of Cancer. It is best to just tell the story, which is based on Andrew Collins's telling of the tale from the *Shahnameh:*

In these days long ago, a king named Sam married a beautiful lady, who gave birth to a boy who was tall and shining with white hair and skin. His mother named him Zal, which means one who is aged. Sam was horrified because he thought Zal was the son of a daeva, Magi, or Demon, so he left Zal on the side of a mountain to be devoured by beasts and birds of prey. The mountain where Zal was left was the legendary home of the Simurgh, some kind of noble female *vulture or unusual bird. When the Simurgh saw the infant Zal lying exposed to the elements, instead of eating the baby or feeding it to her young, she put Zal in her nest. Her baby birds were also kind and loving to Zal, who grew up to be a fine young man. Sam assumed Zal was dead, yet one day he dreamed his son was still alive, so he prayed to the great god, Ahura Mazda, for his son's return. The Simurgh heard his prayer and knew she must return him. But Zal was unhappy because not only had the mysterious bird protected him, it had also taught him many knowledgeable things, including the language and wisdom of his own country.[42] The Simurgh gave Zal one of her wing feathers, so she could appear if ever he needed her. Zal married a foreign priestess, Rudabeh, who was a descendent of a serpent king and was much taller than Zal. She was white as ivory, and her face was like paradise. When Zal's queen was ready to give birth the first time, she was unable to deliver and was in grave danger. With his feather, Zal called in the Simurgh. She came and gave his wife a drug to free her from pain and anxiety, and she used a seer who spoke to lion-boy while he was drawn out by cesarean section!* His mother named him Rustam, and the mother was given another drug that instantly restored her health, and the shining boy became the legendary hero of Iran.*

Collins notes that "the account of the Birth of Zal was almost identical to the miraculous birth of Noah presented in the Book of Enoch," and Zal was married to Rudabeh because "they each bore very specific qualities that were deemed necessary to perpetuate the existing line of divine kings."[43] Because this story is very archaic, and Iranian mythology influenced the later Judaic tradition, Collins suggests that "a much older primary source was responsible for both stories."[44] Then he explores the possibility that with the Simurgh, the myth preserves the story of "a much earlier shamanistic culture" that practiced vulture shamanism.[45] The First Man of Lascaux Cave is bird-headed, and he has a bird on his staff, which he has dropped. Regarding the birth of Zal, his marriage is arranged with another Watcher, he becomes the legendary hero of Iran, and the central player is the Simurgh. Collins argues that the Simurgh was one of many shamans who wore vulture feathers, and I totally agree with him, because this form of

---

* Collins, *From the Ashes of Angels*, 109–22. Where I use the word "seer" for clairvoyant, in his text, Collins uses "hypnotist."

shamanism is still being practiced today. Vulture shamanism would have been critically important for burial needs after the Cataclysm, as well as an ideal shamanic practice for traveling to the otherworld. Collins wonders whether "the Watchers really were distorted memories of a shamanistic culture who had once inhabited a mountainous region, perhaps in Iran, and possessed a knowledge of science and technology well beyond that of the less evolved races of the Near East?"[46] I have no doubt this is true, because many weird archaic tales make sense only by shamanic analysis. Let us imagine this:

Imagine being a family living in the lower levels of Derinkuyu. The Catalcysm has occurred, there are constant small or large earth movements, and way above, the winds are fierce and the cold is numbing. It is the warmer time of year when there are only a few months to plant, harvest, and hunt, and it is your turn to venture out with a small group for food. As you trudge along, keeping an eye out for surface caves for safety, the cloudy sky is darkened by circles of vultures watching to see whether your group brings out a body for excarnation. Not long ago, the land was littered with bodies of animals and people, and the vultures multiplied and cleansed it. If vultures had not consumed the carrion, the people would have died of disease, and so you learned to respect the vulture for cleansing the bodies of your loved ones. Birth and death were intertwined, and the vulture was the great mother who fostered life that she recycled. In turn, she didn't attack healthy animals and people, and after she cleansed the dead bodies, her spirit moved through the higher realms of heaven with their essence returning to the stars. Sometimes she took you on a flying journey to the spirit land, which taught you that death was not to be feared. Sometimes you feared the vulture, which can strip a body clean in an hour, a potent symbol for facing death and undergoing shamanic dismemberment. The vulture teaches that the only indestructable thing in the body is the spirit.

Bird shamans are also found in Sumerian and Babylonian sources, such as the fabulous winged bird-men of Mesopotamia, the Annunaki, sons of heaven and Earth, who were also called shining serpents.[47] The Kharsag Tablets are the oldest texts from Sumeria, and they describe a cataclysm that sounds exactly like the Black Sea Flood. Christopher O'Brien, the scholar

Fig. 7.2.
Vulture Shaman.

who translated the tablets, says that this flood caused a dispersal that resulted in the foundation of the Mesopotamian city-states, which is in agreement with *Noah's Flood.*[48] Collins thinks this occurred around 5500 B.C. and argues that the original homeland was Kurdistan. This is important, because between 9500 and 8000 B.C. Kurdistan "produced some of the first known examples of animal domestication, metallurgy, painted pottery, proto-agriculture, trade, urbanization and written language."[49] Turkish scholar Mehrdad Izady says Kurdistan "went through an unexplained stage of accelerated technological evolution, prompted by yet uncertain forces."[50] Collins proposes that this acceleration was caused by the Watchers, and he substantiates this possibility by reporting on the Shanidar Cave in Kurdistan, which has sixteen levels that have been occupied for 100,000 years. A section of the site dated to 8870 B.C. contains a deposit of "mostly articulated wings of at least seventeen birds, including vultures."[51] The on-site archeologist concluded that they are wings used by bird shamans, and she linked them with vulture shamanism practiced at Çatal Hüyük, where "a human figure dressed in a vulture skin" is depicted.[52]

Are the Watchers derived from the Egyptian Elder culture that survived by living underground at Derinkuyu or underground in Egypt? As we've seen, Çatal Hüyük has much affinity with the Minoans who share attributes with early Dynastic Egypt. Andrew Collins's argument that Nevali Çori was an Elder Culture religious center is very compelling. The

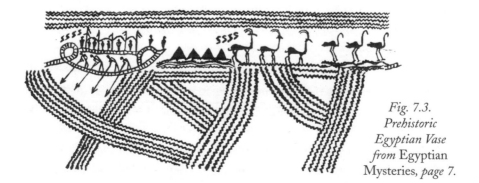

Fig. 7.3.
Prehistoric
Egyptian Vase
from Egyptian
Mysteries, *page 7.*

Blank phase on the Nile suggests that many of the people lived away from the Nile for 5,000 years and returned when it was possible to establish their culture again. Figure 7.3 depicts a painting on a prehistoric vase from at least 5000 B.C. from the Delta region of northern Egypt.[53] These vases are similar to painted pottery from Elam in southeastern Iraq, which points to the time when the Elder Culture left the sites in the Middle East, then dispersed after the Black Sea Flood and returned to the Nile. It shows people taking boats on the Nile all the way to the headwaters of Lake Victoria. The conventional belief is that the four triangles are African mountains. I think they are pyramids, which has obvious implications regarding Giza Plateau. More answers about these early massive waves of cultural dispersal come out when we return to the global seafaring civilization that was breaking down in 10,500 B.C. It was nearly destroyed in 9500 B.C., so there must be other places where people went underground. Next we will consider evidence from the Altiplano of Peru and Bolivia, where the most complete library of a prediluvial culture was found in 1961.

The Mysterious Stone Library of Ica

In 1961, a cache of engraved stones was found near the Nasca Plain in Peru, when a flood of the Ica River uncovered a cave that contained tens of thousands of these stones. In the region where they were found, small and large bones of prehistoric animals have been found on or near the desert surface. The stones are a complete library of the astronomy, geography, medicine, and lifeways of a remote humanity that *coexisted with dinosaurs of the Cenozoic and Mesozoic eras,* that is, as many as 185 million years ago. Soon after the discovery, some of the stones were brought to the distinguished Dr. Cabrera Darquea—who, being a physician, medical professor, founder and director of Casa de la Cultura of Ica, and a biology and anthropology professor at Gonzaga University in Ica—was eminently qualified to evaluate them.[54] After repeatedly attempting to get Peruvian and foreign archeologists and anthropologists to examine the stones to no avail, Cabrera investigated the nearby area in the Ocucaje Desert. He found a full paleontologic measure of fossils of fauna and flora of the Mesozoic era—130 to 185 million years ago—in sedimentary rock a mile from where the cache was found. The strata contain human bones, triceratop bones, and a complete skeleton of a phitosaur, a reptile similar to today's crocodile. This discovery on 14 October 1984 verifies the coexistence of people and dinosaurs, as is depicted on the Stones of Ica. This scientifically confirms that people had lived with saurians at the end of the Mesozoic era.[55] J. B. Delair and E. F. Oppé report on various researchers who have found jumbled remains of Pleistocene animals and humans around the Altiplano, and some of the human skeletons are of gigantic size, suggesting the Giants and the Watchers.[56] Immediately, Dr. Cabrera presented his findings in a lecture for an international academic conference in 1985, and he was ignored.

The cache was found by huaqueros, local indigenous people who search for artifacts to sell, and this find was a goldmine for them. The local people were also fascinated with them. They recognized them as relics of their most distant ancestors, and they began making their own versions, which distorted the credibility of Dr. Cabrera. The Peruvian establishment has been carrying on an ambitious debunking program by setting up the local peasants as the makers. Dr. Cabrera points out that the local peasants would have to be biology professors, surgeons, and master astronomers to craft the stones, and that at first they sold them for much less money than they'd need to charge if they had carved them.[57] Cabrera submitted thirty-three stones to a mining laboratory to analyze the nature of the stone and the antiquity of the engravings. Geologist Eric Wolf reports that the stones were shaped by water in the rivers, and they are andesites—igneous rocks with chemical components that have been mechanically subjected to great pressure, which increased their compactness and specific weight. They are almost as hard as quartz, yet they have the perfect surface for carving, because a fine patina of natural oxidation coated them over time. There is no irregular wear on the incisions, and there is a uniform patina over the carving, which *proves they are very old.*[58] The baffling, gigantic interlocking stones of Tiahuanaco are also andesites.[59]

Other engineers who tested the stones agreed with Eric Wolf. They added that the stones are from lava flows of the Mesozoic, which was terminated by cataclysms, and then the Cenozoic began. In 1966, archeologist Alejandro Pezzia Assereto of the Patronatio Nacional de Archeologia del Peru was present when one of the same engraved stones was discovered in a pre-Incaic grave.[60] This discovery proves that these stones are at least 2,000 years old, but they are probably much older, because the pre-Inca culture frequently buried ancestral power objects in their tombs. The content of the stones indicates they are ancient, but maybe the Ica debunkers would like us to believe people coexisted with dinosaurs only 2,000 years ago. The Ica stones are ancient, they cannot possibly be fakes, and they are one of the *most important archeological discoveries of all time.* The Peruvian establishment forced the local huaqueros to declare publicly they'd made them all. They agreed to this lying because they traffic in archeological objects, which is a sticky trade.[61] The stones are extremely detailed and specific, and it is not at all difficult to differentiate the fakes from the real ones. Fortunately, once Cabrera realized his find was being debunked, he bought every ancient engraved stone he could get his hands on. He has dedicated his life to studying them and getting the world to pay attention. He is the direct descendant of the Spaniard who founded Ica in 1563, and the world is very lucky he cares. He exhibited 5,000 of the stones at the Casa de Cultura to awaken interest, again to little avail. Maybe some of the wakas we discussed in chapter 5 that the Jesuit priests looted when they came into Peru and Bolivia after the conquerors were these same stones. Possibly the Vatican has its own collection.

Dr. Cabrera is an academic biologist and anthropologist, so his dating of the stones and his subsequent interpretation is grounded in the conventional Darwinian paradigm based on the geological column. Based on orthodoxy, the stones depict fauna and flora of the Cenozoic and Mesozoic eras. This means they are a *library of the advanced arts of a civilization more than 185 million years old!* Dr. Cabrera, himself confounded by the stones and the great span of time involved, concluded that the people who carved them must have been a highly advanced race from a planet in the Pleiades. He concludes that they were advanced teachers of the indigenous Peruvians and left for their planet before or during a great cataclysm.[62] However, the mental fog around such fantastic findings lifts when we seek answers about who they were without resorting to the Ancient Astronaut Theory. I have noticed that people who have not experienced shamanic flight journeys in the alternate reality themselves often conclude that fantastic dismemberment or flight images must be signs of spacemen. Although I differ with his hypothesis, the person who knows the most about the stones is Dr. Cabrera, who has studied them for more than thirty years. I have not examined them in person; however, Dr. Cabrera carefully photographed and diagrammed them so that others can consider them. Guy Berthault's suggested revision of the Geological Column and Allan and Delair's Revised Chronology for the Miocene and Pliocene epochs lead to other possibilities for dating this cache. Based on the Revised Chronology, *these stones may be the library of a people at the peak of their evolution circa 15,000 to 10,500 B.C. who were masters of the classic forbidden arts.*

I speculate that the Ica astronomers at some point must have realized a Cataclysm was coming because of the unusual changes 12,500 years ago. The stones might be a library they used for teaching purposes that they buried in a safe place. They might have hoped that they could find it after Earth settled down. The whole region has huge caves in the tufa rock, which were ideal for underground cave shelters or possibly even cities such as Derinkuyu in Turkey. However, unlike the Anatolian Plateau, where Derinkuyu is located, the Altiplano uplifted thousands of feet in the Cataclysm or later. Many caves there have some of the most astonishing Late Pleistocene deposits that contain mixtures of humans and Miocene/ Pliocene deposits, which is evidence that few if any people survived in this location.[63] These stone carvers were not primitive, as can be seen by the information on the stones, and they would have known that stone was the only medium that could survive. I strongly suspect the archaic Icans were the same prediluvial culture as the Tiahuanicans because they both used andesite as their sacred medium, which is very hard to cut, and their remains are so advanced that they are totally baffling. To consider the stones, we will examine an astronomical stone and two global maps of Earth as it was at least 12,000 years ago.

Ancient Astronomers Study
the Sky and Global Maritime Maps

This stone (figure 7.4) has three lateral triangle faces that depict astronomers searching the sky with telescopes, and its triangular superior face is a zodiac encircled by a cometlike object with a long tail. Cabrera has deciphered the symbolic language—"glyptolithics"—by studying 12,000 stones. This is too complex to describe here; however, my analysis is partially based on Cabrera's linguistic decipherment. Readers will not be surprised to hear that Cabrera's books are not available in the United States, so three of the stones are illustrated and discussed. In the top of the first stone, Cabrera sees a thirteen-constellational zodiac, adding the Pleiades to the current twelve constellations based on the gliptolithic symbols for planets and stars. A "comet" coming between Sirius and Regulus in the Leo constellation and traveling out the opposite direction through the Pleiades constellation during a solar eclipse is being observed with *telescopes*.[64] He says, when the comet "passed close to the Earth, it had picked up human life and taken it to the constellation of the Pleiades."[65] Cabrera believes this is gliptolithic man facing an imminent cataclysm on Earth, who returned to the Pleiades. We have to respect this, because many indigenous people around the world claim Pleiadian origins, as well as that they had a calendar that was regulated by the Pleiades before the Cataclysm.* However, according to my training, these Pleiadian connections are not physical—they are in another dimension. Dr. Cabrera had many discussions with astronomers in Paris about his interpretation who agree that this stone depicts truly astonishing levels of astronomical knowledge.[66]

Fig. 7.4. Three views of Phaeton on an Ica Stone, adapted from the cover and illustration pages 41–49 of The Message of the Engraved Stones of Ica.

Could this stone be a depiction of the supernova fragments (Phaeton) moving through space toward the solar system about 12,000 years ago as theorized by Allan and Delair? If so, how did the people have enough time to carve it, as well as the others, during the earth changes? They could have detected the astronomically near supernova, which exploded sometime between 11,000 to 14,000 years ago, because

---

* Vincent H. Gaddis, *American Indian Myths and Mysteries* (New York: Indian Head Books, 1977), 9–10; Richard Rudgley, *The Lost Civilizations of the Stone Age* (New York: The Free Press, 1999), 100. Rudgley notes that the common heritage from the Pleiades is so widespread that it dates back more than 40,000 years.

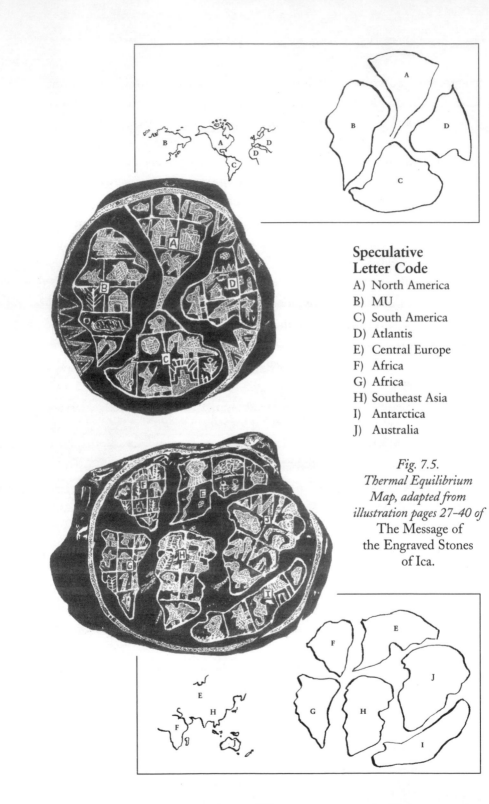

Speculative Letter Code

A) North America
B) MU
C) South America
D) Atlantis
E) Central Europe
F) Africa
G) Africa
H) Southeast Asia
I) Antarctica
J) Australia

Fig. 7.5.
Thermal Equilibrium
Map, adapted from
illustration pages 27–40 of
The Message of
the Engraved Stones
of Ica.

it would have taken from a few hundred years to a thousand years to traverse interstellar space to the edges of the solar system.[67] Next—as a chill creeps up my back—I remember that Allan and Delair say that the persistent connection between the Pleiades and ancient cataclysms exists because it "is an indication of the celestial direction from which Phaeton arrived—*from that of the Pleiades and Orion*."[68] Based on records kept by Arab and Coptic historians regarding the Leo constellation, Andrew Collins says they concluded that the great event took place during the Age of Leo, which fits with Plato's date and Allan and Delair's conclusions.[69] Does this stone depict the ancient Watcher astronomers observing Phaeton arriving?* *This stone may depict Phaeton coming to Earth in the Orion-Pleiadian direction during the Age of Leo.* I realize there is confusion about whether Phaeton is coming in or leaving by the Pleiades, and there is room for interpretation, yet all these elements cannot be just coincidental.

Dr. Cabrera has two stones that are "story" maps of the world—that is, they contain information about the quality of civilization on various continents. Some of Hapgood's maps probably depict the seafaring world during the Early Holocene epoch, when the prediluvial seafarers would also have needed global maps. Because the Ica stones accurately depict fauna and flora going back 185 millions years ago or more, these two maps may depict the prediluvial world sometime within this time frame. Regarding the first stone, Dr. Cabrera believes that it is a map of gliptolithic man's home planet in the Pleiades, and I respectfully disagree. I believe it shows Earth during some phase of the Pliocene or Miocene epochs—from 29 million years ago to about 20,000 years ago—because the proportion of land to sea is great (which is also the case in Allan and Delair's tentative reconstruction of the prediluvial world in figure 2.4). The first Ica stone map shows the Western Hemisphere above and the Eastern below. Above the Western Hemisphere is depicted a letter-coded drawing of Earth, with a corresponding letter-coded drawing of the landmasses on the stone. Similarly, below, the Eastern Hemisphere is shown as a letter-coded drawing with a corresponding letter-coded drawing of the landmasses on the stone. The Ica stone continents are

---

* Allan and Delair, *Cataclysm!*, 210. The authors say that after the Vela supernova exploded, it would have taken between a few hundred to a thousand years to reach the solar system.

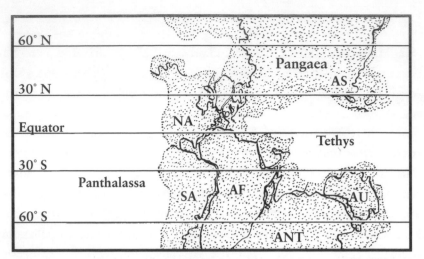

Fig. 7.6. Pangaea, adapted from figure 7.1 of New Views on an Old Planet.

rather accurate for current North and South America, yet they are very different for the Eastern Hemisphere, which suggests greater subduction, uplifting, and splitting apart in that hemisphere, which, in fact, occurred during the past 185 million years.

Figure 7.6 is a speculative map of Pangea, the proposed supercontinent 220 million years ago, by Cambridge geologist Tjeerd H. Van Andel. It is based on conventional geological theory. I ask readers to take a moment to compare Allan and Delair's tentative map of the prediluvial world in figure 2.4 with Van Andel's map of Pangaea, and then compare them with this Ica stone map. The symbols on the continents can be read by glyptolithics (even if it is a map of a planet in the Pleiades), and Cabrera says that this is a map of a *planet in a state of thermic equilibrium* inhabited by humans who are technological and adept at managing its resources. Plants and animals, *including dinosaurs* and domesticated animals, are prevalent, large cities exist, and there are pyramids that capture, accumulate, and distribute energy.[70] Compare the artistic rendition of the pyramids on the 6,000-year-old Egyptian vase depicted in figure 7.3. The glyphs indicate that this is a "planet that is ideal for human life."[71] Like the astronomical stone, men are projecting energy into the cosmos. They are depicted uniting with serpents and assuming various animal forms, which suggests that *they are shamans working with serpentine energy.* It is impossible to exactly date this map, except to say it is precataclysmic, and it is loaded with climatic, paleontological, and geological information.

In the second map (figure 7.7), Earth is in a very different state. The Eastern Hemisphere is radically different, yet the Western Hemisphere, with Mu and Atlantis, is recognizable. The second Ica stone map shows the Western Hemisphere above, and the Eastern Hemisphere below. Above the Western Hemisphere, Earth is depicted with a letter-coded drawing of the landmasses on the stone to the right. Below the Eastern Hemisphere is also a letter-coded depiction of Earth with a letter-coded drawing of the landmasses on the stone to the right. By glyptolithic analysis, Cabrera posits that this is Earth in a *closed thermic system* at a "critical point at which the water vapor precipitated in the form of unending rain that released a correspondingly large amount of mechanical energy that resulted in the beginning of the shift of the enormous continental masses; that is, a cataclysm of monstrous proportions."[72] The closed thermal system is depicted by the thick waves of water around the maps—in the atmosphere—that causes a vapor cap or "black body formed by the clouds;" and the thermic energy of the Sun is captured but cannot radiate back out.* The map depicts even more continental landmass in relation to seas, and it might depict Earth before a great cataclysm in the remote past, or more recently. Possibly it is 10,500 B.C. when the critical earth changes started. By glyptoliths, it records a difficult time for glyptolithic man, and certainly it is a reminder of too much technology. Notice there are no ice caps. Cabrera points out that the pyramids used for power are on the continents in the first map, but in this map, the bottoms of the pyramids aim to the sky, "indicating that part of the energy of the atmosphere is being captured in a complex technological system."[73] The vertices of the pyramids point toward the continents, indicating that humans use the power, and the strange canals seem to be part of this system. Dr. Cabrera is certain that the makers of the Ica stones are the same first people of the Andes who built Tiahuanaco and other Peruvian-Bolivian cyclopean ruins, which suggests a link between the global seafaring culture and the pyramids in these maps. Graham Hancock notes that the "clean-sided

---

* Javier Darquea Cabrera, *The Message of the Engraved Stones of Ica* (Lima: privately published, 1989), 152. I assume readers are aware of the implications of the closed thermic system map regarding current discussions about global warming.

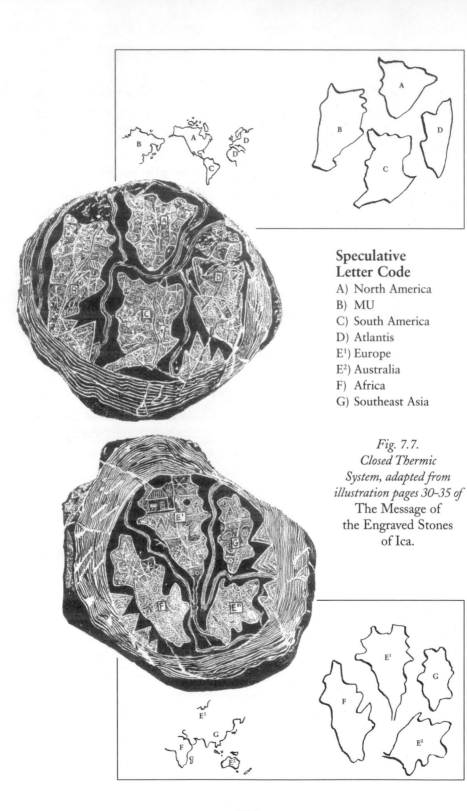

**Speculative
Letter Code**

A) North America
B) MU
C) South America
D) Atlantis
E¹) Europe
E²) Australia
F) Africa
G) Southeast Asia

*Fig. 7.7.
Closed Thermic
System, adapted from
illustration pages 30–35 of*
The Message of
the Engraved Stones
of Ica.

step-pyramid of earth faced with large andesite blocks" at Tiahuanaco "might have functioned as some kind of arcane device or machine" that archeologists think has something to do with fast-flowing water, because it has a "complex network of zigzagging stone channels, lined with fine ashlars."[74] Interpreting the glyphs, Cabrera sees robotic controllers who are dealing with failing, overly managed, controlled agriculture and animal domestication; houses where there are groups of humanoids, called the notharctus, who are having their intelligence raised to the minimal level; and the mysterious scientific, cognitive men who live in the megalopolis, especially in South America.[75] They could fly, and it seems to be a time when humans lived on Earth during an environmental crisis.

Other stones depict advanced surgical methods, such as brain and heart transplants, advanced knowledge of human and animal reproductive cycles, and even dinosaur farms! Gliptolithic man did not quiver in fear of the great reptiles—they understood the dinosaurs' physiology, and they used advanced technology and used them for food![76] I began this chapter by stating that humans have the potential to create reality with thought, yet it would appear that these people were *controlling* the planet with technology, just as today. The mysterious Stones of Ica must be prediluvial, and *I think they may depict the core basis of the forbidden knowledge of the Fallen Angels.* As discussed in chapter 3, engineer Chris Dunn in *The Giza Power Plant* has built a powerful case that the Dynastic Egyptians used power tools, and the Great Pyramid was one of their power plants. The depictions of pyramids as power plants on the Ica stones supports Dunn's theories and even adds more information.

Charles Hapgood investigated a 5,000-year-old ceramic collection found at Acambaro, Mexico, called the Julsrud Collection.[77] It depicts humans interacting with dinosaurs, like the Ica stones; however, carbon dating indicates they are approximately 7,000 years old.[78] In 1972, just before the first edition of *Mystery in Acambaro* was released, Hapgood was visited by a few archeologists who showed him slides of the Ica stones and a few stones that Dr. Cabrera had loaned to them. Hapgood could see many parallels between the two collections. About the Acamboro collection, Hapgood says, "One obtains from the collection itself a sense of the dark forces within the human psyche, an emphasis on the negative power of fear, and a suggestion of witchcraft in an elementary state of development *There may also have been a true, positive rapport with nature that our society does not understand.*"[79] We have reached the point at which researchers must start looking at these kinds of wild findings and seriously evaluate them. This means studying artifacts from human cultures thousands of years ago that suggest levels of advancement contrary to the conventional historical paradigm. One of the most credible new theories is engineer Christopher Dunn's theory that the Great Pyramid of Giza was a power plant.

The Great Pyramid Is a Power Plant!

Like Sir William Flinders Petrie, the great Egyptologist, Chris Dunn studied granite structures and artifacts at Giza Plateau, as well as stone vessels made of diorite, basalt, quartz crystal, and metamorphic schist, some of which are more than 5,000 years old. Both Petrie and Dunn conclude that the makers had used motorized machining.[80] In his day, more than 100 years ago, Petrie could not imagine how they did it, so he wrote detailed descriptions of examples of stonecutting that could not have been accomplished with hand tools or any tool technology of his day. This enabled modern engineer Chris Dunn to examine Petrie's evidence and study the material in Egypt himself. Dunn concludes that ultrasonic machining was the only method they could have used to cut and drill the stone.[81] He has written many articles about his conclusions that have received a lot of notice. He points out that these machine-made artifacts lend support to the theory that the Great Pyramid was built by an advanced civilization.[82] With that in mind, he examined the Florida laboratories of Edward Leedskalnin, who built Coral Castle by lifting and maneuvering blocks of coral weighing as much as *30 tons*. Leedskalnin claimed that he knew the secrets of the ancient Egyptians.[83] Dunn believes that he figured out how to work with Earth's gravitational pull by aligning the magnetic elements within the coral blocks; that is, he built an *antigravity device!*[84] Dunn published more articles and gave interviews about Leedskalnin's discoveries. Then he began working on the big question: What was providing the energy to run the ultrasonic tools 5,000 years ago in Egypt?

The Great Pyramid was built at the center of Earth's landmass, and because the builders used *exactly the dimensions of Earth in its design in that*

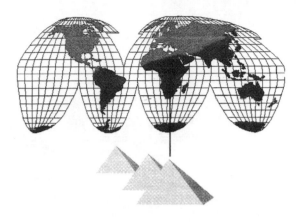

Fig. 7.8.
The Great Pyramid in the
Center of Earth's Landmass,
figure 32 of The Giza
Power Plant.

location, the Pyramid is a harmonic integer of the planet; that is, it responds to Earth's vibrations by resonance and harmonics.[85] Resonance means that it is in sympathetic vibration with the planet, which makes it a *coupled oscillator* that can draw on Earth's energy once it is primed—*the Great Pyramid vibrates with Earth.*[86] Chris Dunn's theory is too complex to cover here; however, he deserves a serious read. As he summarized his work, "The Great Pyramid was a geomechanical power plant that responded sympathetically with the Earth's vibrations and converted that energy into electricity. They used the electricity to power their civilization, which included machine tools with which they shaped hard, igneous rock."[87] Until somebody comes up with some other way that they cut the stone and lifted multiton blocks, Chris Dunn's research must be examined and tested.

This chapter began with some ideas about creating realities with thought; we followed the activities of the Fallen Angels and considered the Ica stones; and we end with the Great Pyramid as a power plant. I have described some truly incredible discoveries that are being covered up by the Global Elite. The question is, Why? Next, we will observe how the Elite chess game is played. Of course, they are the Kings, Queens, Knights, and Bishops, and the common people are the pawns. However, all of us living on the planet are now on the chess board because we are global again. As you can see with the Stones of Ica, when human civilization attained this level before, pyramids were central in the technology. Now that we have considered a technological idea on what the Great Pyramid was used for, and if it is so, *how* did they obtain the technology? This question will be answered in chapter 9; however, we can't approach it until we first understand how the Global Elite game is played. Enter the Global Elite plan for the Age of Aquarius.

8

The Stargate Conspiracy & the Kosmokrater

With the changes that will be wrought,
true Americanism, the universal thought that is
expressed and manifested in the brotherhood of man,
as in the Masonic order, will be the eventual rule
in the settlement of affairs in the world.

—*Edgar Cayce*[1]

Support the Heretics!

The comprehensive cover-up of the real story of the Fallen Angels, the Stones of Ica, and the Acambaro ceramics are all excellent examples of Global Elite information-control programs. The archeological remains of the advanced prediluvial global culture are being lost to the public, and we have been educated with a stupid story about our past that makes us crazy. Great researchers such as Charles Hapgood or Dr. Cabrera are greeted with total silence and debunked. However, in spite of the seeming success of this program, which is now thousands of years old, many people these days are figuring out how the Elite function. There are hundreds of books that report in great detail about the Elite's financial, social, and political programs, such as those by David Icke and William Cooper, which I've included in my bibliography. The details of what the Elite did, where, and when are tedious. No matter how much they are observed, they just change into new forms, because they are *shape-shifters*. The only way out of the control is for the individual to decode the actual program. Later, we will look at how any one of us can transmute this serpentine energy, because it only takes form amid ignorance and confusion. Right now, I want to show how the Global Elite program functions in our times and how it got started in the first place.

The Elite keep one step ahead of people by carrying on an elaborate disinformation campaign. For example, they harass and debunk anyone who gets too close to scientific or spiritual information that can free people. When anybody gets close to divulging the secrets of harmonic resonance, such as Christopher Dunn, one of the Elite creative agents—writers, filmmakers, or media stars—simply picks the most flawed part of a person's research (all research has some weak points) and blows it all out of proportion to make the person look like a fool. Another favorite tactic is to convince the public that an extraordinary happening was faked, such as the Crop Circles in England or the Stones of Ica. The goal of this program is to continually *dishearten and disempower* the public, and then people will lose hope and even forget there is any hope. For example, the book *Giza: The Truth* attempts to take down Christopher Dunn, yet he was able to refute this successfully, and he is not going away.[2] *There is a continual mental wounding going on that tests the fortitude of inventors and avid seekers.* The public gets excited about a new theory and gets turned on by the possibility that they might get some information that could improve the planet or answer some deep questions, and then the theory gets shot down and its inventor is crucified. Always, the most direct route to cosmic resonance is to feel and emote love from our hearts, which is why the disheartening campaign is being run. However, you can bypass all this simply by paying special attention to theories or individuals that the Elite debunk.

The Elite will show you the way! Just turn your attention to the *heretics!* Whenever an exciting discovery is greeted with stone-cold silence by the media and academia, assume it may be of extreme importance. Certain finds, such as the Stones of Ica, are emphasized to teach about how to study in reverse of the Elite program, which stupefies the public. Another tactic of the Elite chess game is to push a dunce into the limelight, such as Thomas Edison, while secretly culling the mind of the real genius, Nicola Tesla. Tesla's resonant energy technologies were stolen, and his discoveries were developed in secret such as the "Philadelphia Experiment" in which a ship and its crew were vibrated into another dimension during the Second World War. Albert Einstein and his bomb were the focus of the twentieth century, whereas Wilhelm Reich's research on the primary life force—orgone energy—was culled. Reich was a psychoanalyst who discovered the organizing force that enables the soul to take bodily form, and his discoveries could have been used to scientifically describe what real health is. Those who go against the official paradigm live a life of great pain, yet everything would shift if smart people turned their attention to the real inventors. Charles Hapgood was shunned by his own colleagues until his death once he published *Maps of the Ancient Sea Kings;* Wilhelm Reich died in prison after his laboratory was destroyed and his books went out of print; and Nicola Tesla died penniless in a ratty hotel. It is ironic that Albert Einstein wrote the foreword for the first edition of *Path of the Pole* by Charles Hapgood.[3]

The Stargate Conspiracy

The Stargate Conspiracy by Lynn Picknett and Clive Prince was published in England in 2000. This deeply disturbing and insightful work deciphers the Elite plans for the new religion of the Age of Aquarius and exposes how "the CIA, Britain's MI5, occult groups, and even some of the world's top scientists" are working together in a vast conspiracy that exploits the human "craving for contact with the numinous and the ineffable."[4] Of course, in light of Egypto-Judaic conflicts of the Age of Aries and Judeo-Christian-Islamic conflicts of the Age of Pisces, this is not new. Whenever the Great Ages shift, the new core beliefs arising among the people seem to be absolutely unique. The latest one is seeking spacemen, but *extra-terrestrials are just a new form of the Fallen Angels and the Watchers.* The way to follow the moves in this elaborate chess match is to never forget for one second that the strategist is a huge political and religious conspiracy that "checkmates" anybody who moves independently. Because humans seek spiritual contact above all other things, *religious movements are where the con-spiracy actually comes from*—politics is merely the front. The last time we arrived at this point was when the Roman Catholic Church superceded Judaism in the West; the obvious question is, "what's the main religion this time?" Like a reverse Exodus, the hot spot is the geodetic center of the plan-et, the Giza Plateau, while riots in Jerusalem distract the public eye. On the Giza Plateau, a fanatical search for the Hall of Records is going on. Millions are hooked into the drama because they seek the almighty dollar with its pyramid capped by the all-seeing eye; *linked by symbolism, millions are energetically involved in this mystical treasure hunt.* Actually, the search for the Hall of Records is a modern form of the Arthurian quest for the Holy Grail, "the ancient, elusive object of the heart's desire," and when it is found, "somehow magically the whole of our civilization will be transformed."[5]

Many new paradigm writers are part of the Egyptological counter-culture that is working to prove that the Sphinx is very ancient and the Pyramids are the relics of an ancient advanced civilization. The conspiracy effectively uses this counterculture, which "has now effectively become a new orthodoxy with an equally unyielding doctrine of its own."[6] Popular writers such as Graham Hancock and Robert Bauval are knights seeking the Holy Grail, and it is nearly impossible to know whether they realize that they've been swept into the mythical quest, or whether they are cynically orchestrating it. I stopped teaching in Egypt in 1996 when I began to realize something very confusing was going on around me. *The Stargate Conspiracy* has made it possible for me to understand my own experiences in Egypt from 1991 through 1996. We are all part of the quest that is taking shape as the Aquarian energy permeates the planetary field. We can grasp our heart's desire, rather than be pawns in a very nasty and transparent global game. Let's have a look at some of the main players.

The Sirius Mystery by Robert Temple (1976) is an erudite book about Egyptian, African, Greek, Babylonian, and Sumerian legends. Temple's main thesis is that the Dogon culture of central Africa were given their symbols and rituals by visitors from the Sirius star system.[7] It gave me some new ideas about what I call the *Sirian mentality;* however, I paid little attention to the spacemen, because any shaman can go to Sirius anytime he or she wants to, which was obviously a favorite sport for the Dogon. Robert Temple radically revised the book for a new edition in 1998, and in it he claims that because of the initial publication, the CIA harassed him for fifteen years, MI5 monitored him; and he was approached by a major Mason, who asked him to join the fraternity so they could discuss his book as equals and keep the discussions private.[8] Regardless of this odd interest in his work by secret societies, *The Sirius Mystery* has greatly influenced the New Age movement because countless people who read it honestly believe the Dogon and Egyptians are extraterrestrial cultures. I thought this was mere silliness on the part of a very intelligent man. I've been in contact with Sirians and other stellar intelligences since childhood, and they are energy forms without bodies.[9] The realms they exist in are nonphysical and nonlocational, which means they are always there and accessible if the doorway can be found. I've seen "spaceships" that were always near military bases or research labs such as Los Alamos, and I am sure that "sightings" are scientific conjurings, which unfortunately are sometimes projected into people's bedrooms. The scariest thing I ever saw in my life was when our family was driving on New Mexico 25 by White Sands testing ground. Suddenly, a mile or two to the left side of the car, a thousand feet high or more, a giant black shining vulture manifested out of thin, clear daylight and flew along by the side of the car! We didn't know what it was until we saw the Stealth Bomber rolling out of a huge hanger and wheeled over a gigantic red pentagram on television a few years later. Mass culture is being conditioned to believe extraterrestrials are real and that they are here now. Maybe so, but I think it is a Global Elite disinformation program.

There also is a widespread belief within the counterculture that Mars hosted an ancient civilization that was connected to the ancient Egyptians. This leads to the conclusion that "the ancient gods were extraterrestrials— *and they're back.*"[10] *The Sirius Mystery* is the grandfather book of many Egyptology books of the new paradigm because it convinced a lot of intelligent people that extraterrestrials influenced Africa.[11] This suggests that the ancient Egyptians could not have built the Pyramids, and such airhead nonsense encourages people to wait for gods in the sky who will come and unleash an apocalypse. *This is advanced catastrophobia all dressed up for the New Age!* The insights offered by Lynn Picknett, Clive Prince, and Andrew Collins have inspired me to clearly describe my own stellar connections. I have not done so until now because these connections are sacred. These authors have helped me realize that the Ancient Astronaut Theory feeds a very dangerous conspiracy that has sucked in countless unwitting people. The agenda is to convince the public that extraterrestrials colonized Earth and Mars, and they are coming back as soon as the Hall of Records is found at Giza. Of course, they will rescue the Chosen People of God before the prophesied cataclysm and take them away in spaceships. How could such silliness ever have gained any credibility? Enter the Sleeping Prophet.

Edgar Cayce and the Search for the Hall of Records

The famed "Sleeping Prophet" Edgar Cayce is the driving force behind the search for the Hall of Records, and he timed this discovery with the *coming* earth changes, which injected fear and urgency into the quest.[12] I ask readers to reread the opening quote for this chapter, which shows that *Cayce's agenda was Masonic.* Cleverly presented to the public as a simple Christian who was deeply disturbed by the weird occult information that came through his trances, Cayce in fact had already been exposed to the information. He had a prodigious memory and worked in bookstores where he read many esoteric books. He was exposed to many occultists who sought him out. Cayce and his father were high enough up in the Masons to found new lodges, and they were salesmen of Masonic insurance.[13] Cayce advised Woodrow Wilson on the formation of the League of Nations. He was introduced to Wilson by Colonel Edmund Starling, then head of the Secret Service, who was a friend and possible fellow Mason along with Cayce's father.[14] The content in Cayce's readings is repackaged, moldy, old esotericism, such as the works of Alice Bailey, Madame Blavatsky, and H. C. Randall Stevens.[15] Channels often bring through material they have already studied, because esoteric data is the perennial wisdom, and this process is a form of teaching and rediscovery for the channels and their groups. The problem with Cayce is that he was presented as an innocent and sleepy Christian, and *ordinary good-hearted people took his occult ideas and prophecies as Gospel truth.* The search for Cayce's fabled Hall of Records is central to the Elite agenda, and the search is a fabulous tool for cloaking the conspiracy. Most people can't believe that intelligence agencies are involved, because such psychic quests are "woo-woo" psychobabble, which the Elite consistently debunk.

Cayce's son, Hugh Lynn Cayce, started the well-funded Association for Research and Enlightenment (ARE) to house, analyze, and promulgate Cayce's readings.* ARE has been deeply involved in explorations in Egypt for the Hall of Records, because Cayce said it would be found there circa

---

* Although I am dubious about Cayce's Atlantis and earth change predictions, he was a fantastic medical intuitive. It would be a shame if that part of his work was discredited because his predictions about earth changes have not manifested according to Cayce's schedule.

1998. Zahi Hawass, director of the Giza Plateau since 1987, was educated in the United States by ARE, and he regularly lectures at their headquarters in Virginia Beach and makes it easy for ARE big shots to explore the plateau.[16] Other projects at Giza have been carried out by the Stanford Research Institute (SRI), which is closely linked with the Department of Defense and the intelligence community.[17] Dr. James J. Hurtak, the author of a bizarre fundamentalist tome, *The Keys of Enoch*, who is a new messiah to millions, has been deeply involved in the Giza explorations.[18] Hurtak had already explored the correlation between the pyramids and Orion in 1973, more than twenty years before the publication of *The Orion Mystery*.[19] In 1977 and 1978, mysteriously, Hurtak was allowed to use lasers to measure the air-shaft angles in the Great Pyramid to see if they align with Orion and Draco; but the results have been kept secret.[20] There are persistent and well-founded rumors that the Egyptians are carrying on clandestine digging all over the Plateau and that many things have already been found but kept secret.[21] In the middle of this bizarre drama is Zahi Hawass, who shows selected "discoveries" on American television that are smoke screens to divert attention from clandestine explorations. Hawass is a classic front man for an elaborate game. These people are shape-shifters, and it is impossible to know what the various players are really doing. The fact is that *affiliations with the intelligence community are always signs of the vast conspiracy that distracts the public by means of rumors and planted lies.*[22] The Internet has brought the heated rumor mill to a boil in cyberspace; meanwhile, the exquisite temples in Egypt are being raided. Sucked unawares into the quest for the Holy Grail, people end up being bitterly disappointed by not finding their heart's desire while they are being subtly conditioned to buy in to the Aquarian Age religion. This culling is more broad based than it may seem: The pyramid on the American dollar, the obelisk in Washington, and other such Masonic symbols have been imprinted in the brains of Americans for more than two hundred years.[23] It is as if the whole American culture is messianic, and millions of unwitting people respond to these thoughtforms because they are so curious about the ancient lost civilization. Recalling the Fallen Angels in the previous chapter, you may notice that J. J. Hurtak's book is titled *The Keys of Enoch*. Next, enter the Martians.

The Lost Civilization on Mars

In 1972, the *Mariner 9* probe took some photographs of an area on Mars called Cydonia, which seem to depict a huge sculpture of a face, some pyramids, and a circular henge and mound that resemble Avebury Henge and Silbury Hill in England.* The possibility that there are ruins of a civilization on Mars that contain a big humanlike face staring at Earth really got the Ancient Astronaut Theory going! J. J. Hurtak linked Cydonia with Giza by describing the Face as "Sphinx-like," even though it has no body, much less a lion's body.[24] Various players made new careers as researchers on the Face on Mars, particularly Richard Hoagland—a NASA consultant, who was once an NBC, ABC, and CNN consultant—who has become the public champion for the Face on Mars.[25] Hoagland is largely responsible for convincing the public that there was an ancient civilization on Mars that was once connected with Giza.[26] Strangely, he said, "The 'Message of Cydonia' could significantly assist the world in a dramatic transition to a real 'new world order'. . . if not a literal New World."[†] Regarding the very real possibility that evidence for an ancient civilization exists on Mars, the Elite are barely more than a step ahead of the pack in space exploration. There are many things the Elite desperately want to figure out before anybody else does. They often persuade brilliant researchers to join up with them, since who wants to end up like Nicola Tesla or Wilhelm Reich? However, once the Faustian pact has been agreed upon, they use the new members as especially lethal weapons for implanting selected data—often the public trusts the knights. In return, the new initiates are published by big publishers and featured on the best-seller lists, they become the stars on the lecture circuit, and they are introduced socially to the Elite.

The big cover-up is that the discovery of the remains of an ancient civilization on Mars—with ruins that are similar to the Giza Plateau and Avebury Circle—that was destroyed *could be the ultimate proof of Allan and*

---

* Graham Hancock, *The Mars Mystery* (New York: Crown, 1998), 91–92. By fractal analysis, there is reason to believe the Cydonia structures were not made by natural forces.

† Quoted in Lynn Picknett and Clive Prince, *The Stargate Conspiracy* (London: Little, Brown, 2000), 128. Notice how these words tie the colonization of the Americas with the New World Order.

Delair's cataclysmic theory. Figure 2.1 indicates that Phaeton ripped close by Mars and changed its orbit. The current slow rotation of Mars—24 hours when it should be 8 hours—suggests that this flyby caused its crust to fracture and its magnetic field to drop. Astronomers say "something quite profound has happened to Mars in the not so distant past."[27] The Martian surface is damaged more profoundly than Earth, yet similar effects suggest that both planets must have been traumatized by an external agency like Phaeton. Allan and Delair note, "Surely these similarities are too close to be products of totally separate events, for all are seemingly united by the insistent underlying theme of a powerful and destructive cosmic assailant."[28] The Martian surface was so destroyed that probably no life survived. Enough Earth species survived so that we have arrived at the point at which, scientifically, we are realizing that *this nightmare recently altered the whole solar system.* Graham Hancock comments, "The notion that the terminal Mars cataclysm might have occurred recently—perhaps less than 20,000 years ago—is an astronomical heresy that raises peculiar resonance for us."[29] In light of what is said here about Cydonia resembling Avebury Henge, readers might want to read the material in appendix D that discusses Ralph Ellis's theory that Avebury Henge is a model of Earth floating in space and *tilted on its axis.*[30]

The Mars Announcement

Regarding the Global Elite's desire to cover up what they know about Mars, on 7 August 1996, NASA mysteriously staged an announcement by a group of scientists that evidence for life on Mars has been found in a meteorite that landed on Antarctica about 13,000 years ago. This event had full media attention, including excited comments by Bill Clinton and Al Gore, which are typical signs of a big Elite plot.[31] This announcement might be part of the program to get the public to buy in to extraterrestrial influence, or possibly it was a smoke screen to distract from Cydonia, or maybe to heighten curiosity about the Face on Mars. This announcement is a perfect example of high-level Elite tactics, which many people recognized instantly, because they knew that the discovery of possible life on Mars had *already occurred and been announced to science* by scientists Vincent Di Pietro, John Brandenburg, and Bartholomew Nagy. Nagy published a paper about the chemical compounds in meteors (although he did not yet know they were Martian) in 1975, and he added the Martian aspect in a paper with scientist Colin Pillinger in *Nature* in July 1989.[32] Nagy died in December 1995, a few months before the Mars announcement validated his research. All scientists in the field know what *Nature* publishes, yet Nagy got the silent treatment. With his Pinnochio nose growing longer on television, Bill Clinton said about the big new discovery, "Its implications are as far-reaching and awe-inspiring as can be imagined."[33] Why was he so surprised? A Washington prostitute, Sherry Rowlands, immediately did press interviews, and she said that Clinton's close adviser, Dick Morris, had told her all about this discovery when it was still a military secret.[34]

What is going on? There is more than meets the public eye. Notice that the mysterious Martian meteor landed on Antarctica *about 13,000 years ago*. Sound familiar? The fact is that Di Pietro, Brandenburg, and Nagy may have gotten too close to the truth; this big distraction was created to make sure nobody figures out that *this is a meteor from the surface of Mars that was flying along with Phaeton 11,500 years ago!* Consider figure 2.1, when Phaeton tangled with Earth, and some Martian meteors fell on Antarctica. The official story is that the meteor formed 4.5 billion years ago when the Martian crust first formed. Then 16 million years ago, a comet or asteroid struck Mars and ejected the piece of rock off the surface; 13,000 years ago, it fell on Antarctica.[35] This is classic Elite disinformation—a useful story that the public will believe because they've been trained to believe that the solar system formed 4.5 billion years ago. The suggestion that a meteor from a Mars impact took 16 million years to land on Antarctica 13,000 years ago is then used to foster the theory that the cataclysmic features of the Martian crust are not recent. The fact is that *the Mars meteors fell on Antarctica 11,500 years ago, and this is a solar-system proof of Allan and Delair's cataclysmic theory.*

What's at stake here? As the magnitude of what happened so recently comes out, many scientists and writers are inventing various cyclical disaster theories. Because the normal human reaction is to assume that if something so horrible happened before, it will happen again, these *cyclical cataclysmic theories are the new scientific catastrophobia.* Meanwhile, as the solar system goes around the galaxy, it moves above, through, and below the galactic plane approximately every 30 million years like a dolphin swimming through stars, molecular clouds, and other bodies. When the solar system moves through the galactic plane, the chance of cataclysmic encounters are much greater than usual. There *were* mass extinctions of species 94.5 million, 65 million, 29 million, and 11,500 years ago. Based on this, Graham Hancock concludes, ". . . this data reminds us that the Earth-Moon system could now enter an episode of bombardment at any time."[36] For Hancock, Cydonia is a "warning that a Mars-like doom lies in wait for the Earth unless we take steps to avert it."[37] Then, of course, we must spend trillions to monitor the skies and build weapons to shoot things out of the sky, which is the stated purpose of star wars technology, the secret agenda of the Elite. Think about it: First, people are mind controlled into believing extraterrestrials are landing, and then star wars weaponry could be used to shoot them out of the sky. Meanwhile, Allan and Delair have already shown that this major cataclysmic phase of the 30-million-year galactic plane cycle *just happened 11,500 years ago.* We probably are in the beginning of 25 to 30 million years of relatively undisturbed evolution as the solar system is reestablishing equilibrium. Regarding the orbital and axial derangements in the solar system, uniformitarian scientists would have us believe that "these anomalies have accumulated over aeons of time," which enables them to convince the public that the solar system is "recurrently catastrophic."[38] If the anomalies are the result of a recent large disaster, the solar system's history "can be best defined as normally quiet and orderly but punctuated recently by a single tremendous cataclysm."[39]

The August 1996 Mars announcement involved all levels, even the subtle ones. Meanwhile, incredibly invigorating cosmic waves are reaching Earth now, which the Elite is measuring.[40] Whether individuals can receive the waves, and whether their subtle glands can activate from these powers, depends on whether they are focused or distracted; that is, whether they are grounded in their bodies. The condition that people will be in during any period of time can only be known by examining astrological patterns that influence the collective mind. Since 1985 and continuing, I have been giving an analysis of these patterns as part of my Friday night lectures, a form of *emotional-body astro-forecasting.* This benefits students while giving me unexpected insights into Elite tactics. Patterns hold for a few days, weeks, or over a few months, and they are of varying potency that can greatly increase or decrease potential freedom for individuals. My students consistently report that by being informed about these patterns, they take greater advantage of these moments. Astrology is one of the most transformative tools available to individuals, and the Elite know that people are strongly affected by astrological patterns.

After a few years of emotional astro-forecasting, I wondered if the Elite were staging managed events during the influential periods I was calling out. Just when there was a period of great opportunity for the public to be inspired by energy, horrible things happened such as the murders of JonBenet Ramsay, Nicole Simpson, and Princess Diana; the Waco and Columbine massacres; the Oklahoma City bombing; and Y2K.* I began to wonder if these were *mass events orchestrated to distract the public from the powerful transformative energy.* Regarding the Mars announcement, I'm sure of it. I had been lecturing from May to early August about the amazing potential of 6–19 August 1996, a time when there was a great cross in the sky formed by lunar nodes (where the Moon crosses the Ecliptic), and Jupiter, Saturn, Chiron, and Mars conjoin Venus. This was a period when there was great potential for men to realize their own participation in female suppression. The potential to heal this Promethean pain directly with the women in their lives and their own "inner female" was so great that it was possible for us to catalyze healthy male-female polarity and sink into intentional love. The Mars announcement was timed to distract men by overwhelming them with martial energy, the vibration that holds them the most captive. In any case, I noticed that some men I knew and many of my students *did* begin removing the armoring around their hearts in August of 1996. I began this book with the premise that Earth is being activated by the Galactic Winter Solstice building up to 2012, so next I wondered if the Elite were creating programs to use these potent forces for their own purposes. Enter the Council of Nine.

---

* David Icke, *The Biggest Secret* (Scottsdale, Ariz.: Bridge of Love Publications, 1999). David Icke and I look at mass events as a tool to control the public very similarly. This comment about managed tragedies mostly comes out of my own experience, as explained in the text.

The Council of Nine

The search for the Hall of Records is driven by the human desire for enlightenment. The *Stargate* authors discovered that noncorporeal intelligences—the Council of Nine, or simply the Nine—hold great power over "top industrialists, cutting-edge scientists, popular entertainers, radical parapsychologists, and key figures in military and intelligence circles."[41] Both Richard Hoagland and J. J. Hurtak have been heavily influenced by the Nine. In fact, the Nine is Hurtak's source for *The Keys of Enoch*, which then causes millions to be open to the Nine.[42] What is the Nine and where did they come from? A primary source is Andrija Puharich, a parapsychologist who began the Round Table Foundation in Glen Cove, Maine, which is devoted to channeling and other esoteric pursuits.[43] At the Round Table, Puharich set up channeling sessions for an Indian mystic, Dr. D. G. Vinod. The Nine Principles or Forces identified themselves and explained that they are a group of nine entities who make up a whole that is godlike.[44] The Nine through Dr. Vinod never said they were extraterrestrials, but Puharich declared this was so after channelings by a young psychic convinced him.[45] Notice how this leap blocks our free access to the numinous and ineffable, because it concretizes divine beings who are not meant to be material. Because of the awesome size and power of these beings, the contactee becomes confused and eventually becomes a fanatic. Puharich was initiated as a full-fledged Hawaiian Kahuna; he studied many methods for altering consciousness, including the use of psychedelic drugs; and he may have been a real seeker. Regardless of his merits, he was deeply involved with the Elite.[46] He used hypnosis to cull the minds of many brilliant psychics, such as Uri Geller, and he was involved in SRI experiments on Geller during the same period that the CIA was involved in remote-viewing experiments with SRI.[47] Speaking of strange bedfellows, Lab Nine was founded at Puharich's estate in Ossining, New York, with J. J. Hurtak as his second in command.[48] This spawned a series of people who were primarily channeling extraterrestrials with wealthy backers, celebrities, and SRI physicists hanging around.[49] Books were written; the Nine gave seminars through a channel at Esalen; the group continued even after Puharich died in 1995; and channelers around the world, including me, brought in the Nine with no knowledge of each other.[50]

The gods of the Egyptian Heliopolitan Mysteries were called the Nine, and they still are potent cosmic forces.[51] The level of interpretation of these forces is in direct proportion to the spiritual level of the channel. Because individuals, groups, and cultures are in a very low state of moral and spiritual consciousness, often what comes through channels is distorted. Through the Round Table channels, the Nine claimed that they were going to return to save humankind, whose salvation is mixed up with apocalyptic fear, racism, the Chosen People, and the battle between good and evil. Humans are flawed because extraterrestrials messed up our genetic programming. The Nine have come to fix all this, because we humans are so helpless.[52] How will the Nine fix everything? First, the apocalypse will cleanse the planet, and then, according to Hurtak, America will be the location of a new "Spiritual Administration," the rise of the new "JerUSalem."* The big problem with Puharich's presence in the midst of this is that he "was also carrying out secret research for the defense and intelligence establishments in two main areas: techniques of psychological manipulation using hallucinogenic drugs; and the military and intelligence capabilities of psychic skills."[53] He was deeply involved in the mind-control experimentation projects of the military and CIA for many years, and his "use of hypnosis was unethical and dangerous."[54] This is a classic example of how the Elite co-opts greatly needed healing methods: for example, hypnosis is an incredible tool for removing phobias, clearing emotional blocks, and sharpening intelligence.

The Nine are the center of an orchestrated plot to implant a series of ideas into individuals, cults, and the culture to create a new religion. This has spawned organizations, such as the Institute of Noetic Sciences at Palo Alto, that are used as intelligence organs to influence powerful individuals and the world.[55] Why? The *Stargate* authors note that Puharich "was obsessed with the space gods," he was fascinated with the Heliopolitan Mysteries, and he believed that "it was possible to open the stargate," which would force extraterrestrials to enter this reality so he could meet with them.[56] This is conjuring, which can call in energies that are normally non-

---

* Picknett and Prince, *The Stargate Conspiracy*, 197. Word formation—"JerUSalem"—is by J. J. Hurtak.

physical into the physical plane. These forces operate by their own laws, and properly trained indigenous shamans are very wary and respectful of them. Puharich and Uri Geller carried on so many weird experiments at the Lawrence Livermore Laboratory in California that the physicists began to see apparitions of huge, ravenlike birds and flying saucers.[57] They caused a temporary break in the barriers between dimensions, something that physicists play around with when they split matter.[58]

I report on the Nine extensively here because it is a hideous spiritual distortion. The Heliopolitan Mysteries are eternal and available, and contemplation of their structure and laws can gift anyone with exquisite mystical communion. Because of the personalized interpretations of Puharich, Cayce, Hurtak, and others, very real spiritual skills are perverted just when they are the most needed. The plan seems to be that once the extraterrestrials have been conjured, then they will be the new messiahs. The buildup of communication links since 1900—such as phone, radio, television, and Internet—have increased connectivity. Most channels obsess on the coming earth changes, and people think it must be true because everybody says the same things. The herd mentality on the Internet blinds people. Meanwhile, there is a deeper and more profound contact with spirit that is building. For example, Spiritualism was a huge movement in the nineteenth century that was devoted to reaching people who had died to comfort their loved ones by helping them experience loved ones in the nonphysical state. First, this is comforting, and it also helps living people experience the numinous quality of life in other dimensions. There is a great difference between Spiritualism and occult conjuring, yet distortions like the Nine take away respect for legitimate contact with other dimensions.

Symbols as Transmitters of the Divine Mind

The working hypothesis of this book is that Earth's axis was tilted by Phaeton 11,500 years ago, which began an entirely new form of human evolution. Approximately 10,000 years ago, abstract symbols began to appear, and by studying the mythology and artifacts during this time frame, the influence of the Great Ages can be detected. But, what are symbols? I think they form in other dimensions and are a two-way street. Symbols *translate ideas from other worlds into ours,* as if they are a vertical axis tunnel. The sages saw that they have great power, and people are creatively inspired to make art with them. Before the Cataclysm, people seemed to have been in direct contact with a huge library of complex astral mythology that penetrated ordinary reality, and then our access into the library system was shattered. Afterward, symbols were found that were a doorway into these complex stellar holograms. The myths that have come down from that time right after the disaster long ago—which are contained within more recent myths like cosmic seeds—are garbled, stripped-down versions of the great dramas in the night sky. What is different now is that *we live these myths out in our personal dramas because so many people are unaware of the life in the other world.* This has been overwhelming and the astral realm has been a gigantic theater looming over the world, and the sages observed this development with amazement. Soon kosmokraters, or lords of Time, appeared, because by the Age of Gemini the sages could see that the symbols changed when the ages shifted. Based on the Çatal Hüyük discussion in chapter 6, the symbolism for the Age of Gemini was available in toto exactly when the age opened. It was obvious to them that the symbols could be used to influence how people create realities with thought. For example, the great reformer of human civilization, Zarathustra, used symbols to encourage people to improve life on Earth by adopting agriculture. Anthropologist Felicitas Goodman says, "What all agriculturalists have in common is the illusion of power, of being able to exert control over the habitat."[59] During the Age of Gemini, cultures developed exquisite and complex symbolism, and its inherent control potential was utilized.

People can feel the inherent numinousness of symbols, and they are lured by them. Responding to symbols became an unconscious process for people during the Age of Cancer, perhaps because they were still numbed. Now the time has come for *many* people to understand these gateways to other worlds. Why shouldn't they, to develop their awesome individuality? It is important to see how symbols affect people in general. After all, the Internet could create global waves of positive connections or set off a collective insanity—the potential "cataclysm" this time, not periodic destructive agents in the sky. Because symbols bridge realities, they are *divinized;* they can manifest out of nowhere because they are formed by pure thought. Great beings like the Nine have no problem returning at this time, but there are few vehicles who can receive their vibrations, because most vehicles distort spirituality with their egos. Where are our Michelangelos, Beethovens, and Bachs? It is easy to answer that question. The culture used to support Renaissance artists; today it supports Edison, Einstein, Steven King, and sex online.

Each Great Age births a body of potent symbols that are doorways to numinous worlds. During the past 12,000 years, artifacts that have symbols can be accurately dated and their makers identified. Just as there are layers of time in myths, symbols all over the planet manifest in geographic zones by Time; they are *geomorphic*. Amazingly, the symbolic system shows up in toto right when the age opens. Symbols have been used to inspire beautiful potentials, and they've been used to limit and pervert human potential, which is what Hitler did with the swastika. But, where does beauty or evil come from? I think evil manifests through control programs: *Evil comes into the world when symbols are used to manipulate and mind-control humans by a select few who happen to know how this process works.* Kosmokraters figured out the game. They enjoy playing it, so they keep it secret because they'd rather be a king than a pawn. In other words, *what if evil always begins with thought manipulation?* This is one of the ways, if not the greatest way, that evil enters our world. Those who have become impervious to these evil influences by seeing what the control forces are intending observe every single thought that comes into their heads. We have seen how symbols, such as the all-seeing eye in the capstone of the pyramid on the dollar, can be used for good or evil. There are great forces operating that are using symbols and manipulating thoughtforms for their own purposes. We live in an age in which it is obvious that huge forces are controlling people for power, money, and sex. Most people even know exactly who is doing it! The information we need now is how did this happen to our world and when? The master program that enslaved the world during the Piscean Age is from the Roman Empire.

Perseus Slays the Medusa

Mysteriously, about 200 years before the beginning of this era, when the Age of Aries melted away, a mysterious brew of forces in the ancient classical world—Stoic philosophers, Greek astronomers, and Cilician pirates—

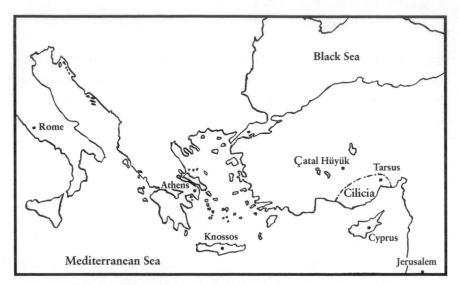

Fig. 8.1. The Black Sea Region and the Eastern Mediterranean.

created a new religion called *Mithraism*. Mithraism and Christianity arose at the same time and spread through the Roman Empire in the same places, because they were "two responses to the same set of cultural forces."[60] Mithraic scholar David Ulansey says that Mithraism was the "road not taken" by Western civilization.[61] However, I think it is *the secret road running deep in the bowels of Roman Catholicism,* a road they would just as soon keep private. The Cilician pirates were 20,000 sailors who controlled the Mediterrenean Sea during the Roman Empire, and the new religion spread like fire through their ranks and the Roman legions. This religion of soldiers was the inheritance of the Age of Aries, when the battleground was the favorite sport for 2,000 years. The Cilician pirates were wealthy men of illustrious lineage who used the stars for navigation. They believed that they possessed superior intelligence as bluebloods; they had inherited the right to live adventurous lives and pursue knowledge.[62] These strapping pirates burned with occult curiosity, just like the Cayce knights today.

Tarsus was the capital of Cilicia, and during Hellenistic and Roman times, it rivaled Athens and Alexandria. An exciting intellectual community developed around the Stoic philosophers, because the natives were fond of learning. Tarsus hosted many famous Stoic philosophers. Among them were both Posidonius and Athenodorus, and the famous Zeno of Tarsus, who was influenced by the famous astronomer Aratos of Soli

(315–240 B.C.).[63] According to the Stoics, stellar patterns greatly influence human affairs. They believed in the Great Year that was determined by stellar patterns, and they preached that the "entire cosmos was periodically destroyed by a great conflagration *(ekpyrosis)* and subsequently re-created *(palingenesis)*."[64] They allegorized gods and mythical figures to represent cosmic and natural forces; they had mastered symbolism and mystery plays. For example, Phaeton was an allegorical being who drives the chariot of the Sun at the end of an age, the agent of ekpyrosis.[65] In other words, the scientists of today who preach that a cyclical cataclysm will be coming soon are Stoics.

Stoicism was the primary philosophy of Tarsus, the city of the Cilician pirates. Therefore, when Hipparchus supposedly discovered precession in 128 B.C., it had a huge impact on both the Stoics and the pirates because of their interest in the stars.[66] In fact, I have pointed out throughout this book that precession was understood in some form at least 10,000 years ago, but it was the way that Hipparchus *described* this influence that matters. Of course, Hipparchus was the dunce shoved into the public eye. Because he believed that Earth was fixed in space and everything in the cosmos moved around it, then precession was the movement of the *"structure of the entire cosmos"* around a cosmic axis.[67] Because the current belief was that stars were fixed and unchanging, and because the real precessional knowledge was hidden within secret cabals, the announcement by Hipparchus would have been shocking to the public. However, just like the Mars announcement, this was merely what the public was being told. I am suggesting that this form of lying and public manipulation has been endemic for more than 2,000 years. Meanwhile, the real power brokers— Cilician pirates, Roman soldiers, and Stoics—took these new ideas and formulated a potent religion. The Stoics allegorized divine beings to carry natural forces. Which great god would then be selected as the mover of the cosmos, the kosmokrater? It is actually easy to imagine this wild mixing, since we are seeing the same thing today on the Giza Plateau. When the Age of Pisces began more than 2,100 years ago, everything was in flux, and there were many strange bedfellows. If we keep the *Stargate Conspiracy* in mind, it is possible to imagine what I will call the *Tauroctony Conspiracy. Tauroctony* means "bull slaying."

The Stoics searched for a suitable archetype to embody the kosmokrater, the awesome force that moves the heavens. Ulansey argues that *they used Mithra in public and Perseus covertly.*[68] Out of the exquisite Mediterranean blue sky, the great god Perseus—who looms over Taurus, Aries, and Pisces on the Ecliptic and holds the severed head of the Medusa in one hand and the sword of Damocles in the other—became numinous. Impelled by the great cosmic whirlwind as the Age of Aries ended, Perseus was seen as the force that had ended Taurus and Aries, and his sword even points to Pisces. Contemplate figure 8.2 and imagine the potency of this warrior god wearing a Phrygian hat (meaning that he is a Magi) as he looms over two or three Great Ages and slays the Medusa. The Perseus constellation is in the Milky Way, possibly the axis the cosmos turns on, where the last remnants of the ancient Goddess culture, the Medusa, is decapitated.* Medusa represented the ancient snake shamans, who were often females like the vulture shamans, and she turned people to stone just by looking at them. However, after thousands of years of war and oppression that eventually destroyed the inner feminine, Medusa's shamanic powers would be stolen during the Age of Pisces.

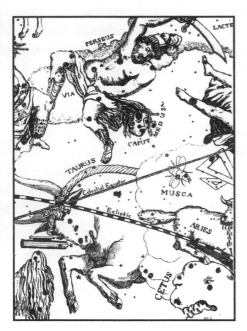

Fig. 8.2. Perseus Hovering Over the Ecliptic, adapted from figure 3.1 of The Origins of the Mithraic Mysteries.

Perseus turns the wheel of time with bull and woman slaying, and a divinity of such power could control Earth,

---

*J. B. Delair, personal letter, 22 November 2000. Regarding my discussion of Perseus, Delair notes that the Perseus legends have been established as Oriental (they are even known in Siberia). Regarding the Medusa, he says, "The oldest creation legends place Medusa's birth *before* that of Earth and man (some scholars suggesting she was an early form of *Tiamat*), and located her domain in a place distant from Earth." She may be Tiamat as located between Mars and Jupiter. Perseus slayed her, so Perseus is a "cataclysm" figure. This means he was the ideal archetype for power and control of Time by the Mithraists.

which was the agenda of the Roman Empire. Exactly how the Cilician pirates and the Stoics got together and developed the Mithraic rituals is not clear. We know more about the actual rites than we do about most secret religions, because they built Mithraeums in Roman towns and cities from northern Scotland to Libya. These are undergound, cavelike temples with huge altars called *tauroctonies,* which depict Mithra slaying the bull surrounded by numerous astral and mythological symbols. Why was Mithra the public hero and Perseus the covert hero? Perseus was an ancient Greek and Persian god, and his birth and life are very similar to the story

Fig. 8.3. The Narmer Pallette, from Hieraconpolis.

of Zal in chapter 7. The mother of Perseus, Danae, was seduced by her uncle, a rival twin to her father, and her father locked her away in a tower. Zeus seduced Danae in the tower, Perseus was born, and he was sent away, like Zal. This is an early Greek version that goes back to the earliest phases of Iranian and Indian religion, back at least 10,000 years to the survival phase after the Cataclysm during the Age of Cancer. Perseus and the tauroctony were chosen because they are potent archaic archetypes that were needed to numb the people during the Age of Pisces. Perseus as kosmokrater created the need for the central core initiates to work with this force very secretly. The sacrificial rituals in caves or underground temples made the outer members feel like they were participating in a great mystery.

The Predynastic Narmer Palette from Hieraconpolis (Nekhen) is dated circa 3500 B.C. and is a very early rendition of the Pharaoh slaying his enemies—in this case, Semites—who came to the Nile periodically.* The

---

* W. B. Emery, *Archaic Egypt* (London: Penguin Books, 1961), 38–49. Found with the Narmer Palette was the mace head of the Scorpion King (Narmer). In this rendition, he is protected by the vulture goddess, Nekhet (also known as Nekhbet), which adds to the vulture shamanism theory. One of the editors for this book, Nicholas Dalton, believes the vulture headdress of Isis hearkens back to vulture shamanism, and I agree.

Palette is made with such exquisite skill, and the concepts expressed are so clear and complete, that I speculate that it depicts pharaonic kingship at the opening of Taurus in 4480 B.C. I have included it here for comparison with figure 8.2 because I believe that the Mithraists adopted Perseus because the Dynastic Egyptians had already used this archetype to depict the *Pharaoh as Perseus slaying his enemy*. The Mithraists would have selected this archetype because Rome planned to conquer Egypt. This is important, because first, it is more proof that the Egyptians used the precessional ages to organize their empire; second, the one being slayed here is an invader of Egypt, but the Mithraists use Medusa; and third, because this constellation is named Perseus, an archaic Iranian god. The Narmer Palette may be a record of the sojourn of the Elder Culture in the Middle East that commemorates their return to the Nile. Clearly, this religion was going to be very powerful. Recall how conspiracies operate through religion, yet politics is on the outside.

Mithridates VI Eupater, the king who controlled Asia Minor, had the religion named after him. Perseus was an ancestor of the Iranian line of kings begun by Zal, from which Mithridates descended, and Mithra was an ancient Iranian bull-slaying god. Mithridates was also a great rival of Rome during the Mithridatic Wars, and he used the Cilician pirates as allies against Rome. Perseus was the secret divinity, and naming the god after a great king empowered the cult. Because Mithra was a god way back during the horrible time of the struggle with the Watchers, the cult was *chthonic*—imbued with powers from the inner Earth.[69] Once the Stoics had formulated this potent allegorized deity with the King in hand, then the Cilician pirates adopted Mithra as their god. The bull-slaying rituals activated massive chthonic forces, and amid the blood, great thoughtforms were formed and imprinted with potent astral symbols. That is, forces were conjured that still possess the dark side of Roman Christianity: the Mass is a symbolic sacrificial eating ritual. There is a hidden tauroctony exactly below the altar of the Vatican Church, just as there are hidden caves under the altars of many old churches that may have Mithraeums.*

---

* The existence of ritual caves with a tauroctony directly below the Vatican altar was revealed to me by a Jesuit, who said Mass there. This information was given based on my promise to keep his identity confidential.

Fig. 8.4. Tauroctony, adapted from figure 5.5 of The Origins of the Mithraic Mysteries.

The tauroctony in figure 8.4 is typical of tauroctonies in general—note that the bull is dying an agonizing death, and the sword of Perseus sprouts wheat in the wound. The followers of Mithra did bull-slaying rituals in front of tauroctonies such as this one; and because this was done in caves, it revived distant Paleolithic and Early Holocene memories when humanity was forced to live underground. *Mithraism was incredibly atavistic,* as the Nazis were. As we've seen, because of the horrible struggle to survive during the Age of Cancer, the early myths of the Fallen Angels suggest that people endured lives that numbed and desensitized them. Sacrificial and orgiastic cults—such as the Orphics and Dionysiacs, which existed in the distant past—were religions that helped people process chthonic powers, but they were probably not used to conjure forces. The Mithraic rituals and iconography have many of the symbols of old orgiastic religions, which they used to cull atavistic powers. We have to wonder why such a potent cult was developed by soldiers who carried out blood rituals that obviously conjured up very great chthonic forces. One thing we can be sure of: These soldiers and their esoteric masters created an intense wave of misogyny, which still grips the Roman Catholic Church and other powerful organizations today. As long as women are Medusa, men will be stones, and eventually the world will run out of mothers.

Zoroaster and the Age of Asa

During the Age of Gemini, when the earth changes were settling down and people moved out of the survival level, reforms came naturally. Most people prefer a more refined approach to life than basic survivalism. Shamans, as mediators between Earth and sky, work with these forces for collective balance, and ordinary people can go about their business. *People do not seek or want these chthonic powers in their lives except when they are afflicted with catastrophobia.* The Age of Cancer was ending, and various spiritual teachers and sages came forth to create new religions to diminish chthonic practices and help people animate their lives with finer vibrations. For example, Zarathustra of India or Zoroaster of Iran was this kind of great reformer. He goes all the way back through the Great Ages, and there was probably a series of Zoroasters who assumed this lineage. Zoroaster/Zarathrustra means "watching the stars," so this is a lineage of astronomers, who obviously knew about precession as we've seen with Çatal Hüyük. Following Zoroaster through the stages of Time by symbols and mythology is a great way to see how the patterns of the Great Ages change, because the many forms he took reflect the evolution of humanity. Magiism may be the earliest form, because in later times, Magi priests were wild rainmaking shamans, which points to the Age of Cancer. The next form was Zervanism, as we've seen in the discussion of the double axe and the wheeled cross of Çatal Hüyük, which may actually depict the opening of the Age of Gemini. Settegast believes Çatal Hüyük was one of many sites where Zervanism was actually taught, possibly by the prophet himself.[70]

Zoroaster was a very successful reformer during the Age of Gemini. Agriculture was sorely needed because of the condition of the land and the burgeoning population, and he and his emissaries taught people how to care for the land and to work hard and value a simple life. He encouraged people to cease invoking chthonic forces in orgiastic rituals, and he taught them how to live in a state of order by being a good person enjoying a good life. He called the principle of order and peace *Asa,* and his concept of it was the same as the Tao and Maat. "The cultivation of the earth was looked upon by Zarathustra's followers as a kind of worship."[71] Settegast argues successfully that the Samarran and Halafan cultures, who established farming communities from Greece through Turkey to Iraq and Iran exactly when the Age of Gemini began, were inspired by the religion of Zarathustra.[72] As you can see in the illustrations, their pottery designs are very geometrical and have great contrast between dark and light; they are so beautiful and inspiring that religious awe must have inspired them. Because Zarathustra taught about bringing in the light and encouraged people to not invoke dark forces, pottery was used as art in the household to teach people how to blend these forces in their lives. Asa and Maat are similar concepts, and these cultures both used exquisite art to bring high spiritual forces into the people's everyday lives. The Egyptian Elder Culture may have built Derinkuyu as an underground refuge 12,000 years ago, and then the people fanned out and settled Anatolia, Kurdistan, and even Iran. Zarathustra/Zoroaster may represent the Elder Culture in the Age of Gemini.

Fig. 8.5. Halafian Geometrical Pottery Designs, adapted from figure 138 of Plato Prehistorian.

In the previous chapter, I commented that Zoroaster stifled further discussions about Angels being involved with humans; however, they remained in the sacred literature and folk tales. *This suppression of the dark forces may have been the beginning of the cover-up of the Fallen Angels.* This phase in Zoroaster's teachings probably comes from the beginning of the Age of Taurus, when theocracies began that created places and temples where priests and kings could conspire. It is interesting that modern Zoroastrians keep priestly control and rituals to a minimum, and, as Andrew Collins notes, "over the centuries the Muslims of the Middle East had systematically attempted to eradicate their faith completely."[73] As we know, there are difficult tensions in the world today in the Middle East, which may be the result of early suppression of the dark forces. Collins visited a Yezidi sacred cave on the Turkish border with Syria. The Yezidis are *zaddik* priests who are ecstatic nomadic rainmakers who claim descent from Noah, and their records go back at least 10,000 years.* On the floor, Collins saw a rendering of an early zodiac, and he saw shrines with ancient figures wearing conical caps like the ones the Tibetans wear. This conical cap is the earliest version of the Phrygian cap that Perseus wears. We will return to Perseus/Mithra, now that we can see how ancient and potent these archetypes really are. They are the forces that were hidden totally during the Piscean Age after being progressively suppressed in previous ages.

Blood Rituals and the Ahriman

Considering the tauroctony in figure 8.4 again, notice that there is a scorpion pinching the genitals of the bull, a long snake under the bull's right leg, and wheat coming out of the bull's body where Mithra slays him. Hundreds of tauroctonies have been found, and they all contain the same grouping of symbols. In this tauroctony, the scorpion on the genitals of the bull suggests that his sexuality is part of the energy of the ritual, and the long snake under his leg is astronomical. The bull's leg or thigh commonly depicted the Great Bear constellation, and the snake is Draco writhing around the North Pole. Notice the twins, who represent the Ecliptic and the Age of Gemini. On many tauroctonies, one carries a scepter at a 90-degree upright angle, and the other tilts his about 23½ degrees.[74] Based on Iranian mythology, the dagger in the shoulder means that the slain bull is creational as he bleeds out the plants and herbs as he dies. If we look at the Perseus constellation astronomically in figure 8.2, Ulansey says that the Pleiades are located right where the dagger goes into the bull's shoulder. The knowledge that Phaeton came in through the Pleiades was part of the Mithraic secret teachings.[75] Because they carried out the bull sacrifices hidden away in caves, they were free to reveal what they knew by symbolism.

---

* Collins, *From the Ashes of Angels,* 185–87. J. B. Delair notes in his 22 November 2000 letter to the author that the Noah element also exists in the "lore of the Turkish Kurds who associate certain topographical features with his memory."

When we conceive of the darkly shamanic Age of Cancer as a survival and struggle period, then the process of reform during the Age of Gemini shows that it was a heroic age for humanity and a time when many of the great religions began. It was an age when people strived for peaceful community and artistic and mental freedom after a very dark and mystical experience with Earth's powers during the Age of Cancer. When considering Zoroaster as an agricultural and religious reformer who influenced religions in the Middle East, including Judaism, we have to ask: Isn't it odd that Mithraism, which is based on the older chthonic forces from the Age of Cancer and Leo, would be reinvoked at the beginning of the Age of Pisces? This sacrificial ritual religion of soldiers, which centers on the slaying of the female, would have horrified Zoroaster: *It represents everything he and his followers reformed thousands of years before.* I am not the first or the last person to wonder if the dark forces—the Ahriman of Zarathustra—rule the Roman Catholic Church. I would not even mention this without offering some solutions in the final chapter. The most important thing to recognize here is that *evil forces are real, yet they cannot come into this world unless somebody conjures them.* Powerful forces were invoked in the Mithraeums as the Piscean Age began. From a positive point of view, this proces may have relieved some of the subconscious pressures in people's minds from the the time of survival during the Age of Cancer. This conjuring sucked up the archetypal forces of the previous five Great Ages and loaded them directly into the Piscean Age. *These are the occulted forces of the Elite that humanity is becoming objective about now.*

Christianity may have been the light force and Mithraism the dark force during the Piscean Age; however, as we consider these forces in our present age, they are both fundamentally misogynist. The long-lasting Elder Cultures of the Athenians and the Egyptians, and the prediluvial Goddess culture of the Magdalenians were adamant about one thing: the importance of the veneration of the Goddess. As the Aquarian vibrations penetrate our planet today, we have some grand opportunities. First, the Age of Aquarius will form a trine to the Age of Gemini, which means it will naturally foster enlightenment and leadership by sages. Second, the Aquarian energy is so androgynous that it will tend to balance male and female powers. Third, and most importantly, the great data convergence described in this book suggests that *humanity is on the verge of being able to transmute the control forces that have been building for thousands of years.* It is doubtful that very many people will be swept along in *The Stargate Conspiracy* because it is so transparent and sophomoric. The knights might chase the grail all the way to the end, since Faustian pacts are lucrative, but the people will not follow if they are informed. The great challenge is to invoke the Great Goddess in balance with the new harmony of Earth that is forming as the planet establishes equilibrium. The greatest challenge will be to bring the Goddess back into our world without conjuring chthonic forces. She is best found in the love between people, in our journeys with animals, in the eyes of children, and in the natural world around us.

9

Goddess Alchemy & the Heliopolitan Mysteries

Feelings are the only way you can move yourselves
outside of linear space and time while you are in body,
since they are the access point for beings in other
realities to communicate with you.
　　　　　—*Barbara Hand Clow*[1]

The Pleiadian Agenda Model and Interactive Time

The central consciousness model of *The Pleiadian Agenda: A New Cosmology for the Age of Light* shows how our bodies receive frequencies from nine dimensions simultaneously when we are grounded in linear space and time (3D).[2] It is a *schema of the awakened human.* The first dimension (1D) is the iron-core crystal in the center of Earth, which pulses 7.8 times per second, or 7.8 hertz. This pulse moves out into the rocks, magma, and microbial essences that live in the area beneath the surface of Earth—the *telluric elemental world* (2D)—as magnetic waves. On Earth's surface, the magnetic waves are charged by electricity in the atmosphere, and they become electromagnetic fields that support all living beings, such as the person shown lying on a massage table in figure 9.1. This person is in 3D and emotes thoughts and feelings that all weave together into the collective consciousness. The collective consciousness (4D) makes an etheric energy dome over the individual and all communities. We all participate in this group mind, which is not solid or physical. This group mind is *real* but less dense than our bodies, and it is textured and colored by each person's sense of Time and history; it is fluid and changes as cultures and people

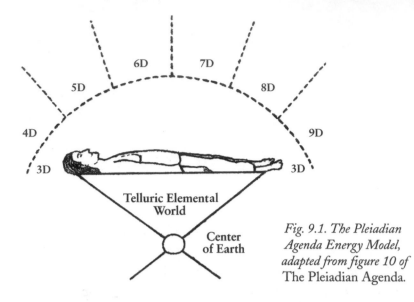

Fig. 9.1. The Pleiadian Agenda Energy Model, adapted from figure 10 of The Pleiadian Agenda.

evolve. The 4D emotional body is greatly shaped by events in 3D, such as events staged to manipulate people, like the so-called search for the Hall of Records. These quests incite people to take actions or influence them to shut themselves down, but only if they are unaware a game is being played. Any person can read these etheric energies and choose to work with 4D consciously, which means accessing many realities through feelings.

Egyptian sacred science teaches us how to detect the 4D archetypal realm in 3D by learning to recognize the activities of the gods or neters in ordinary reality. When Earth's field is balanced and people live in cultures that hold the field of the Tao, Asa, or Maat, the individual is profoundly grounded, intensely stimulated by feelings, and can read events brilliantly. When cultures achieve these levels, people spend most of their time telling stories, making art, and carrying out ceremonies that bring the gods into life on Earth. At present, humanity is grossly unbalanced and out of touch with these spiritual realms. This is why I chose to explore how we can reestablish Paradise on Earth—Maat/Tao/Asa. Simply by tuning ourselves to the frequencies we all are capable of holding, we invite the divine intelligences into the human world. We have forgotten about them, and they are lonely when they cannot play in this dimension. In this sense, new creation is always at the edge of our senses; the divine is immanent. This form is a simple and accessible new method that is inspired by the Heliopolitan Mystery School.

All existence is a matter of perspective, which is why my nine-dimensional model views realities as dimensions in which our consciousness locates itself. These days most people view reality from their 4D emotional bodies—*they are not located in their 3D physical bodies.* This causes them to swirl around totally confused in the archetypal realms, where they are available to be manipulated or allured by various minds. When a person is profoundly grounded in body, he or she has tremendous flowing energy from Earth, and the 4D dome becomes diaphanous and easily permutated by cosmic consciousness. Clear and open feelings are the bridge between the tangible and intangible—between body and spirit. Then our 4D feeling bodies access cosmic frequencies of the fifth through ninth dimensions (5D through 9D), and we can actually comprehend the spirit world by becoming adept at reading divine manifestations in our world. We are designed to live in a delicious cocoon of subtle impulses that soften 4D while our cells regenerate by potent lower forces, such as crustal movements, magnetism, and microbial life-forms. In the Pleiadian Agenda model, 5D through 9D are shown as lines coming right into our 4D domes, because this shows how these frequencies activate the 4D dome. *We receive cosmic information first by feelings in our bodies.* Simply put, we are designed to play with the gods all day by first noticing how we feel, and then by expressing these forces through art and ceremony. According to the ancient Egyptians, these gods like to eat, have sex, work, and organize realities! We are *designed to have total access to divine essences.* Reducing these intelligences to extraterrestrials, the Ancient Astronaut Theory is childish and demeans our innate divinity.

I show a person lying on a healing table because so many of us have first detected these feelings while in a healing session with a guide; however, this person could be standing, sitting, or swimming. The dimensions that humans can interact with are progressive, such as moving from 1D to 9D, yet here we are interested in how we can detect these dimensions with our bodies.*

The lower dimensions are the most dense and have the most intense energy. The higher dimensions vibrate with progressively faster frequencies

---

* If readers are interested in the specific qualities of each dimension, that is the subject matter of *The Pleiadian Agenda: A New Cosmology for the Age of Light* (Santa Fe: Bear & Company, 1995).

and are less dense, and they translate down into our bodies through the 4D dome. That is, this dome is a gateway for the higher dimensions that opens or shuts according to our feelings. *Radical density differentials are the cause of the split between body and spirit; yet, ironically, there is no split in someone who is emotionally clear.* As the iron-core crystal pulses Earth, we in 3D vibrate with waves coming through the telluric realm (2D), and by these waves we take physical form by our soul's intention.* Meanwhile the pulses in the sky penetrate Earth by waves, such as gamma rays, which vibrate at much higher frequencies than 1D through 4D and contain amazing intelligences who usually are sourced from various cosmic worlds, such as the Pleiadian, Sirian, or Orion star systems. Our 4D bodies feel these higher dimensional vibrations, and each is characterized by certain divine qualities that have been identified by the perennial wisdom communicated by our ancestors and wisdom teachers.

We pick up these signals by our *feelings*, and if we do not understand our own emotional response patterns, the 4D collective mind tends to dualize us, which blocks our reception of higher frequencies. For example, feeling an awesome presence, a fundamentalist of any religion might think the Archangel Michael has just arrived; a New Age fool might think an extraterrestrial from Zeta Reticulae is at the end of the bed; and both might be certain a demon is in the room. Yet, this person is just being contacted by a spirit in another dimension who wants to communicate, which is a marvelous opportunity for playing and learning. Most people are out of their physical bodies and stuck in 4D, where divine forces are reduced to dark/light, good/evil, and positive/negative. They are thrown into *dualistic confusion* by appearances of the scintillating archetypal realms, especially because we live in a culture that debunks the perennial wisdom, which teaches us how to befriend these forces. All embodied humans are naturally able to see, hear, touch, read, or smell these frequencies; yet many, if not all, avenues are dormant because of the education system. Usually, a person has at least one doorway open and can receive the intensity of one or more of the higher dimensions. For example, you may be able to hear

---

* We can heal ourselves by slowing down the frequencies in our bodies to the level of 2D. See chapter 3 of *The Pleiadian Agenda* (Barbara Hand Clow, 1995) for this information.

the divine in a Beethoven late quartet, yet the 5D emotional domain of the heart may be too complex for you because there are so many ways we can love each other. Many of us who contemplate the realm of 6D divine forms may be easily transported by its symbols and geometrical patterns that impulse creation in this world, yet we might have a heart attack if we *really* fell in love! The Pleiadian Agenda model indicates that we are capable of receiving any one of the five higher dimensions, and once we learn to hold one form of divinity, the others can open.

Bringing the Divine into Everyday Life

You might be able to discover the numinous in the idealized 6D forms or hear God in the 7D sound codes, yet you might be almost incapable of finding the divine in passionate 5D love. However, once you experience how the divine *feels*, eventually other forms of this exquisite elixir become available to you. The seventh dimension structures itself by vertical octaves, and its waves are measurable as the musical scale. Regarding sound's ability to create forms in 6D, this has been demonstrated by cymatics, the study of sound, which show patterns forming out of grains of sand as they are actually moved by sound waves.* In the eighth dimension, sound becomes the voice of higher orders and we can hear God/ Goddess, a dialogue we lived by when our brains were bicameral. Earlier, I discussed Julian Jaynes's research extensively because I think the most successful Elite debunking program of the past 4,000 years was the loss of our bicameral brain skills. We have been heavily conditioned in our times to think we are crazy if we hear voices in our heads—"bicameral"—yet *each one of us can hear divine sages*. When a person is in a conversational relationship with the sages, then the political and religious agendas of the Elite are easy to decode because they operate in the fourth dimension (4D), and they are much less complex than the immanent divine mind. The eighth dimension actually creates the material world by clear intentionality—the

---

* The cymatics machine was demonstrated by John Beaulieu during a BioSonics Repatterning Workshop I attended at Stone Ridge, New York, in October 1999. The sand moves around and makes patterns on a metal disk that is vibrated by sound tones. This machine demonstrates how 7D sound waves form 6D geometry!

divine word—and when we hear these words, we know the divine plan and our role in it.

In the ninth dimension (9D) we experience cosmic Time, which links our world with the Milky Way Galaxy; knowing this realm helps us know when it is *time* to take action. The sages suddenly materialize when we are conversant in this dimension, and they move into the temples to create with us. The ancient Egyptian stories about the activities of the neters—such as Osiris, Isis, Horus, and Seth—are great examples of sages existing on Earth.

This all makes more sense when we go from the top down: The Galaxy pulses from its center where the 9D divine intelligences live, and they speak to humans through 8D councils, which offer excellent advice.* If we absorb this advice, it generates 7D waves of intelligence that are the sounds of creation. These tones form into 6D geometrical morphogenetic fields, which are allured into pulsing 5D biological fields of love that are so intense that they are split by our 4D feelings. Once we know our feelings, we are seized in a creative vortex that invites the divine into the material world. At any moment, you may be pierced by 5D love, carry this into resonant harmony in 6D geometry, be transported by the 7D music of the spheres, find communion with 8D divine beings or guides, and meet the 9D sages from the center of the Milky Way Galaxy.

The Pleiadian Agenda model is a living system that describes how cosmic awareness enters the material world. It also shows how stars in our galaxy periodically awaken Nature and act as our keepers. For example, the Pleiades are the *keepers of the human heart;* the Sirius star system, *sacred geometry;* Andromeda Galaxy, *sound;* the Orion star system, *karma;* the Milky Way Galaxy, *the divine.* We humans are the keepers of Earth, a place where all these intelligences may visit and play. As Nature awakens, the polarity is intense because the higher dimensions are activating the 4D archetypal realm by stellar archetypes, and the telluric is activating our bodies, and we are sandwiched between. During the cataclysms, our 4D emotional bodies went into shock, and we locked out higher frequencies because we were so afraid of these cataclysmic forces. Now the *light is moving into all the shadows and clearing catastrophobia.* This makes us feel

---

* Often these councils are circles of animals, trees, or stones, and even groups of microbes.

overenergized, and millions drug themselves just to calm down. However, drugs move awareness out of the body and into the 4D archetypal realm, which subverts our 3D body's ability to be regenerated by the 2D telluric powers. *Drugs steal the will, which is our mind's ability to heal, and people become zombies—pawns of the collective mind.*

As the Pleiadian Agenda model shows, we can be conscious receivers of many dimensions, which is how we differ from animals.* As higher dimensional forces arrive, we polarize them by our feelings in order to understand the energies. Our minds play with the issues, such as considering that the Angels once walked among us; suddenly, in the midst of the mundane world, exquisite dramas and mystery plays emerge like huge emotional mushrooms. We become children in a dark room peering at a puppet box as the forms on the strings begin to dance. Our minds awaken by the primordial archetypal forms, such as the Minotaur or Medusa, when we perceive that these beings can reveal the depths of the characters and events in our ordinary lives. Did you see the Medusa when you met your future mate's mother? Or, was the Minotaur in bed on your wedding night? Did you see the great big green lizard in Washington, D.C., last week? Our mundane world is too small without expansion by the higher dimensions. Because we are so fearful, we lessen and belittle the awesomeness of our personal dramas and monsters. We remain small and fearful beings who hide in our little personal worlds and look out through periscopes into the great 4D emotional realm, yet we are ready to have more courage. Instead, we must stretch our emotional bodies by staying grounded in our physical bodies so we can contain these great forces to be free of manipulation. Otherwise, our 3D lives are hysterical theaters for events that actually only exist in other dimensions.

In our lives, we are always on one side or the other of any drama and this misplaced duality splits 3D into all good or all bad. In this darkened theater of life, lower dimensional (2D) forms seeking freedom are

---

* Each animal embodies a specific faculty—such as sight in the hawk or hearing in the fox—that is superior to human capability. We are an aggregate of the animal faculties, and we are inferior to them, especially if we destroy their home on Earth, thereby losing the specific faculty they hold.

sucked into this world to occupy the side that is judged and denied, because they exist to energize 3D. These are materialized archetypes that will work through us in 3D, and cancer is a very good example of this process. These forces would rather emote great energy in the 4D dome and be there in us to open doorways for higher-dimensional spirits. This telluric invasion of the material realm causes disease and violence in the material world, which *will not cease until each one of us recognizes that the realm of dark and light simply expresses both the positive and negative aspects of ourselves.* If we work with these aspects of ourselves emotionally without succumbing to actions in the physical world, authentic creativity will emerge that makes the real world a joyful home to play in. This is why the ancient Egyptians created constant stories about the gods and dialogued with them in the temples. The gods lived with them and made their lives bigger. In the Celtic and Balinese worlds, the gods are everywhere in the house helping to solve problems with herbs and critters, and home is a magical place. Divine forces only become demonic when they are denied creative participation. The second and fourth dimensions work together to energize 3D, and this process is integrated in people who have matured their emotions.

The archetypes that filter divine forces into this world reveal themselves by art and symbolism, the library of collective human evolution that links us to the divine realms. Higher dimensions are simultaneous realities that penetrate our world with waves that we may or may not receive. To detect these waves, we each need to learn to feel their specific vibrational frequencies, because our feelings can decode them, just as a radio or a screen downloads certain waves. *The Pleiadian Agenda model decodes how humans can be receptive devices for multidimensional frequencies when emotional bodies are not dualized and our deep memories awaken.* This is why Egyptian sacred science says that the first step is Maat, or balancing the polarities, and the goal is stellar access to Sirius and Orion.

As one Great Age ends and another begins, the great sages return to this world with the perennial wisdom. Then, it is up to us to bring in an age of enlightenment, such as the Age of Gemini, which can only happen if everyone participates. Without knowing the feelings of archaic people, we cannot imagine that they were in contact with greater realms of being.

However, our intuition knows something else by tuning in to their art and symbolism. That is why we are moved by the art of the Paleolithic, who were at the end of tens of thousands of years of cosmic contact when the link was shattered.

The Collective Awakening

When we have a clear and responsive emotional body and receive higher frequencies, we have tremendous energy and vibrational force. If we are emotionally split, eventually we become possessed by the archetypal forces that are trapped in our emotional bodies and finally become exhausted and deenergized. According to the wisdom of the sages, we are completing 11,500 years of a collective degeneration, and we are rapidly shifting into an exciting regenerative phase. The key to the whole process is the awakening of each individual, because each one of us has incredible creative gifts to offer that hold resonance in the morphogenetic field of ideas. The great creative gods are returning and looking for meetings in our reality; yet, will there be anybody home they can meet with? This book discusses the heart of secret, arcane, and superhuman abilities that are being explored by many researchers. Clearly, *we are preparing for the return of ancient wisdom.* However, something is still missing, and I think it is understanding that we each live many lifetimes. Reincarnation was eliminated by the Church in the West so that people would feel the knowledge they've attained in each lifetime dies with them, but it does not. As we've seen, anybody can go into a trance and easily report the "secrets"—the Hall of Records. When our planet achieves global consciousness, everyone participates in the awakening because each one of us has gifts for the gods. For example, Egyptian sacred science actually describes how the gifts of the gods are seeds contained in mundane human activities. Their culture was profoundly sacred because each individual—farmer, priestess, architect, or Pharaoh—was an artist. These days, people resist the movement of creative energy through themselves because they are conditioned by religion to be unsure whether the forces are dark or light. These forces will not go away as long a humans exist, so wouldn't we handle chthonic upwellings better by realizing that *the black frenzy can only penetrate dualized emotional bodies?* Mass psychotic hypnosis is what I fear, not the magical awakening of individuals. Let us look at what goes on when an individual responds to the collective mind.

People who clear inner psychological blocks stimulate a *group alchemy*, and then they can support those who continue to struggle. Actually, I am very optimistic about our future, but we are right in the middle of a most difficult passage because humanity is facing the true depths of its wounds. As people clear pain, archaic memory from old wounds is awakened, and some of it is bizarre, such as the antics of the Giants and the Nephilim described in chapter 7. Egyptian sacred science is the best source for understanding this because of how the Egyptians understood the antics of the gods in the human realm. The myths say Osiris was more than 15 feet tall, which means his energy was huge, and his presence was something for the individual to aspire to.[3] Stories about the sexual behavior, eating habits, or sickness and suffering of the gods contain brilliant instructional information because they were based on how developed beings handle problems, which offers humans more developed and complex solutions.[4] The gods aspire to a more ideal order because their dimensions are without space and time, which offers perspective in human dilemmas. This information was freely available to everyone through storytelling, and it often enabled people to heal themselves. For example, symptoms were a sign from the gods, and they interpreted these messages by reading their own bodies as much as possible. It was a matter of concern if anybody was suffering or unbalanced because this could destabilize Maat, so the strong people looked out for the weaker ones. They knew the gods were acutely sensitive and that their higher vibrational qualities could only exist in happy and kind homes. Altars were kept in the home to invite the divine into ordinary reality.

The perennial wisdom has been taken into secrecy by the Elite over the past 2,500 years; however, suddenly people who aren't even aware of occult ideas find themselves flooded with rich, arcane memories. Those of us who actually understand what is happening must have great compassion and courage for those who are still in shock. When we awaken inner memory, our nervous systems reconnect with the planetary mind, and our bodies have to learn how to handle greater flows of energy. Each receiver grounds these forces for the alchemy of the whole. Through a spinning module of biological intelligence, plants and animal species know when it is time to

*Fig. 9.2. Megalithic Spirals from the entrance stone
at Newgrange Temple in Ireland.*

regenerate within an ecological zone. The human ecological zone is the collective mind, which is calling us to regenerate, and many of us gravitate naturally toward the times and experiences needed for growth. When we find a way to be in harmonic resonance with Earth, our bodies, emotions, minds, and souls activate or quicken. Our personal energy fields change profoundly according to the qualities of the planetary mind. As more of us come to terms with emotional blocks and physical traumas from the past that are inhibiting growth in the present, the collective is flooded with memorable intelligence. Using reincarnation as a concept enables most people to be participatory in the collective mind through great spans of time, and it is an idea that even a little child understands.

By traveling back into the past by means of past-life regression, I found that archaic Egyptian, Minoan, and Paleolithic initiates were always guided through their previous lifetimes. Their method of reactivating past knowledge was used to advance their own cultures. This method of memory recall was how the oral tradition was maintained, especially after the Cataclysm. It also was how cultures avoided making the same mistakes over and over again. As a result, certain cultures experienced *spiralic evolution,* not cyclical Time, which is why spirals are so common in their megalithic art, as well as labyrinths. As we regain memory, the coils on the spiral thicken, and we become serpentine. We have forgotten this excellent venue of cultural transmission until recently. Cultural continuity will be lost unless we remember who we have already been. We need to lie down on our beds and reweave the time dream.

Past-Life Regression under Hypnosis

Past-life regression (PLR) is a therapeutic method for our "past lives," and whether these stories are thought of as "real" does not really matter. PLR helps us access the themes of our lives and see the lineage as a cosmic journey as it activates all nine dimensions in our consciousness maps. In a typical regression session, clients are hypnotized, or induced into a light trance, and they are encouraged to go back in time to seek information that might assist them in their current life. Often, by simply remembering key themes in the past, we can experience psychological breakthroughs that stimulate new growth in our current life. Crippling phobias can be conquered—such as fear of water or heights—by having the client reexperience a drowning or a fall in a past life; and sometimes overweight people achieve their normal weight after experiencing a past life in which they starved to death. Many clients also recover lifetimes in which they experience terrifying cataclysms. *PLR significantly reduces catastrophobia.**

PLR emerged out of standard hypnotic therapy and psychological counseling during the 1960s, and now it is widely used by therapists to help clients access deep emotional themes. Beyond receiving symptomatic relief, some clients seek spiritual growth and transformation from PLR sessions. When spiritual growth is the goal, PLR is greatly facilitated by using the concepts of karma and reincarnation, which teach us that we are reborn many times to work out karmic issues. We return again and again, guided by our soul's desire to learn, express love, and find spiritual meaning. I've lectured to thousands of people about reincarnation and karma, and so far the biggest objection to the concept is that people say they hate the idea because *they never want to be born again!* This is why Western culture is ecocidal. Why bother to care for the forests and streams, the ani-

---

* So many people have reported significant relief from PLR that it is sometimes covered by medical insurance.

mals and insects, and the fertility of the soil if you believe you will not return again to this world? In India, each major temple maintains a perfect habitat for selected animal and bird families, no matter how crowded the villages become.

Gregory Paxson of Chicago was my first PLR therapist. He comments that although PLR is a recent practice in our culture, it is actually an ancient and sacred tradition that was used to train adepts for thousands of years.[5] Most people who do PLR sessions report their past experiences by using linear space and time, and many are surprised to find themselves doing this. This is what makes me think there is a central, time-coded library that contains all our past experiences—*the* Hall of Records—that anybody can visit at any time. In chapter 3, I discussed the inner stellar chronometer, which is essentially a timepiece for our souls; it is very active in the archetypal realm—our gateway to higher awareness—and I am sure it can't function if we have an incorrect time line. We seem to be souls who create experiences amid collective events, as if being alive is like being in a movie. Computer technology is making it easier to consider ideas like this, because computer files are organized by linear time based on crystalline clocks. By traveling through various times and experiencing the qualities of their energy fields, I encoded the mental-vibrational qualities of those times in my brain, including the quality of being bicameral. Anyone can reawaken these dormant capacities. PLR is tremendously helpful for clearing your emotional body and going beyond duality, because the therapist is trained to help you see all the aspects around a particular dilemma and seek resolution.

Greg Paxson thinks of memory as a "power of refreshment, of new life in harmonic resonance with the ancient earth of the heart."[6] I would like to add that when we explore this harmonic resonance, we experience ourselves as vibrational, pure energy, which is what happens when we have a clear, diaphanous emotional body. Realizing that your feelings are the energy field that holds you in physical form is very liberating and expansive. I hardly need mention that millions of meditators attain these levels of awareness day after day. Paxson calls our bodies of consciousness—physical, emotional, mental, and soul—"holograms of different densities, co-occupying the same physical space, vibrating independently and in harmonic interaction around the reference—frequency of Self."[7] To him, an initiation is "an event in which higher energies are received into the person, permanently changing the energy frequency and functioning of that personality"—that is, accessing nine dimensions simultaneously.[8] For me, memories are like imagistic musical chords, and when we experience them again, we enrich our current resonant frequency. For example, think how we are forever enlarged by listening to Beethoven's late quartets or Bach's fugues. By feeling past vibratory fields existing deep within our brains, our current nine-dimensional structure tunes up. Like an old violin in the attic that is oiled, restrung, and played again, we become cosmic instruments. To accomplish this, PLR leads the client to experience the body, feelings, thoughts, and spirit aspects of forgotten lifetimes that lurk deep within us, waiting to tell their stories. Paxson discovered that the easiest way to *advance* a client's consciousness was to have him or her experience past initiations, because those were the previous times that we had advanced our consciousness.

As I relived past initiations, I began to see how the vibratory fields around my body were responding to this activation. We know that everyone has experienced initiations in the past, because ancient cultures were initiatory. Initiations are encoded in our bodies, and anyone can relive them. When I went out to interact with my readers, I was amazed to hear them tell me that while reading my Mind Chronicles Trilogy, they experienced their own initiations, which were often the same initiations as mine! Many readers said they were fascinated by the shifting vibratory fields, and they sometimes went into altered states of consciousness or trance as they read my descriptions. They felt they were attaining initiatic levels right along with me, and I am sure they were. A few students described initiations that they experienced in therapy thousands of miles away from where I was. I noticed that some described initiations I had just gone through in PLR sessions with Greg that had not yet been published. This is a great example of group alchemy—we must have all been tapping in to an awakening collective mind. Initiation is a process that follows certain laws of progressive levels of attainment that alter the group mind; this is why indigenous cultures use it. Eventually I got to the point at which all my lifetimes became interactive: My current reality kept changing whenever I removed a block in the past, and finally I fell into a resonant field that is quite remarkably connected to others. If we want to wake up and be whole, one way is to process dormant personalities that still want to grow. No one can free that entity except you; free your soul now, and offer your current state of mind a much wider view. The ancient Egyptians described this process as embodying your *ka,* which enables you to eliminate useless old traits and open space for new parts of the self that carry forgotten wisdom. Eventually, these lifetimes all meld into this life as you become a well-traveled person who is dressed and perfumed by exotic places—even if you never left home.

The recovery of PLR in the midtwentieth century began a clearing in the collective mind, because Judeo-Christian theologians removed reincarnation from doctrine 1,600 years ago, and the one-lifetime mentality has built a great dam made of unprocessed emotions. Individuals erupt evermore ferociously and irrationally with desperate and violent cries for help because they feel they must do it all—get married, have children, succeed at work, be famous—in this life. They are drugged, the dam gets higher, and the weight of the water means it will be breached. These intense inner complexes must be expressed eventually, which is why the initiation process has always been used in healthy cultures. As Paxson puts it,

An existential schizophrenia has evolved in our own society which is manifested in the inner lives of many of its inhabitants. Judeo-Christian culture is founded on the accounts of men to whom God spoke directly, or through a burning bush, or prophesied through their dreams, and reaches its height of fervence in the Teacher who raised the dead, restored sight to the blind, and, as a climax in a long series of miracles, resurrected himself after death. The binding thread that runs throughout is that there is a higher source and value to our existence than we can perceive by physically objective means. The chasm between these fundamental roots in "the Seen and Unseen" and the realm of scientific, rational knowledge of the tangible world "where we actually live" is broad and deep. This polarity in our minds and bodies has been expanding and intensifying for the last two centuries.[9]

Dancing on Turtle's Back

Many respected scholars, such as Joscelyn Godwin and Julian Jaynes, have feared that awakening the powers of the dark and light drives people to racism and collective insanity.[10] Mass movements have polarized cultures by getting people obsessed with great archetypes, such as National Socialism and Aryan Supremacy in Nazi Germany. Many thoughtful people fear that people will become possessed by these forces if they expand their awareness. I believe we must all awaken and understand how these powers influence our reality; otherwise someone else will use them to control humanity. The concept behind the Pleiadian Agenda model—that we must be totally grounded in our bodies—offers a surprisingly simple solution for possession by dark forces: It cannot happen unless our perspective is buried in the collective 4D mind. As we've seen, the Global Elite insidiously divides and conquers people and countries by triggering dualistic forces. Once divided, people are victims or victimizers, and neighbor will kill neighbor or brother will kill brother. However, *the Elite can not trigger people into fighting each other if people understand these forces within themselves.* If you think about the world wars in the twentieth century, the vast majority of people on the planet participated in them physically or emotionally. This generated a huge collective insanity that fed the flames of conflict while the Elite used the world as a game board. If there had been less emotional involvement in the collective, peace might have been found sooner, and the general public would have been able to see the moves of the game masters. Things are different now because many people realize that the only winners of wars are the financiers and manufacturers of weapons.

Sages have helped people discover the sweetness of peaceful vibrations within themselves once they have cleared their own emotional conflicts. In the early twenty-first century, the Elite are again trying to whip up the deadly whirlwind of dark and light forces. Each person and country that holds both sides of the dilemma in the heart reduces anger, judgment, and hatred. *The world needs to become intelligent about the sources of the conflicts.* For example, what if the genesis of the Arab/Israeli conflict is actually the unresolved battles between the Fallen Angels and the Nephilim trapped in the emotional bodies of Judeo-Christian-Islamic people, who are involved in or reacting to the dilemma? What if the Elite selected the land of Palestine for this arcane conflict because it is suspended over tectonically active caves and faults that are greased by microbial oil powers in this geomorphic zone? What if participants in this conflict are caught in the survival mentality of the Age of Cancer, and the dust would clear for them if they got a history lesson in the New Paradigm? Possessed by the survival times and praying for the end of Time, people fight over the caves and portals to the underworld like vultures stripping a carcass. How can anyone who lives in such a battle zone deal with this totally dualistic and covert field without clearing their own emotions first?

People outside this field must emote compassion and observe their own participation by their thoughts in this vortex. This part of the world seems to hold the ultimate wounding of humanity, and who would dare visit the sacred sites in Jerusalem without full shamanic initiatory guidance? Assuming that the people who are fighting it out there are fed by energy in the collective mind and the vortex, what if dualized emotions from the outside were removed? What if the only support to live in or go to the Middle East is for the people who were born there? After thousands of years of migrations, this whirlwind, or any other whirlwind on the planet, exists to be accessed by people in physical bodies in these places. Harmony arises when each one of us cares for the land where we live.

Earth once hosted a global maritime civilization that mastered geomancy, resonant forces, astronomy, geography, and community. This world collapsed 11,500 years ago, and the survivors settled around the planet and attempted to renew their cultures while they coped with more cataclysms. Quickly they realized that the position of the stars in the sky had changed, and the amount of heat coming from the Sun now varied and caused seasonality. Highly shamanic hunter-gatherer cultures adopted agriculture and became less free. In spite of many great changes, these people saved the great knowledge of the Elders, and temples were built everywhere to save these records and to continue the ritual practices. Today, as we consider that humanity was once highly developed, we can see that the knowledge that the ancients developed—such as using vibrational energy, sound, contact with very advanced beings in other dimensions, and dimensional laws for technology—is critical for balanced life on Earth. Many are participating in a massive awakening of Earth's intelligence by using harmonic resonance, and they know the place to find Earth's "mind" is right at home.

Turtle Medicine teaches us that it is time to withdraw our consciousness from the global field temporarily so that people in each field can feel the building intensity of the second dimension in our own geomorphic field. This brings a new aliveness in our bodies that triggers astonishing waves of feelings. As our bodies vibrate with this intensified dome of archetypal forces coming from our own hearts, the great emotions—forms, sounds, words, and light of the higher dimensions—will guide us into embodying our own reality. This great confusion about being home in our own bodies must be resolved first before we push our consciousness into other places, especially into places as juicy and coded as Palestine, which the Elite use as distraction to keep our eyes away from Egypt. Most people are easily drawn away by the Great Angels and the survival times, yet the activated field of Egypt encourages us to plug into Earth right where we are located. The Holy Land is the most difficult zone on the planet because the Global Elite have selected it as ground zero for the massive collective insanity: catastrophobia. In truth, we are like Osiris experiencing a great global dismemberment. Just as the goddess Isis found the parts of Osiris's body and made temples in each place on the Nile, so too we put ourselves back together again—we will not be whole unless we are *home.* Instead of being torn apart by vultures in the land of duality that will trigger the dark and light until the land is pacified, we can heal our own pain and move our consciousness into the vertical axis of enlightenment. The divine will enter into our peaceful and loving emotions.

Osiris was the most popular god in Egypt because he modeled dismemberment in life and eternal renewal of the soul in time. Osiris, by his battle with his brother Seth, is a teacher for facing the dark within and living to make peace with it. The Sethian nature represents the powers of the second dimension that we all must learn to pacify. These dark vibrations pulse deeply in our bodies and connect us to Earth, and when we realize that making peace with them enables us to ascend to spiritual realms, we learn to love the dark. The fetish of Abydos (figure 5.6) was carried through the crowds of people to the temple, because it taught them how the vertical axis forms by the activation of the lower dimensions. They were allowed to see how Earth energies are born out of the lower and deeper dimensions, and how living in the third dimension and praying to the four directions propels our consciousness into contact with the divine. It was during this festival that the common person was allowed to contemplate the most potent path to enlightenment. The ancient Egyptians all knew that their land—Khemet—was the sacred land, yet the teaching was not actually about Egypt. They are located in the geographic center of Earth; they realized it was possible for everyone on the planet to be at home in their own geomorphic zones. As was true in ancient Egypt, *Maat can be created today only by the people*. Osiris was a popular god because he was a male who was made whole by the goddess, his wife. The rest of this book is devoted to offering my own techniques for establishing Maat, and we begin with how to do it using astrology.

Chiron as the Wounded Healer

The tangible and intangible have been split by Western rationalism; our bodies have become so bound in material things that many of us cannot feel the surrounding vibratory fields. Mysteriously, in November 1977, a cosmic vehicle for healing this split was sighted by astronomer Charles Kowal at the Pasadena Observatory. Kowal sighted a new planet, which orbits the Sun between Uranus and Saturn, and named it Chiron. With a highly eliptical orbit, Chiron also travels inside Jupiter's orbit for a few years during its 51-year solar journey.* Immediately upon sighting the planet, a group of astrologers investigated Chiron's mythology, for whenever a new planet is sighted, a new archetypal field opens in human consciousness. Mythologically, Chiron was a centaur (half horse and half human), and in Greek prehistory before 1600 B.C. he was an astrologer who initiated healers, astrologers, and warriors. He was the founder of natural medicine and energetic healing, and he was a guide for adepts who went out on the alchemical quest.[11] "Chir"—or the Greek form, "Cheir"—means "hand" and is the root word for many healing modalities, such as chiropracty, chiromancy (divination), the chiral wave (the energy that moves between the hands of healers), and choroid plexus, which should be *chiroid* (the deep cranial wave). Surgery is *chirurgery* in French, as it was in English until the twentieth century, but it is difficult

---

* Kowal first called Chiron a small planet. Since then, astronomers have also said that Chiron is an asteroid or a comet. As you can see in the story of the Cataclysm in chapter 2, the Akkadian epic, the *Enuma Elish*, actually defines what Chiron is: a moon of Saturn that was propelled into a planetary orbit 11,500 years ago.

to pronounce. In historic Greek times, Asclepius claimed Chiron's healing mantle and founded allopathic medicine in 600 B.C., which was based on the idea that the doctor heals the patient. Chiron was the founder of natural healing and medicine, which posits that individuals heal themselves, and Chiron's sighting heralds the return of subtle-healing modalities in the West, such as the emerging forms of vibrational medicine.[12] The Greeks had forgotten their own past, just as Plato said; and when they came out of their dark age around 600 B.C., Asclepius replaced Chiron. Now *we* are asked to swallow this bitter pill. This was the beginning of the split between our bodies and minds, which intensified within Judeo-Christian culture, especially during the past 500 years. This split, however, is finally ending.

The body/mind dichotomy in the West began to heal in 1977 when psychologists realized what goes on in people's *bodies* is relevant to what is going on in their *heads*. Simultaneously, bodyworkers realized that what was going on with people's feelings and thoughts is very relevant to what happens when they stimulate their bodies. Suddenly, in the late 1970s, like Humpty Dumpty putting himself back together again, we began rebuilding our fractured selves. The last few hundred years of the body/mind split have been so disturbing for most people that nothing will stop this holistic fusion. Chiron was known as the "Wounded Healer" because he was poisoned by one of Hercules's arrows, and he had to live in his pained body because he was immortal. Finally, Chiron wanted to die, and in exchange for his descent into Hades, Zeus freed Prometheus, the fire god, who was hanging on a cliff while vultures ate his liver. Of course, this legend reaches way back into the survival times. By this exchange, Zeus liberated the Promethean creative fires, and the centaur healer died when nothing was left in his body except pain. Aren't these still big issues for us now? Our creativity is bound within our angry livers, and millions are trapped in bodies tortured by allopathic medicine. The medical system makes a person feel guilty unless they battle against their inevitable end with chemical and radioactive weapons, and replace worn-out parts in their bodies with donated organs. *We must regain power over our own bodies to be free to choose our time and way of death; we were not born to be fodder for the medical system.*

In the ancient world, Chiron initiated the warriors during the survival times. He goes back to the earliest times, and amazingly, Chiron was born when Phaeton smashed through the solar system 11,500 years ago! Phaeton is the same as Marduk in the *Enuma Elish*. Marduk pulled Gaga, a moon of Saturn, free from its orbit, and Gaga assumed a new orbit as Chiron.* That is, *Chiron became a planet during the Cataclysm and became known as the Wounded Healer 11,500 years ago.* Chiron was sighted for the first time by modern astronomers in 1977, exactly when the body/mind healing movement really got going; therefore, *Chiron is the planetary archetype for healing catastrophobia!* According to astrology, the planetary archetype that is being born comes during the first orbit of that planet since its sighting. Chiron will complete its first orbit around the Sun since its discovery in August 2027, when the world will have again established a global initiatory culture. Chiron was the astrologer's astrologer, so how can many of us use astrology to enhance our lives?

The Liquid Light Principle

Most people who use astrology have a natal reading done, and then they periodically keep track of current planetary aspects (transits and progressions) in relation to their birth chart. Because I spent so much time watching general patterns (astro-forecasting), I noticed a larger cycle in everyone's lives—the liquid light principle—that is easy to understand and is extremely influential. This is the cycle of major life passages: (1) *Saturn return* at about age 30, when people set a direction for their whole lives; (2) *Uranus opposition* between ages 38 and 44, when we face midlife crisis and clear our emotional conflicts or begin losing energy; and (3) *Chiron return* around age 50 to 51, when we face our mortality and redirect our consciousness into

---

* D. S. Allan and J. B. Delair, *Cataclysm! Compelling Evidence of a Cosmic Catastrophe in 9500 B.C.* (Santa Fe: Bear & Company, 1997), 204, 222. Allan and Delair believe Gaga is Chiron, which I'd already concluded myself in 1986 by consulting the key Akkadian Seal—VA/243—and studying the *Enuma Elish*. VA/243 shows the whole solar system *after* the Cataclysm, and Earth and its moon are clearly represented. Allan and Delair note that the key section of the Ninevah tablets, the Third Tablet, describes Gaga/Chiron being pulled out of its orbit as a moon of Saturn and then gaining its own orbit. See L. W. King, *Enuma Elish: The Seven Tablets of Creation* (London: Luzac and Co., 1902), the Third Tablet.

spiritual pursuits.* These issues are very important for each individual, and group awareness of these phases is even more beneficial for community. The liquid light principle occurs because we are all like plants on Earth growing in the Sun, and it describes how the life force—kundalini energy—activates by the planets going around the Sun. This triggers the growth stages that shape community. For example, everybody benefits by recognizing that individuals are ready to assume responsibility at age 29 to 30. When we understand that people are working out their lives by three key stages, then knowing how and when to support them becomes more apparent. Richard Gerber, M.D., author of *Vibrational Medicine*, notes that "Barbara Hand Clow's interpretations of astrological cycles and their implications for midlife crisis are quite remarkable in that they lead us to a whole new way of understanding the process of growth and transformation as a part of everyday life."[13]

Thinking of ourselves as plants with the Sun shining down, whether young men and women approaching age 30 have the opportunity to set their direction in life by work, marriage, having children, or serving society, is a major issue for achieving peace in the world. Many people would be more concerned about the lost youth of Earth if they could feel this need in their hearts. Also, individuals around the young people would tend to not pressure them too much when they are in their early twenties. When individuals approach midlife crisis, extremely potent and regenerative kundalini energy flows through their bodies, and they can clear their emotional bodies, fine-tune their minds, and direct their lives with their souls. Many people almost become psychotic at this point because the culture does not value this quest; in fact, it denies it. Yet, whether people can transmute their essence during midlife is the key to human health and enhanced character. When many people near age 50, a huge chasm of despair opens up. They are realizing they will someday leave this world by death, and they have no idea where they will go because the culture denies the reality of the spirit world. *The spirit world must be experienced while we are alive to have the courage to face our mortality*, and sages and

---

* Barbara Hand Clow, *The Liquid Light of Sex: Kundalini, Astrology, and the Key Life Transitions* (Santa Fe: Bear & Company, 1991). I have created the phrase *liquid light principle* to encompass the process of kundalini energy integration during the three key life passages.

shamans have always helped people to experience the other worlds so they will not despair.

I stopped doing natal readings in 1991 because the liquid light principle enables me to simply feel the energy flow moving in people's bodies without analyzing charts. Of course, natal astrology is very valuable; yet over the years, after participating in many ceremonial teachings, I've become more interested in community because it is so lacking on the planet. I worked in a New Moon group in New Mexico for about ten years, which is a very easy and fun way for people to find community. We gathered at each New Moon, and we created ceremonies, mystery plays, gossip circles, and medicine objects. Through this experience, gradually I began to heal one of the deepest woundings that many indigenous people suffer in North America: Our blood lines are thinning out as more time goes by. For me this is a Celtic issue as well as a Native American one. As more time went by, I realized it wasn't really the blood issue, it was more the *clan* issue. Clans are groupings of people by blood, specific interest, or geographical affinity who explore realities together. Then, in the early 1990s, I began to see that clans group together in ordinary reality to explore other dimensions together, much like little children playing in the sandbox. I found Felicitas Goodman of the Cuyamungue Institute in New Mexico, and I realized she'd discovered an incredible technique for modern people to access the alternate reality that can play a major role in healing the world. Shamans and medicine people universally understand that they contact an alternate reality that is "the twin of the ordinary secular one, a sacred reality where the spirits dwell."[14] Assuming ritual postures while in trance is a great way for modern people to connect with archaic consciousness because *these same postures were used by shamanic cultures for thousands of years.*

The Alternate Reality and Ecstatic Body Postures

Dr. Felicitas Goodman discovered that assuming a ritual posture and going into trance is how archaic shamanic cultures met with the spirits and sought information for solving problems. Once she discovered this by accident in 1977 (Chiron's discovery year), she then discovered that often figurines and rock art around the world "are not simply expressions of creativity, but in fact are ritual instructions."[15] If the posture of one of these artifacts is combined with rhythmic stimulation, "the body temporarily undergoes dramatic neurophysiological changes, and visionary experiences arise that are specific to the particular posture in question."[16] Neurophysiological changes include stress-related hormones in the blood that initially rise and then drop dramatically during the rest of the trance, and blood pressure that drops while the pulse increases. This is what usually happens when you die, which may be why many shamans say that they die in trance.[17] Goodman found that the trance should be maintained for 15 minutes, and the induction and cessation instructions teach people how to go in and then out of the other world safely. She has researched and developed the easiest, fastest, safest, and most direct way to enter and leave the alternate reality. While doing PLR work, our psyche always selects a past life that can give us the solution for a current dilemma. When doing a sacred posture, our body experiences journeys, cultures, or meetings with animals and spirits that we need at the time. The postures are a great way to bring in the sages and learn from them because they tap in to archaic sacred cultures that always worked with the spirits. They are also an ideal way to maintain your constant self-awareness while in ordinary reality. The first dimension is the iron-core crystal, which vibrates at 7.6 cycles per second, and remarkably, while in trance, the brain waves have been measured at *exactly the same frequency! The person in trance is synchronizing with the center of Earth.*[18] Remember, Greg Paxson said that memory is "new life in harmonic resonance with the ancient earth of the heart," as if he too was intuiting the pulse of Earth's center. As far as I can see, the alternate reality just opens up when humans pulse with the planet, which is what Chris Dunn says happens when the Great Pyramid resonates with Earth.

Statues or drawings of the Bear Spirit Posture, which is used for healing, have been found at hundreds of sites around the planet and are as many as 8,000 years old, and thirty-four examples were found on the Cyclades alone.[19] Some postures are more than 30,000 years old, such as the Venus of Galgenberg, which means that this ritual art form began way before the Cataclysm. The Cuyamungue Institute is still finding new postures and testing them in groups, and as of 1996, more than fifty significant postures were being used by students and teachers. The postures access nine different realities: healing, divination, metamorphosis, spirit journeys, death and rebirth initiations, living myths, and celebration.[20] For example, if you or someone you love is ill, you can assume *the bear spirit posture* or six or seven other healing postures, each of which have special spirits attached to them that are known by the Institute's research. If you need to let go of old realities and just allow change to come, you can undertake a metamorphosis posture, such as the *Olmec prince*. All the postures are shown and the technique described in *Ecstatic Body Postures*, written by Belinda Gore, who is a psychologist and director of the Cuyamungue Institute.

The points of interest are: *What* is the alternate reality and *why* would we want to enter it? Chapters 7 and 8 show that there is a titanic struggle going on over human access to the ancient wisdom records. Those caught up in this game are obsessed with the end of the world and afflicted with "ecstasy deprivation."[21] We are cut off from an ancient lineage of spiritual contact that goes back at least 40,000 years when we were "gathering hunters," who were in balance and harmony with their environment. We were in balance because we sought the advice of the spirits, which is the same as being able to hear the voices of the 8D sages, and it leads us to being in tune with Earth. As Belinda Gore notes, "It is a powerful lesson to realize that today, when we are at the

Fig. 9.3. The Bear Spirit Posture from Ecstatic Body Postures, page 49.

brink of ecological disaster, it is within our human power to enact rituals that can help bring the natural world back into harmony."[22] The alternate reality where the spirits live is eternally there and available just by assuming a posture and using your body as a magic carpet to enter nonordinary reality.

Felicitas Goodman noticed that the postures came from only two kinds of societies—either hunting societies or horticulturist—and although pastoralists and agriculuralists had poses during religious ceremonies, "they are symbolic, and do not mediate entrance into alternate reality."[23] Changes came in the Early Neolithic period, and as populations increased, people began to control the cycle of plants and regulate their societies more;

they "seemed to lose the deep sense of unity with the natural world that has characterized their hunter-gathering ancestors."[24] Gore believes people in Neolithic societies refined the postures to restore their connection to the more free life of the past, and Goodman sees this as a system they passed along to us so we can enter the alternate reality.[25] Eventually, large-scale agriculture took over in many places and control over the natural world dominated; as Gore puts it, "Duality became the focus in spiritual and secular visioning of the world. . . . The world of ordinary reality and the spirit world were split between good and evil, heaven and hell, above and below, spirit and body, God and Devil."* This primal duality is what splits our emotional bodies and cuts off access to the spirits.

Fig. 9.4. The Empowerment Posture from Ecstatic Body Postures, *page 74.*

The conspiracy grows because people are starved for the numinous and the ineffable, for shamanic access to other worlds. Modern tribal shamans access these worlds by drug-induced ecstasy, and the shamanic Egyptian priests contacted other worlds as the Pyramid Texts describe ascension to other worlds.[26] During ayahuasca journeys in the Amazon, when the processed plant is ingested, creating psychotropic effects, the women sit with the ayahuasqueros and go into the other realms with them, yet they do not take the drug, because they "have no need of chemical aid for their spiritual flights."[26]

Those of us who use ecstatic trance, whether we are male or female, also do not need to use drugs. Amazonian shamans receive specific answers to

---

* Belinda Gore, *Ecstatic Body Postures: An Alternate Reality Workbook* (Santa Fe: Bear & Company, 1995), 18. Geologist Andrew Sherratt wrote about the genesis of agriculture and plate tectonics in *The Origins and Spread of Agriculture and Pastoralism in Eurasia* (David R. Harris, ed. [Washington, D.C.: Smithsonian Press, 1996]) on pages 133–40. He believes that prehistory is *structural* as the outcome of rare and important accidents—that is, the effects of plate tectonics. Of course, I posit that this began 11,500 years ago, as do Allan and Delair *(Cataclysm!).* Sherratt shows that agriculture began within three tectonic global bottlenecks: Central America, the Middle East, and the Far East. His theory is relevant here because it emphasizes the traumatic genesis of the Holocene.

specific questions in their trances; likewise, the postures are so specific that one can select a certain posture for a specific purpose.

At the Cuyamungue Institute and at other locations where sacred postures are taught, students participate in masked trance dances. A group of fifteen or twenty of us go into sensory deprivation by a simple diet, withdrawal from the outside world, praying with the sunrise and sunset, and exhaustion by doing trances and making art all day and into the night. We have come to create a dance of the spirits, and this is only possible if we live with them in their world for many days, which happens by gradually withdrawing our attention from ordinary reality. We go into trances in specific postures, often divination, to learn about the story of the dance from the spirits. That is, *the spirits teach us the elements of a dance that will bring them into our world.* We discover what animal, plant, or being each one of us will be in the dance, and for days we learn to become the animal by making a clay mask and using various materials to become our animal from head to toe. We no longer conceive of ourselves as humans. We divine more together to understand the story coming in through all the dancers, and a new story for Earth emerges that will be danced, a teaching from the alternate reality for our world. When our costumes are made and the dance has been woven into a form by the spirits through the teacher, then it is time to dance in the sacred field while the drummers beat the drums. I have done this on two occasions, and both times the story of the dance was happening out in the so-called real world while we were dancing. For example, in August 1994, the spirits taught us the dance of the birth of the White Buffalo from Lakota tradition. When we went home after the dance, we read in the newspapers that the sacred White Buffalo calf was born near Janesville, Wisconsin. This was seen by the Lakota as a sign of new hope coming to Earth. This calf was born while we were dancing in New Mexico at the Cuyamungue Institute.

The nine dimensions described in *The Pleiadian Agenda* show how the divine manifests as sound and forms geometrical fields that create life. We know this creation in our bodies when beings, animal and plant spirits, and cosmic forces visit, play with us, teach us wisdom, and heal us. The spiritual and cosmic forces can enter our world especially easily during special times, and the Galactic Winter Solstice is one such special time according to the Mayan Calendar. However, we are the portals to our world, Earth is our home, and the spirits will only enter if we invite them. The dances of indigenous people at the Cuyamungue Institute, the Egyptian mysteries, art and music, shamanism and meditation are all ways to bring the spirits into our worlds. Most of the archaic sources illustrated and discussed in this book existed after the Cataclysm, such as Çatal Hüyük, megalithic cultures, and the Dynastic Egyptians. We have a glimpse into the world before the Cataclysm by the Magdalenian cave painters and the Ica stones. I think I will always be haunted by wondering what Earth was like before reality suddenly became so much more complex, possibly caused by the tilting axis. If it is true that the disaster began the split between the ordinary reality and the alternate reality, then perhaps the spirits enjoy our complex, emotional experience. From my experiences in masked trance dances, I already know that they think our world is better than ever. Regardless, if we invite them in and learn their wisdom, our experience with Earth can be peaceful, harmonic, blissful and much more fun!

Appendix A:
Egyptian Time Line

- 39,000 to about 9500 B.C.—The **First Time,** or *Zep Tepi,* when great mythical sages called the Shemsu Hor ruled Egypt.[1]

- 9500 to about 4000 B.*C.*—The **Egyptian Elder Culture exile** in the eastern and western deserts and in the Middle East.[2]

- 5500 to about 3200 B.C.—The **predynastic archaic period** when the Egyptians reemerged by the Nile, first as the Gerzean culture, who by predynastic times had claimed descent from the Shemsu Hor, the mythic gods and goddesses of the First Time. The tomb of Uadji was built during this period.[3]

- 3150 B.C.—The **Unification** of Upper and Lower Egypt under Menes (who may be Narmer) when the First Time was reestablished by the Nile and continued for 3,000 years.[4]

- 3150 to 2700 B.C.—The **Archaic Period,** which encompasses the First and Second dynasties with named pharaohs such as Narmer, Menes, and Djer.

- 2700 to 2200 B.C.—The **Old Kingdom,** which encompasses the Third through Sixth Dynasties. This is known as the Pyramid Age, when the power of Egypt greatly intensified, whether the pyramids were built during that time or not. Djoser was a famous Third Dynasty pharaoh, who built the pyramid of Saqqara, which was said to have been designed by the great sage Imhotep. Khufu was a famous Fourth Dynasty pharaoh who supposedly built the Great Pyramid. Unas was a famous Fifth Dynasty pharaoh who built a pyramid temple at Saqqara, which is incized with the earliest version of the Pyramid Texts. The Old Kingdom was characterize by the religious practices of the Heliopolitan, Hermopolitan, and Memphite mystery schools mostly directed from Lower Egypt.

- 2200 to 2000 B.C.—The **First Intermediate Period,** which encompasses the Seventh through Tenth Dynasties, when royal power declined and there was much anarchy and chaos and Upper and Lower Egypt divided.

- 2000 to 1750 B.C.—The **Middle Kingdom,** which encompasses the Eleventh and Twelfth Dynasties, when Egypt was reunified and Thebes became a new capital where the priesthood of the god Amun became a political and theological power that rivaled the Old Kingdom mystery schools.

- 1750 to 1550 B.C.—The **Second Intermediate Period,** which encompasses the Fourteenth through Seventeenth Dynasties, when unity was broken down again and the Hyksos occupied much of Egypt from their kingdom at Avaris in the Delta. This movement of people was probably caused by massive earth changes in the Middle East.

- 1550 to 1070 B.C.—The **New Kingdom,** which encompasses the Eighteenth through Twentieth Dynasties, when Egypt carried on organized warfare for the first time in its history. Some call this period the Golden Age of Egypt. Egypt unified again, and possibly because of the previous occupation by the Hyksos, it conquered territories beyond its borders by campaigns in the Middle East. Famous pharaohs were the Tutmosids I–IV, Amenhoteps I–III, Hatshepsut, Akhenaton (who was Amenhotep IV but changed his name), Tutankhamen, and Seti I and his son Ramses the Great. This period was characterized by constant power struggles between the pharaohs and the priesthood of Amun.

- 1070 to 525 B.C.—The **Third Intermediate Period,** which encompasses the Twenty-first through Twenty-sixth Dynasties, when pharaonic power declined and the Amun priests ruled Egypt from Thebes.

- 525 to 332 B.C.—The **Late Period,** which encompasses the Twenty-seventh through Thirty-first Dynasties until Alexander the Great conquered Egypt in 322 B.C.

Appendix B:
Earth Changes During the Holocene Epoch

A Holocene Snapshot by J. B. Delair[1]

Even a cursory glance at the Holocene record shows that, coming after the allegedly glacial 2 million-year-long Pleistocene epoch, its duration has been exceptionally short: only about 11,500 years. This dating and the epoch's brevity are confirmed by field evidence straddling several disciplines. Within this brief period, however, a whole series of profound environmental and climatic changes has occurred in quick succession. Naturalists have coined names to distinguish the different episodes, while prehistorians, studying them from anthropological and social perspectives, have given them other names. Appendix C tabulates these chronologically.

Outstanding among these changes have been globally rising sea levels, oscillating water-tables, fluctuating glaciers and snow-lines, recurrent volcanic and seismic episodes and cycles of desertification. All these have either engendered or resulted from often quite acute climate changes— including monsoonal shifts—with widespread effects on plant and animal life and also human activity. Superficially of great permanence, many existing environmental systems initiated by these changes have been accorded great antiquity but modern researches tend to demonstrate the opposite: *with few exceptions these systems have been proved to be remarkably youthful and anything but permanent.* [italics mine]

Particularly prominent examples are the North Sea, the Saharan and Arabian deserts, the bed of the Persian Gulf, the Indonesian archipelago, North America's Great Lakes and the Amazon jungle. Indeed, in their present guises, none of these "permanent" geographical features actually predates the Holocene.

The North Sea, resutling from progressive subsidence of its site (40), only achieved its present configuration about 6500 B.C. (41) Before that date, men could walk across continuous dry land from Flamborough Head to western Germany's Elbe estuary. In those days the Isle of Man was still joined to mainland Britain (42), the present Bristol Channel remained land-filled as far West as Westward Ho and Cardigan Bay's western coast followed a nearly straight North-South line from western Anglesey to the furthest extremity of the Pembroke peninsula. (43)

A network of river channels on the sea floor between Sumatra, Java, and Borneo (44) and other Indonesian islands (45), many of them submerged extensions of the rivers still active on those islands, testify with drowned offshore peats and undisturbed tree stumps (46) to the estreme geological recency of a crustal subsidence and marine invasion of huge tracts of Southeast Asia (47) around 8000 B.C.

Generally coeval analogous effects also separated northern Australia from the island of New Guinea (48, 49, 50), while the slightly earlier drowning of the territory now submerged between eastern New Guinea and Melanesia (Bismarck Archipelago and the Solomon Islands) and extending northwards to neighboring Micronesia (now mostly represented by the Caroline Islands) is part of the same story. (51) Not surprisingly, marked sea level changes accompanied these developments in French Polynesia (52) and as far eastwards as the Society and Tuamotu Islands. (53) The disappearance of so much continuous terrain (collectively almost as extensive as Australia) represents a land loss of continental dimensions.

Similar changes involved the separation of Sri Lanka (Ceylon) from mainland India approximately 9,000 years ago (54) and, perhaps a little before then, the drowning of much land now occupied by the Persian Gulf (55, 56), as well as of the Atlantic Coast of Canada's Maritime provinces. (57)

In geological parlance the terms "Holocene" and "postglacial" are essentially interchangeable. It is significant that, more or less coevally with the aforenoted crustal susidences, "post-glacial" uplifts of the lithosphere occurred in North America (58, 59), Scandinavia (60, 61)—including the Gulf of Bothnia (62)—and northern Estonia (63, 64), to list just four examples.

Of these, the Scandinavian uplift in particular was uneven and apparently quite abrupt, insofar as huge portions of Earth's crust supporting large lakes were, especially in Norway and Sweden heaved up *en bloc*. Otherwise undisturbed, the lakes were brought to rest with differently-tilted shorelines. (65, 66) The exact postions of the pre-tilt shorelines are clearly visible on the adjacent hillsides. Several millennia later, many of the great Alpine lakes were also tilted but in their case on two separate occasions. (67) Lake-village communities grouped around these lakes were severely disrupted by these events.

Still further South, far away in upland Peru and Bolivia, tilted strand lines noted for extraordinary "freshness" (68) were left on the flanks of the Andes by a formerly much greater and deeper Lake Titicaca. Interestingly, Titicaca's water level has fluctuated quite markedly several times during the past 7,500 years (69) and even today it submerges the impressive ruins of cyclopean stone structures made by some ancient, now forgotten, civilisation.

With tectonic (crustal) movements of this magnitude, it is hardly surprising that the sole egress of the waters of North America's Lake Michigan was, until some 10,000 years ago, the Mississippi River (figure B.1). Following a temporary coalescence of the waters of the Great Lakes some 8,000 years ago, when they formed super-lake Algonquin, the seawards flow of Michigan's waters was along a now defunct channel known as the Ottowa Outlet. A further 4,000 years elapsed before the Great Lakes began to assume their modern outlines and Michigan's waters reached the sea by their present route—Lakes Huron, Erie, and Ottawa, Niagara Falls, and the St. Lawrence River. (70) Niagara Falls, incidentally, are actually little more than 5,000 years old (71, 72), no older than Sargon-of-Agade's unification of the early Mesopotamian kingdoms of Sumer and Akkad! (73,74)

These crustal and lake changes inevitably affected local hydrographies. Among other effects, the Alpine tilts diverted the original courses of

Tyrolean rivers (75), damned others to produce new waterfalls as at Jajce in Bosnia (76), or altered Holcene water-tables at innumerable localities, causing rechannelling or draining of countless rivers and minor streams. Of these we may note the hydrographic changes in Zambia's Kafue valley (77), the extinct waterways of the English fens (78, 79, 80), a now dry former channel of the River Lea near Wheathampstead, Hertfordshire (81) and the successive changes in the course of China's mighty Yellow River,

---

Fig. B.1. *Lake Algonquin and the Great Lakes (E=L. Erie, F=Finger Lakes of New York State, H=L. Huron, IS=Icesheet, M=L. Michigan, S=L. Superior, O=L. Ontario.)*

Fig. B.1a. *The ancestors of Lakes Superior, Michigan, Erie and Huron forming at the southern edge of the Laurentian icesheet about 10,000 years ago. Lakes Michigan and Superior drained into the Mississippi River and Lakes Huron and Erie into the Hudson River.*

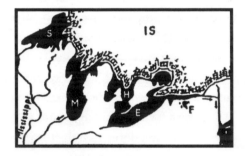

Fig. B.1b. *Lake Algonquin in its heyday about 8,000 years ago, formed by the meltwater of the retreating Laurentian icesheet and emptying into the swollen St. Lawrence seaway. Lake Erie had become separated from Lake Algonquin though it also drained into the St. Lawrence valley.*

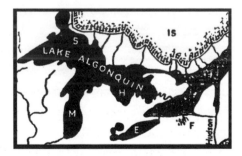

Fig. B.1c. *The Great Lakes began to assume their present outlines about 4,000 years ago, as the icesheet retreated still further and Lake Algonquin diminished in size. The upper lakes still drained into the St. Lawrence seaway, though via the Ottawa River valley. Lake Ontario and Niagara Falls had formed by this stage.*

some of which relocated large sections almost 100 miles from their previous route. (82, 83)

These hydrological changes had widespread repercussions. In many instances—including inland Australia (84, 85), Africa's Namibian (86) and Kalahari (87) areas, Syria (88), Arabia (89, 90, 91, 92, 93) and virtually the whole of the Sahara—entire, often extensive, lake and river systems disappeared.

The immense size of some of these networks was highlighted in 1981 when ground penetrating radar sweeps of the Sahara by the Columbia Space Shuttle "discovered" several of them buried just below the desiccated surfaces of southern Libya and western Egypt. (94) Similar defunct systems had been found earlier in the western Sahara (95) and were traced in the desert's central region as far back as the 1920s. (96)

Elsewhere, as with the bygone sources of various still extant rivers such as the Nile, tributaries shrank, reversed their direction of flow, or altogether ceased supplying the original parent rivers. (97, 98)

Lakes as large as the huge freshwater one occupying Egypt's celebrated Fayum vanished only around the close of Neolithic times. (99) Unfossilised remnants of modern animals and plants congregated in the beds of these extinct lakes and rivers reveal the equally recent demise of the organic life sustained by these lost hydrological systems. They show that, just a short geological time ago within our own (Holocene) epoch, large areas of these now desert regions hosted thriving fauna and flora. Even as late as 4000 B.C., woods still flourished in now dehydrated areas of the Sudan (100), the Nubian sector of which has had no continuous rainfall since about 3500 B.C. (101)

Before then, in Neolithic (middle Holocene) times, the (currently bare) Red Sea Hills were well wooded and irrigated by rivers—now nearly all dry—well stocked with fish. Several distinct predynastic Egyptian cultures successfully availed themselves of those conditions. (102) As now known to us, much of the Saharan desert regime dates from only around the astonishingly recent datum of 5,000 years ago. (103) The desertification process developed unevenly, since a few oaks and cedars, which formerly dominated many Saharan districts, contrived to survive in small isolated pockets, e.g., South of El Daba, in Egypt's Qattara Depression as late as 500 B.C. (104)

To the East, a similar story unfolds in Arabia where, in middle Holocene times, vanished civilised peoples utilised the once active river and lake networks in the peninsula's currently parched "Empty Quarter" and environs. (105, 106)

These developments were unquestionably connected with a northwards pan-Asian shift of the early Holocene's monsoon belt (107) about 5000 B.C., before it slowly returned to its present latitude in late-Atlantic times or by 3500 B.C. Of particular interest is the sensitivity of the monsoon system to orbital changes. (108) As already noted, the Earth's rotational speed varies and its orbit is eccentric. All these factors are inextricably linked.

While extensive early Holocene desertification was seriously affecting contemporary vegetation in the Old World, quite different developments occurred in the New.

Earth's largest rain forest fills South America's Amazon basin. Modern studies of fossil pollen there reveal that, until very recently, large areas of the forest were occupied by typical savannah flora and that the similarities of the plants in the still extant but widely sundered patches of savannah actually demand a former continuous contact between them. (109, 110) This conclusion parallels that of ornithologists investigating Amazonian bird speciation (111), herpetologists investigating lizard evolution (112) and archaeo-ethnological studies across the region. (113)

This environmental change appears to have proceeded in stages. Radiocarbon dates of masses of fallen subfossil timber underlying today's rain forest, examined at several widely separated localities, show that generally speaking three main episodes of sudden change have occurred, involving destructive violent flooding quite unlike the region's present seasonal flooding. (114, 115) These arose around 8000 B.C., 5200 B.C. and 3600 B.C. (116) Before those dates, the Brazilian rain forest, as we know it, with its extensions into lowland Venezuela, Colombia, Peru and Bolivia, simply did not exist. This "snapshot" of the Holocene does no more than highlight the remarkable geological modernity of many of the world's most celebrated natural features and indicates dates for when at least some began life.

[J. B. Delair's notes for this article are included in the notes section for those who wish to consult them. They are an excellent example of the extensiveness of the recent worldwide data convergence discussed in my text, and the short text reproduced here is such a remakable synthesis of broad data.]

Appendix C: *Holocene Chronological Highlights*

Dates B.C.	BIOGEOGRAPHICAL		ARCHAEOLOGICAL			
	Episodes	Significant Events	Egypt/Nubia	Levant	Mesopotamia/Iran	India
c. 687		• Acute meteorological upsets			Sennacherib's army destroyed	
c. 1000	SubAtlantic		NEW KINGDOM Dynasties VII–onward			Indus Valley civilization ends
c. 1630		• Thera (Santorini) erupts				
c. 1700	Transitional					
c. 2300			OLD KINGDOM Dynasties III–VI		Ur-Larsa Akkadian	
c. 2500		• Niagara Falls begin life	EARLY DYNASTIC Dynasties I–II		Early Dynastic I–III Jemdet Nasr	Apogee of Indus Valley civilization
c. 3000			Pre-dynastic / Nagadian Gerzean		Late Uruk	
c. 3500		• Asian monsoon belt shifts back to the South		Chalcolithic	Early Urrk	
c. 3600	SubBoreal	• Catastrophic land floods in lowland South America	Amratian	Chassulian		
c. 4000		• Scandinavian lake beds tilted/Woods still flourish in Nubia	Badarian / Late Fayum	Jericho (*level viii*)	Late Ubaid	
c. 5000		• Saharan/Arabian deserts assume modern images	Early Faylum		Ubaid	Indus Valley civilization begins
c. 5250	Atlantic	• Asian monsoon belt shifts northward				

IRON AGE   BRONZE AGE   NEOLITHIC

Chronological chart (read vertically):

Date	Period	Climatic / geographic events	Egypt / N. Africa	Mesopotamia / Iran	Levant
		assume present form			
c. 6000–	Atlantic	• Saharan/Arabian/Australian lakes/rivers begin to dry up		Ubaid (Eridu)	
c. 6500–		• Britian severed from mainland Europe			
c. 7000–		• Sri Lanka severed from South India	QUARUNIAN	Khuzistan	
c. 7500–	Boreal	• General retreat of glaciers/snowfields	TASIAN	Jamo	
c. 8000–		• Indonesian archipelago forms			
c. 8200–		• Catastrophic floods in lowland South America			Jericho (level i)
c. 8300–	PreBoreal	• Australia/New Guinea/Melanesia become islands		Zawi-Chemi & Karim Shahir	Natufian
c. 8600–		• Apogee of 'Little Ice Age'		Ali Kosh	Mallaha
c. 8700–		• Slow sea level rise begins globally			
c. 9000–	Younger Dryas			Shanidar cave dwellers	
c. 9400–		• Glaciers/snowfields form on most elevated areas			
c. 9500–			——Global Disruption——		
c. 9550–	Pleistocene	• Sea level much lower than now			

NEOLITHIC   MESOLITHIC   PALEOLITHIC

Appendix D:
Reflections on
Earth's Tilting Axis

J. B. Delair's thoughts about why Earth's axis must have tilted 11,500 years ago from his recent "Planet in Crisis" article are next.[1] I also describe Alexander Marshack's research on Paleolithic and Neolithic bone markings as well as some very avant garde Neolithic astronomical research by a few other scholars. This material could have been a whole chapter, but I chose to put it in an appendix because of its highly technical quality and because Axial Tilt Theory is a working hypothesis that I have by no means proven. We begin with J. B. Delair.

"The most immediately striking image of the Earth is that it rotates on an axis inclined at 23½ degrees from the vertical. Its orbit is not a perfect circle and it is not strictly concentric with the Sun. The axial tilt accounts for the variation in daylight hours per day between different parts of the world through the year. Combined with the Earth's eccentric year-long revolution around the Sun, the tilt accounts for the seasons and the difference between the average summer temperature North and South of the equator. Earth's axis of rotation does not coincide with its magnetic axis. This is also apparently connected with Earth's variable rotation, which fluctuates over a 10-year period. (28, 29)

"While following its orbit, Earth also oscillates cyclically: the 'Chandler Wobble,' with a cycle of 14 months. (30, 31, 32) This wobble is also associated with viscosity at the Earth's Core (33), so it is an intimate part of Earth's present internal mechanism.

"Because the Earth ought, theoretically, to rotate on a vertical axis and may actually have done so in the geologically recent past (34, 35), *these details suggest a planet which, in not very remote times, has been seriously disturbed.* [italics mine] If true, these 'ill-fitting terrestrial cogs' [i.e., Earth's inner Core rotates significantly faster than the rest of the planet], which appear to function only through the presence and action of inner-Earth viscosity, may be regarded as abnormalities.

"Yet a number of these features, including axial inclinations and eccentric orbital paths, are shared by several of Earth's planetary neighbors, so are the terrestrial equivalents really 'normal' ones? The evidence suggests otherwise. A selection of this evidence and its pan-solar ramifications, has been discussed by Allan and Delair (36) [and further considered in the main text of this book, especially chapter 2].

"*There ought to be no reason why any Earth-like planet undisturbed for untold ages should not have a vertically positioned axis.* [italics mine] This would unify the locations of the geographical and magnetic poles, ensure equal daylight hours in all latitudes and virtually eliminate the seasons. There would be no necessity for various subcrustal layers to function differentially and the present rheological mechanism would not be required. However, an equatorial bulge would remain as an essential stabilising feature and the retention of a non-circular and non-concentric orbit would probably still cause small 'seasonal' climatic differences when Earth was nearer or further from the Sun."

What follows next in "Planet in Crisis" is a few comments about the implications of these abnormalities, and then Delair describes the Holocene earth changes in detail, which is in appendix B. He notes that these relatively recent global earth changes must be the result of other forces operating deep within Earth, and he speculates on the "cause or causes of the Holocene cluster of catastrophes" in this section, which is titled "Rupture."

"Earth's essential instability, as mirrored by its structural and behavioral 'abnormalities' must reflect some persistent internal imbalance not yet fully accounted for. However we have already seen that the boundary of the solid Mantle with the liquid outer Core is irregular, perhaps to the point of being topographic (119), and that the outer surface of the solid inner Core is also not smooth. (120) Indeed, it is uncertain whether the inner Core is actually spherical: as it moves within the viscous medium of the outer Core it need not necessarily be. A non-spherical or iregularly surfaced inner Core would, however, generate further instabilities.

"Given these details and the inner Core's higher rotational speed [four or five hundred years for one complete turn by the inner Core!], its surface irregularities must be in continuously varying opposition to those of the slower moving Mantle's inner boundary. The plastic material of the intervening outer Core must therefore undergo displacement as the distances between the opposing irregularities alter. Continuous compression and release of this material must occur as the outcome of such differential rotation. Inner Earth movements of this kind are now being investigated deductively. (121)

"It is not unreasonable to infer that peaks of acute outer Core compression and troughs of compensatory relaxation should alternately develop to differing subsurface intensities at different times in different hemispheres. Likely results, which could sometimes arise quite suddenly, would include events which have often been termed mid-Holocene catastrophes. Lithospheric adjustments such as the Scandinavian, Alpine and South American lake tilts, extensive regional subsidences such as the Indonesian/Australasian/Melanesian area [see appendix B], large-scale water table changes as in the Arabian and Saharan regions and earthquakes and severe vulcanism, such as the Santorini eruption and its widespread aftermath effects (122), are typical examples. There is also no doubt that large earthquakes such as at one time racked the Roman Empire are closely associated with the Chandler Wobble (123, 124), itself intimately connected with viscosity activity at the Earth's core. (125)

"Why does the inner Core rotate faster than the rest of the planet and why doesn't the inclination of its axis coincide with that of Earth as a whole (cf. the different locations of the geographic and magnetic poles)? *It strains credulity to suppose that any Earth-like planet, undisturbed by external influences for millions of years, could have naturally acquired, unaided, a tilted axis, an offset magnetic field, variable rotation, or a Chandler Wobble.* [italics mine]

"Most geoscientists who have studied this broadly agree that any event or series of events resulting in characteristics as profound as these would almost certainly have to involve some influential outside agency. In other words Earth would need to be subjected to some powerful extraterrestrial force—a force severe enough to rupture its previous internal mechanism without actually destroying it.

"Down the centuries precisely such a source has been repeatedly advocated to account for traditionally catastrophic events like Noah's Deluge, the loss of a primaeval Golden Age, the advent and also the demise of the Ice Age, the sudden refrigeration of the Siberian/Alaskan mammoth fauna and even the foundering of legendary realms such as Atlantis, Lyonesse, etc. (126–135)"

Next the article discusses the main catastrophic scenario, which is already synthesized in my main text, and advances these events as the cause of Earth's abnormalities, such as the axial tilt.

"After apparently adversely affecting many of the Sun's outer planets, the postulated cosmic visitor was seemingly able to temporarily retard the rotation of Earth's Mantle and lithosphere but could not halt the rotation of the inner Core, due to the viscosity of the outer Core. As a consequence of this disruption, Earth's thermal and electromagnetic levels increased enormously, with all kinds of unwelcome effects. Among these appear to have been an *axial slewing of the Mantle and crust to an inclination differing from that of the solid inner Core.* [italics mine] Indeed, the latter may itself have been wrenched, gravitationally, within the liquid outer Core to an off-centre position, causing the Earth to yaw or tremble (or both), as some traditions recalling the events actually state. Such movements were *only* possible because of the viscosity of the outer Core. It is also probable that the cosmic assailant pulled the entire Earth over to its present inclination, since any former *normal* planetary regime *must* have developed over a more vertical axis.

"The resumed rotation of the Mantle/Lithosphere around a still rotating but slight off-centre inner Core (the liquid outer Core is immaterial at this point) at different speeds round different axes (the geographical and magnetic poles) imposed huge strains and stresses on the Earth. Prominent were fluctuating rotation and the Chandler Wobble. An off-centre Core would ensure only a very slow and stuttering return to planetary normality, punctuated sporadically by catastrophic terrestial adjustments. Holocene history is littered with these. While often alarming, they are really the coughs and wheezes of a world still in crisis."

Catastrophobia is the psychological syndrome resulting from these earth changes over 11,500 years. This book posits that the syndrome can be healed by remembering the original event and recognizing the valiant adjustments to the new Earth by the Neolithic people. The memories of these catastrophes were saved because the people they knew their ancestors—us—would need this information to be able to achieve the next stage of our evolution. This is Turtle Medicine. Recently, some amazing new theories about ancient astronomy have been advanced that highlight how Neolithic humans came to terms with the new Earth. I will cover some of these new theories very briefly, since these new ideas may end up being fertile ground for others who may want to consider whether Earth's axis may have tilted recently and made life on Earth into a whole new ball game.

Science writer Alexander Marshack was asked in 1962 by leaders in the space program to co-write a book that would explain how humankind had reached the point of planning a Moon-landing. When Marshack interviewed many of the key movers and shakers in the space program, he realized none of them knew *why* we were going into space; all that mattered was they had the skills to do it. He was supposed to write a few pages on the dawn of civilization and how the development of mathematics, astronomy, and science leads up to entering space. He studied the orthodox interpretation of our historical emergence and ran right into all the "suddenlies" that begin 10,000 years ago, such as the instant-flowering model of Egyptian civilization.[2] He went back into Paleolithic cultures, and then he had the big awakening that changed his whole life, as well as our current understanding of Paleolithic and Neolithic science: Marshack discovered he could read and decode the markings by early humans on ancient bones. Ironically, he was working on a project that was to explain how we could get to the Moon, and he discovered that Paleolithic and Neolithic carved bones are lunar calendars! Eventually he became intrigued by the fact that from the earliest times until 9000 B.C. (Early Neolithic) the bones are lunar calendars, and then about 10,000 years ago, the solar factor is added to the lunar notations. The lunar phases are divided into six-month phases, which are either equinoxes or solstices.[3] *Marshack's research and the research of many other paleoscientists indicates that early humans show no signs of being aware of the existence of the four seasons until 10,000 years ago.* I think it is unrealistic to surmise they just didn't notice the Sun traveling back and forth on the horizon and the changing seasons, especially since they suddenly became obsessed with this factor approximately 10,000 years ago.

Marshack's laborious decodings of the bone markings as lunar calendars from before 10,000 B.C. have been widely accepted over the past forty years by most prehistorians.[4] Eventually, he focused on the fact that the bone notations were lunar calendars until the end of the Paleolithic and then added the solar factor 10,000 years ago. He spent twenty years trying to decipher the marking of a plaque found in 1969 at the Grotte du Tai that is 10,000 to 11,000 years old because it has the typical lunar cycles with some new elements. Marshack decoded it by using all of his knowledge of Upper Palaeolithic notations and art combined with the art and notations of Neolithic preliterate cultures. This plaque is one of the earliest and most complex scientific Early Neolithic objects, and it probably is one of the first objects that records attempts by humans to show that there are about six lunar cycles between the solstices and equinoxes.[5] Anthropolgist Richard Rudgley notes that the Tai notation fills the vacuum "before the apparently sudden development of astronomical observations in the Neolithic period in north-western Europe, epitomized by alignment of megalithic monuments, such as Stonehenge."[6] Regarding Early Neolithic astronomical notations, what strikes me the most is the wall art of Çatal Hüyük, the complex geometrical Natufian designs, and the incised spirals and chevrons of New Grange, which show the year divided into the light and dark halves with the phases of the Moon deliniated.[7]

We have only barely begun to realize how advanced Neolithic astronomy was because we only now are deciphering their monuments, notations, and artifacts. It is very hard for us to take their obsession with the sky seriously because we can barely see the night sky in our modern cities. A great change is evident in Neolithic renditions of the sky, and I believe it was the tilting of the axis that caused the equinoxes and solstices. I think we suddenly can see things that were right under our noses because our own perspective is expanding. For example, Robert Temple, the author of *The Sirius Mystery*, described in chapter 8, has just published a brilliant book, *The Crystal Sun*, that definitively proves people have been using telescopes and lenses for improving eyesight for thousands of years, and many of the lenses have been on view in museums all over the world for hundreds of years.[8] I mentioned in chapter 5 that Ralph Ellis, author of *Thoth*, makes a strong case that Avebury Circle is a representation of Earth floating in space. Also according to Ellis, *Avebury Circle exhibits Earth's axial tilt!*[9] The diagrams and text by Ellis need to be studied by interested readers. In the 1980s, I noticed that the north/south avenues coming into Avebury tilt about 23 degrees to the east/west avenues, and I wondered why. Why would they go to so much trouble to model Earth in space tilted in its solar orbit? Megalithic astronomy exhibits a virtual obsession with the solstices and equinoxes. For example, New Grange captures the first light of the winter solstice when the Sun sends daggers of light deep into its chambers that illuminate the centers of complex spirals. Many other megalithic chambers capture the light at the exact moment of the spring or fall equinox. Even the center of the Vatican is constructed to capture the spring equinox light.*

In *Uriel's Machine*, Christopher Knight and Robert Lomas have shown how early cultures went to almost unbelievable lengths to comprehend, record, and anticipate light from the Sun and Venus. They have demonstrated that the shapes of various lozenges depicted on Neolithic Grooved Ware pottery and incized stone balls actually convey astronomical information. The shape of the lozenges created by sunrise and sunset through the year changes with latitude; they believe these lozenges depict the latitude of the makers![10] Suddenly latitude became important because the solar angles by season change so dramatically in the northern latitudes. Although there are theories in *Uriel's Machine* that need much testing, their conclusions about the megalithic stone chamber Bryn Celli Ddu on the Isle of Anglesey (3500 B.C.) merit serious attention. The authors

---

* I noticed this orientation when I visited the Vatican in 1979.

demonstrate by archeoastronomy that Bryn Celli Ddu is a sophisticated chamber that was used to correct the time drift in solar and lunar calendars by callibrating the time of year by the 8-year Venus synodic return cycle with the winter solstice. Venus shines a bright dagger of light every eighth year into the chamber at Bryn Celli Ddu when it is the brightest. According to the Roman historian Tacitus, this was when the Goddess appeared, and since Venus is the most accurate indicator of the time of the year, what does Time have to do with the Goddess?[11]

In *The Dawn of Astronomy* Sir J. Norman Lockyer reported in his exhaustive study of the star temples of ancient Egypt that various temples are aligned to certain key stars as far back as 6400 B.C. (see chapter 3). He also demonstrated that the "apertures in the pylons and separating walls of Egyptian temples exactly represent the diaphragms in the modern telescope," and comments that they "knew nothing about telescopes."[12] Robert Temple has subsequently demonstrated that the ancient Egyptians *did* have telescopes, so perhaps their temples were used like the large telescopes in modern observatories.[13]

I bring together these related details here because I believe that *the tilting axis inspired a preliterate scientific revolution* that we are decoding in our times. The axial tilt changed the way we receive light on Earth. Alexander Marshack was asked to find the source of humanity's ability to get to the Moon, and he discovered that archaic people were already profoundly in touch with the Moon in their times. I suggest the way beyond catastrophobia is to awaken this archaic intelligence, which I find is encoded in the Light itself. According to indigenous traditions, the Light is infused with cosmic information, and modern science has discovered that photons carry cosmic information. Megalithic astronomy, as well as indigenous astronomy, suggests that the Light is more potent and transmutative for humans during the equinoxes, solstices, and new and full moons. Perhaps that intentional attunement awakens cosmic intelligence. A new evolutionary form began when the tilting axis cracked Earth open, as if Earth is a cosmic egg ready to hatch in the universe. As the scientists peel the egg, perhaps it might be wise for them to come up with a reason.

Notes

CHAPTER ONE

1. John Major Jenkins, *Maya Cosmogenesis 2012* (Santa Fe: Bear & Company, 1998), 332.

2. Matt Ridley, *Genome: The Autobiography of a Species in 23 Chapters* (New York: HarperCollins, 1999), 122–35.

3. D. S. Allan and J. B. Delair, *Cataclysm! Compelling Evidence of a Cosmic Catastrophe in 9500 B.C.* (Santa Fe: Bear & Company, 1987), 15.

4. Ibid., 215–16.

5. Ibid., 207–11.

6. See E. C. Krupp, *Beyond the Blue Horizon: Myths, Legends of the Sun, Moon, Stars, and Planets* (New York: HarperCollins, 1991); John North, *Stonehenge: A New Interpretation of Prehistoric Man and the Cosmos* (New York: The Free Press, 1996); and John Major Jenkins, *Maya Cosmogenesis 2012* (Santa Fe: Bear & Company, 1998).

7. Robert M. Schoch, *Voices of the Rocks: A Scientist Looks at Catastrophes and Ancient Civilizations* (New York: Harmony Books, 1999), 33–51.

8. J. B. Delair, letter to the author, 3 August 1999.

9. Robert Bauval and Adrian Gilbert, *The Orion Mystery: Unlocking the Secrets of the Pyramids* (New York: Crown Publishers, 1994), 179–96.

10. Daniel Giamario, "May 1988 and the Great Galactic Alignment," *The Mountain Astrologer* 82 (1998): 57–64; Jenkins, *Maya Cosmogenesis 2012*, 105–14, 324–26; Nick Anthony Fiorenza, *Erection of the Holy Cross: Astronomical Earth-Grid Spacetime Mapping* (Fort Collins, Colo.: IANS, 1995) 14; Michio Kushi, *The Era of Humanity* (Berkeley, Calif.: East West Journal, 1977), 98–100.

11. Kushi, *The Era of Humanity*, 104.

12. Giuseppe Maria Sesti, *The Glorious Constellations* (New York: Harry N. Abrams, 1987), 447.

13. William Ryan and Walter Pitman, *Noah's Flood: The New Scientific Discoveries about the Event that Changed History* (New York: Touchstone, 1998); Stephen

Oppenheimer, *Eden in the East: The Drowned Continent of Southeast Asia* (London: Weidenfeld and Nicolson, 1998).

14. Kushi, *The Era of Humanity,* 105.

15. Allan and Delair, *Cataclysm!,* 83–137.

16. Felicitas D. Goodman, *Where the Spirits Ride the Wind: Trance Journeys and Other Ecstatic Experiences* (Bloomington, Ind.: Indiana University Press, 1990), 19–23.

17. Jenkins, *Maya Cosmogenesis 2012,* 116.

CHAPTER TWO

1. Hertha Von Dechend and Giorgio de Santillana, *Hamlet's Mill: An Essay on Myth and the Frame of Time* (Boston: David R. Godine, 1977), 145.

2. D. S. Allan and J. B. Delair, *Cataclysm! Compelling Evidence of a Cosmic Catastrophe in 9500 B.C.* (Santa Fe: Bear & Company, 1987), 149–51, 161–64.

3. John Major Jenkins, *Maya Cosmogenesis 2012* (Santa Fe: Bear & Company); Norman J. Lockyer, *The Dawn of Astronomy* (London: Macmillan, 1894); John North, *Stonehenge: A New Interpretation of Prehistoric Man and the Cosmos* (New York: The Free Press, 1996); William Sullivan, *The Secret of the Incas: Myth, Astronomy, and the War against Time* (New York: Crown Publisher, 1996).

4. Allan and Delair, *Cataclysm!,* 254.

5. Ibid., 149–68. See also Rand Flem-Ath and Rose Flem-Ath, *When the Sky Fell: In Search of Atlantis* (New York: St. Martin's Press, 1995), 53–72.

6. Allan and Delair, *Cataclysm!,* 263.

7. Ibid., 265.

8. Tjeerd H. Van Andel, *New Views on an Old Planet* (Cambridge: Cambridge University Press, 1994) 107–8; and John A. Stewart, *Drifting Continents and Colliding Paradigms* (Bloomington: Indiana University Press, 1990), 29–34, 181.

9. Allan and Delair, *Cataclysm!,* 267.

10. Ibid., 267–68.

11. Ibid., 268.

12. Flem-Ath and Flem-Ath, *When the Sky Fell,* 1–6; Charles Hapgood, *Maps of the Ancient Sea Kings: Evidence of Advanced Civilization in the Ice Age* (London: Turnstone Books, 1966), 174–88; Charles Hapgood, *The Path of the Pole* (Kempton, Ill.: Adventures Unlimited Press, 1999), 1–45, 185–92.

13. Guy Berthault quoted in John Milton, *Shattering the Myths of Darwinism* (Rochester, Vt.: Park Street Press, 1992), 68.

14. Allan and Delair, *Cataclysm!,* 136.

15. Ibid., 241.

16. Ibid., 12–17.

17. Michio Kushi, *Forgotten Worlds: Guide to Lost Civilizations and the Coming One World* (Becket, Mass.: One Peaceful World Press, 1992), 64.

18. Allan and Delair, *Cataclysm!*, 54.

19. Ibid., 136–37.

20. Ibid., 135.

21. Ibid., 136.

22. Hapgood, *Maps of the Ancient Sea Kings.*

23. Ibid.

24. Graham Hancock, *Fingerprints of the Gods* (New York: Crown Publishers, 1995), 22–23.

25. Hapgood, *Maps of the Ancient Sea Kings,* 178.

26. Ibid., 188, brackets mine.

27. Flem-Ath and Flem-Ath, *When the Sky Fell,* 73–88.

28. Hapgood, *Maps of the Ancient Sea Kings,* 187.

29. Ibid.

30. Allan and Delair, *Cataclysm!*, 53.

CHAPTER THREE

1. John Milton, *Paradise Lost* (Norwalk, Conn.: Eastern Press, 1976), 254.

2. Julian Jaynes, *The Origin of Consciousness in the Breakdown of the Bicameral Mind* (Boston: Houghton Mifflin, 1976), 105.

3. Jaynes, *The Origin of Consciousness,* 101–25.

4. Felicitas D. Goodman, discussion during Masked Trance Dance, Cuyamungue, N. Mex., July 1994.

5. Jaynes, *The Origin of Consciousness,* 255–92.

6. Mary Settegast, *Plato Prehistorian: 10,000 to 5000 B.C.—Myth, Religion, Archaeology* (Hudson, N.Y.: Lindisfarne Press, 1990), 1–5.

7. Robert Bauval and Adrian Gilbert, *The Orion Mystery: Unlocking the Secrets of the Pyramids* (New York: Crown Publishers, 1994), 69.

8. Ibid., 189–96.

9. Graham Hancock, *Fingerprints of the Gods* (New York: Crown Publishers, 1995), 383–87. See also W. B. Emery, *Archaic Egypt* (London: Penguin Books, 1961), 21–37.

10. Bauval and Gilbert, *The Orion Mystery,* 187.

11. Hancock, *Fingerprints of the Gods,* 382–87.

12. Ibid., 382.

13. Plato, *Timaeus and Critias,* trans. Desmond Lee (London: Penguin, 1965), 33–36.

14. Peter Tompkins, *Secrets of the Great Pyramid* (New York: Harper & Row, 1971); Kurt Mendelssohn, *The Riddle of the Pyramids* (London: Thames and Hudson, 1974).

15. Michael A. Hoffman, *Egypt before the Pharaohs: The Prehistoric Foundations of Egyptian Civilization* (New York: Dorset Press, 1979), 102.

16. John Anthony West, *Serpent in the Sky* (New York: Harper & Row, 1979), 196–232.

17. Hancock, *Fingerprints of the Gods,* 396.

18. Hoffman, *Egypt before the Pharaohs,* 102.

19. Karl W. Butzer, *Early Hydraulic Civilization in Egypt: A Study in Cultural Ecology* (Chicago: University of Chicago Press, 1976), 56.

20. Hoffman, *Egypt before the Pharaohs,* 40.

21. Butzer, *Early Hydraulic Civilization in Egypt,* 35.

22. Ibid., 39.

23. Ibid., 12–56, and Norman J. Lockyer, *The Dawn of Astronomy* (London: Macmillan, 1894), 235–42.

24. Butzer, *Early Hydraulic Civilization,* 26–36.

25. Hapgood, *Fingerprints of the Gods,* 107–8.

26. Hoffman, *Egypt before the Pharaohs,* 28.

27. Settegast, *Plato Prehistorian,* 97–101; Henri Lhote, *Frescoes* (New York: Dutton, 1959), the insert between 88–89 and the insert between 96–97.

28. Glenda Cooper, "Why We Must Now Rethink Civilization," *London Daily News,* 28 December 2000, 26–27.

29. Butzer, *Early Hydraulic Civilization,* 23.

30. Bauval and Gilbert, *The Orion Mystery,* 196.

31. Ibid., 97–104.

32. Ian Lawton and Chris Ogilvie-Herald, *Giza: The Truth* (London: Virgin Publishing), 323–25.

33. Lockyer, *The Dawn of Astronomy.*

34. Robert Bauval and Graham Hancock, *Keeper of Genesis: A Quest for the Hidden Legacy of Mankind* (London: Heinemann, 1996), 194.

35. Bauval and Gilbert, *The Orion Mystery,* 80–104.

36. Steven J. Dick, *The Biological Universe: The Twentieth Century Extraterrestrial Life Debate and the Limits of Science* (Cambridge: Cambridge University Press, 1996), 215.

37. Jane B. Sellers, *The Death of the Gods in Ancient Egypt* (London: Penguin Books, 1992), 700.

38. Lockyer, *The Dawn of Astronomy,* 352–53.

39. Bauval and Gilbert, *The Orion Mystery,* 179–96.

40. Sellers, *The Death of the Gods,* 93.

41. Hancock, *Fingerprint of the Gods,* 372.

42. Christopher Dunn, *The Giza Power Plant: Technologies of Ancient Egypt* (Santa Fe: Bear & Company, 1998), 134–50.

43. Jeremy Naydler, *Temple of the Cosmos: The Ancient Egyptian Science of the Sacred* (Rochester, Vt.: Inner Traditions, 1996), 80; Lucie Lamy, *Egyptian Mysteries: New Light on Ancient Knowledge* (London: Thames and Hudson, 1981), 35–46.

44. Dunn, *The Giza Power Plant,* 125–50; Barbara Hand Clow, *The Pleiadian Agenda: A New Cosmology for the Ages of Light* (Santa Fe: Bear & Company, 1995).

CHAPTER FOUR

1. Immanuel Velikovsy, *Mankind in Amnesia* (New York: Doubleday, 1982), 30–31.

2. Editors of Pensée, *Velikovsky Reconsidered* (New York: Doubleday, 1976), 7.

3. Velikovsky, *Mankind in Amnesia,* 30.

4. Rand Flem-Ath and Rose Flem-Ath, *When the Sky Fell: In Search of Atlantis* (New York: St. Martin's Press), 14.

5. Thomas D. Dillehay, *The Settlement of the Americas: A New Prehistory* (New York: Basic Books, 2000), 36.

6. Flem-Ath and Flem-Ath, *When the Sky Fell,* 61.

7. Ibid.

8. D. S. Allan and J. B. Delair, *Cataclysm! Compelling Evidence of a Cosmic Catastrophe in 9500 B.C.* (Santa Fe: Bear & Company, 1987), 133–34; Charles Hapgood, *Maps of the Ancient Sea Kings: Evidence of Advanced Civilization in the Ice Age* (London: Turnstone Books, 1966), 182.

9. Mary Settegast, *Plato Prehistorian: 10,000 to 5000 B.C.—Myth, Religion, Archaeology* (Hudson, N.Y.: Lindisfarne Press, 1990), 17.

10. Flem-Ath and Flem-Ath, *When the Sky Fell,* 107–8; Hapgood, *Maps of the Ancient Sea Kings,* 126–36.

11. Graham Hancock, *Fingerprints of the Gods* (New York: Crown Publishers, 1995), 409.

12. Richard Rudgley, *The Lost Civilizations of the Stone Age* (New York: The Free Press, 1999), 69–71.

13. Settegast, *Plato Prehistorian,* 108.

14. Ibid., 106.

15. Ibid., 107–11.

16. Stephen Oppenheimer, *Eden in the East: The Drowned Continent of Southeast Asia* (London: Weidenfeld and Nicolson, 1998), 430.

17. Jean Clottes and Jean Courtin, *Cave Beneath the Sea: Paleolithic Images at Cosquer* (New York: Harry N.Abrams, 1996), 34–35.

18. Settegast, *Plato Prehistorian,* 106–110.

19. Ibid., 109. See also Hapgood, *Maps of the Ancient Sea Kings,* 124–33.

20. Oppenheimer, *Eden in the East,* 441–74.

21. Settegast, *Plato Prehistorian,* 110.

22. Brian Clark, "Gemini: Searching for the Missing Twin," *The Mountain Astrologer Magazine* 91 (2000): 3223.

23. Settegast, *Plato Prehistorian,* 110.

24. Felicitas D. Goodman, *Where the Spirits Ride the Wind: Trance Journeys and Other Ecstatic Experiences* (Bloomington, Ind.: Indiana University Press, 1990), 23.

25. Plato, *Timaeus and Critias,* trans. Desmond Lee (London: Penguin, 1965), 156.

26. Tjeerd H. Van Andel, *New Views on and Old Planet: A History of Global Change* (Cambridge: Cambridge University Press, 1994), 85–87.

27. Dillehay, *The Settlement of the Americas.*

28. Dr. Walter Neves, quoted in Larry Rohter, "An Ancient Skull Challenges Long-Held Theories," *New York Times,* 26 October 1999, sec. F, pp. 1, 5.

29. Sourcebook Project, *Science Frontiers* 1, no. 126.

30. Oppenheimer, *Eden in the East.*

31. Hapgood, *Maps of the Ancient Sea Kings,* 218.

32. Plato, *Timaeus and Critias,* 34–36.

33. Ibid., 136–37.

34. Marija Gimbutas, *The Language of the Goddess* (San Francisco: Harper & Row, 1989), 321.

35. Plato, *Timaeus and Critias,* 35–36.

36. Norman J. Lockyer, *The Dawn of Astronomy* (London: Macmillan, 1894), 329, 414–18.

37. Rudgley, *The Lost Civilizations of the Stone Age,* 100.

38. Plato, *Timaeus and Critias,* 36–37.

CHAPTER FIVE

1. Marija Gimbutas, *The Language of the Goddess* (San Francisco: Harper & Row, 1989), 321.

2. John Michell, *Old Stones of Land's End* (Bristol, England: Pentacle Books, 1979), 6.

3. John Michell, *The New View over Atlantis* (San Francisco: Harper & Row, 1983), 83–105.

4. David Cowan and Anne Silk, *Ancient Energies of the Earth* (London: Thorsons, 1999), 8–23.

5. Michell, *Old Stones of Land's End*, 11–27.

6. Ibid., 11.

7. Ibid., 11–27.

8. Tom Graves, *Needles of Stone* (London: Granada, 1980), 99–100. See also Francis Hitching, *Earth Magic* (New York: William Morrow, 1977).

9. Michell, *The New View over Atlantis*, 47–58.

10. Michael Dames, *The Silbury Treasure: The Great Goddess Rediscovered* (London: Thames and Hudson, 1976).

11. Ralph Ellis, *Thoth: Architect of the Universe* (Dorset, England: Edfu Books, 1997), 104–29.

12. Ibid., 50.

13. William Sullivan, *The Secret of the Incas: Myth, Astronomy, and the War against Time* (New York: Crown Publishers, 1996), 23–24.

14. Michell, *The New View over Atlantis*, 94.

15. P. C. W. Davies and J. Brown, *Superstrings* (Cambridge: Cambridge University Press, 1988).

16. Michell, *The New View over Atlantis*, 39.

17. Georg Feuerstein, Subhash Kak, and David Frawley, *In Search of the Cradle of Civilization* (Wheaton, Ill.: Quest Books, 1995) 76–99.

18. Tom Van Flandern, *Dark Matter, Missing Planets, and New Comets: Paradoxes Resolved, Origins Illuminated* (Berkeley, Calif.: North Atlantic Books, 1993), 155–236.

19. Richard Rudgley, *The Lost Civilizations of the Stone Age* (New York: The Free Press, 1999), 8–9. See also Felicitas D. Goodman, *Where the Spirits Ride the Wind: Trance Journeys and Other Ecstatic Experiences* (Bloomington, Ind.: Indiana University Press, 1990), 219–23.

20. Jeremy Naydler, *Temple of the Cosmos: The Ancient Egyptian Science of the Sacred* (Rochester, Vt.: Inner Traditions, 1996), vii.

21. Michell, *The New View over Atlantis*, 94.

22. Norman J. .Lockyer, *The Dawn of Astronomy* (London: Macmillan, 1894), 235–36.

23. Barbara Hand Clow, *The Mind Chronicles Trilogy: Eye of the Centaur* (Santa Fe: Bear & Company, 1990), 37–40.

24. Graham Hancock, *Fingerprints of the Gods* (New York: Crown, 1995), 400–407.

25. Miriam Lichtheim, *Ancient Egyptian Literature, Vol. II: New Kingdom* (Berkeley, Calif.: University of California Press, 1980), 197–99.

26. Dimitri Meeks and Christine Favard-Meeks, *Daily Life of the Egyptian Gods* (Ithaca, N.Y.: Cornell University Press, 1993), 26.

27. Henri Frankfort, *Kingship and the Gods: A Study of Ancient Near Eastern Religion and the Integration of Society and Nature* (London: University of Chicago Press, 1948), 101–23.

28. Frankfort, *Kingship and the Gods,* 19.

29. Ibid, 20.

30. Ibid., 23.

31. Ibid., 112, 126.

32. Ibid., 128–29.

33. Ibid., 91–129.

34. Ibid., 130.

35. Ibid., 133.

36. Ibid., 134.

37. Ibid., 79.

38. Brian Fagan, *From Black Land to Fifth Sun* (Reading, Mass.: Perseus Books, 1998), 74.

39. Frankfort, *Kingship and the Gods,* 86.

40. Ibid., 207.

41. Citing C. H. Wilkinson in Alan F. Alford, *The Phoenix Solution: Secrets of a Lost Civilisation* (London: Hodder and Stoughton, 1998), 322.

42. Ibid., 327–28.

43. Naydler, *Temple of the Cosmos,* 13.

CHAPTER SIX

1. Aeschylus, *Prometheus Bound,* trans. E. H. Plumptre, 1868. Full citation not available, but an alternate translation can be found in Albert Cook and Edwin Dolan, *Greek Tragedy,* (Dallas: Spring Publications, 1972), 80–81.

2. Mary Settegast, *Plato Prehistorian: 10,000 to 5000 B.C.—Myth, Religion, Archaeology* (Hudson, N.Y.: Lindisfarne Press, 1990), 30–34.

3. W. B. Emery, *Archaic Egypt* (London: Penguin Books, 1961), 152, fig. 8.

4. Adrian Barnett, "Written in Stone," *New Scientist,* 4 October 1997, p. 11.

5. Andrew Collins, *From the Ashes of Angels: The Forbidden Legacy of a Fallen Race* (London: Signet, 1997), 327–47.

6. Ibid., 344.

7. Settegast, *Plato Prehistorian,* 94–105.

8. Charles Pellegrino, *Unearthing Atlantis: An Archaeological Odyssey* (New York: Vintage Books, 1993), 246. See also Michael Hoffman, *Egypt before the Pharoahs: The Prehistoric Foundations of Egyptian Civilization* (New York, Dorset Press, 1979), 23–32.

9.   George Rapp Jr. and Christopher L. Hill, *Geoarchaeology: The Earth-Science Approach to Archaeological Interpretation* (New Haven, Conn.: Yale University Press, 1998), 159.

10. Settegast, *Plato Prehistorian*, 46.

11. Ibid., 46–49.

12. Ibid., 50.

13. Plato, *Timaeus and Critias,* trans. Desmond Lee (London: Penguin, 1965) 134.

14. Settegast, *Plato Prehistorian,* 42.

15. Ibid., 42–51.

16. Ibid., 141.

17. William Ryan and Walter Pitman, *Noah's Flood: The New Scientific Discoveries about the Event that Changed History* (New York: Touchstone, 1998).

18. Ryan and Pitman, *Noah's Flood,* 188–201.

19. Andrew Collins, *Gods of Eden: Egypt's Lost Legacy and the Genesis of Civilization* (London: Headline, 1998), 312–17; Stephen Oppenheimer, *Eden in the East: The Drowned Continent of Southeast Asia* (London: Weidenfeld and Nicolson, 1998), 60–61.

20. Charles Hapgood, *Maps of the Ancient Sea Kings: Evidence of Advanced Civilization in the Ice Age* (London: Turnstone Books, 1966), 186–87.

21. Georg Feuerstein, Subhash Kak, and David Frawley, *In Search of the Cradle of Civilization* (Wheaton, Ill.: Quest Books, 1995), 87–99.

22. A. G. Galanopoulos and Edward Bacon, *Atlantis: The Truth behind the Legend* (New York: Bobbs-Merrill, 1969), 112.

23. James W. Mavor, *Voyage to Atlantis* (Rochester, Vt.: Park Street Press, 1990), 46.

24. Plato, *Timaeus and Critias,* 36.

25. J. B. Delair, "Planet in Crisis," *Chronology and Catastrophism Review,* 2 (1997): 2.

26. Jane Hamblin and the Time-Life Editors, *The First Cities* (New York: Time-Life Books, 1973), 43–67.

27. Settegast, *Plato Prehistorian,* 163–71.

28. Ibid., 169.

29. Ryan and Pitman, *Noah's Flood,* 184.

30. Collins, *From the Ashes of Angels: The Forbidden Legacy of a Fallen Race* (London: Signet, 1997), 266–70.

31. Settegast, *Plato Prehistorian,* 189.

32. Ibid., 201–03.

33. Brian Fagan, *From Black Land to Fifth Sun* (Reading, Mass.: Perseus Books, 1998), 69.

34. Ibid., 92.

35. Settegast, *Plato Prehistorian*, 201, 215–16.

36. Hertha Von Dechend and Georgio de Santillana, *Hamlet's Mill: An Essay on Myth and the Frame of Time* (Boston: David R. Godine, 1977), 62–63.

37. Settegast, *Plato Prehistorian*, 9, 215–21.

38. Ibid., 201. See also David Ulansey, *The Origins of the Mithraic Mysteries* (Oxford: Oxford University Press, 1989), 9.

39. Settegast, *Plato Prehistorian*, 205.

40. Malcolm W. Browne, "Harnessing a Molecule's Explosive Powers," *New York Times*, 25 January 2000, sec. F, p. 3.

41. Richard Rudgley, *The Lost Civilizations of the Stone Age* (New York: The Free Press, 1999), 50–57.

42. Ibid., 86–105.

43. Ibid., 87.

CHAPTER SEVEN

1. Elémire Zolla in Giuseppe Maria Sesti, *The Glorious Constellations* (New York: Harry N. Abrams, 1987), 14–15.

2. Michio Kushi, *The Era of Humanity* (Berkeley, Calif.: East West Journal, 1977), 100.

3. Kushi, *The Era of Humanity*, 65–69.

4. Ibid., 105.

5. Ibid., 104.

6. Ibid., 104–5.

7. Mary Scott, *Kundalini in the Physical West* (London: Routledge & Kegan Paul, 1983), 236–37.

8. David Icke, *The Biggest Secret* (Scottsdale, Ariz.: Bridge of Love Publications, 1999); Christopher Knight and Robert Lomas, *The Hiram Key: Pharoahs, Freemasons, and the Discovery of the Secret Scrolls of Jesus* (Boston: Element, 1999); Louis Pauwels and Jacques Bergier, *The Morning of the Magicians* (New York: Stein and Day, 1964); and Trevor Ravenscroft, *The Spear of Destiny* (York Beach, Me.: Weiser, 1982).

9. Andrew Collins, *From the Ashes of Angels: The Forbidden Legacy of a Fallen Race* (London: Signet, 1997), 10.

10. Ibid.

11. Andrew Collins, *The Gods of Eden: Egypt's Lost Legacy and the Genesis of Civilization* (London: Headline, 1998), 261.

12. Collins, *From the Ashes of Angels*, 283–85.

13. Ibid.

14. James Mellaart, *Çatal Hüyük: A Neolithic Town in Anatolia* (New York: McGraw-Hill, 1967), 66.

15. Collins, *From the Ashes of Angels*, 286.

16. Ibid., 345.

17. D. S. Allan and J. B. Delair, *Cataclysm! Compelling Evidence of a Cosmic Catastrophe in 9500 B.C.* (Santa Fe: Bear & Company, 1997), 183–90; Tjeerd H. Van Andel, *New Views on an Old Planet: A History of Global Change* (Cambridge: Cambridge University Press, 1994), 36, 86, 96–97.

18. Allan and Delair, 101–5.

19. Collins, *From the Ashes of Angels*, 290.

20. J. B. Delair and E. F. Oppé, "The Evidence of Violent Extinction in South America," in *The Path of the Pole*, ed. Charles Hapgood (Kempton, Ill.: Adventures Unlimited Press, 1970), 280–97; Hershel Shanks, "Everything You Ever Knew about Jerusalem Is Wrong (Well, Almost)," *Biblical Archaeology Review* 65, no. 6 (1999): 20–29.

21. Collins, *From the Ashes of Angels*, 102.

22. Ibid., 92.

23. Ibid., 98. Mary Settegast, *Plato Prehistorian: 10,000 to 5000 B.C.—Myth, Religion, Archaeology* (Hudson, N.Y.: Lindisfarne Press, 1990), 211–25.

24. Collins, *From the Ashes of Angels*, 100.

25. Ibid., 101.

26. Ibid., 103.

27. Ibid., 105.

28. Ibid., 116.

29. Ibid., 51–54.

30. James M. Robinson, ed., *The Nag Hamadi Library* (San Francisco: Harper & Row, 1977).

31. Collins, *From the Ashes of Angels*, 23–24.

32. Ibid., 24–25.

33. Ibid., 25–27.

34. Ibid., 63.

35. Ibid., 62–73.

36. Ibid., 38–45.

37. Ibid., 41.

38. Margaret Starbird, *The Woman with the Alabaster Jar: Mary Magdalen and the Holy Grail* (Santa Fe: Bear & Company, 1993), 27–30.

39. Matthew Fox, *Original Blessing: A Primer in Creation Spirituality* (Santa Fe: Bear & Company, 1983), 18, 232–38.

40. Collins, *From the Ashes of Angels,* 56–61.

41. Ibid., 109–22.

42. Ibid., 114.

43. Ibid., 111–15.

44. Ibid., 112.

45. Ibid., 127–34.

46. Ibid., 140.

47. Ibid., 205–7.

48. Christopher O'Brien and Barbara Joy O'Brien, *The Genius of the Few: The Story of Those Who Founded the Garden in Eden* (Northhamptonshire, England: Turnstone, 1985), 68–70.

49. Collins, *From the Ashes of Angels,* 244.

50. Ibid., 245.

51. Ibid., 247–48.

52. Ibid., 249.

53. Lucie Lamy, *Egyptian Mysteries: New Light on Ancient Knowledge* (London: Thames and Hudson, 1981), 7.

54. Javier Darquea Cabrera, *The Message of the Engraved Stones of Ica* (Lima: privately published, 1988).

55. Delair and Oppé, "The Evidence of Violent Extinctions in South America," 280–97.

56. Ibid., 286–91.

57. Cabrera, *The Message of the Engraved Stones of Ica,* 87–102.

58. Ibid., 40–42.

59. H. S. Bellamy, *Built Before the Flood: The Problem of the Tiahuanaco Ruins* (London: Faber and Faber, 1947), 35; and Graham Hancock, *Fingerprints of the Gods* (New York: Crown, 1995), 76.

60. Cabrera, *The Message of the Engraved Stones of Ica,* 24.

61. Ibid., 87–102.

62. Ibid., 64–74, 200.

63. Delair and Oppé, "The Evidence of Violent Extinctions in South America," 281–94.

64. Cabrera, *The Message of the Engraved Stones of Ica,* 189–92.

65. Ibid., 196.

66. Ibid., 190–97.

67. Allan and Delair, *Cataclysm!,* 207–11.

68. Ibid., 317.

69. Collins, *The Gods of Eden,* 338–41.

70. Cabrera, *The Message of the Engraved Stones of Ica,* 164–67.

71. Ibid., 166.

72. Ibid., 152.

73. Ibid., 142.

74. Hancock, *Fingerprints of the Gods,* 76.

75. Cabrera, *The Message of the Engraved Stones of Ica,* 151–64.

76. Ibid., 173.

77. Charles Hapgood, *Mystery in Acamboro* (Kempton, Ill.: Adventures Unlimited Press, 2000), 72–153.

78. Ibid., 93.

79. Ibid., 96 (italics mine).

80. Christopher Dunn, *The Giza Power Plant: Technologies of Ancient Egypt* (Santa Fe: Bear & Company), 103–70.

81. Ibid., 87.

82. Ibid., 105.

83. Ibid., 109–19.

84. Ibid., 109–24.

85. Ibid., 134–35.

86. Ibid., 138–39.

87. Ibid., 151.

CHAPTER EIGHT

1. Edgar Cayce cited in Lynn Picknett and Clive Prince, *The Stargate Conspiracy* (London: Little, Brown, 2000), 59.

2. Ian Lawton and Chris Ogilvie-Herald, *Giza: The Truth* (London: Virgin Publishing, 2000), 214–16, 476–78; Christopher Dunn, "Petrie on Trial," *Atlantis Rising* 24 (2000): 24–25, 60–61.

3. Charles Hapgood, *The Path of the Pole* (Kempton, Ill.: Adventures Unlimited Press, 1970), xiv–xv.

4. Picknett and Prince, *The Stargate Conspiracy,* xv.

5. Ibid., 59.

6. Ibid., 13.

7. Robert K. G. Temple, *The Sirius Mystery* (New York: St. Martin's Press, 1976).

8. Picknett and Prince, *The Stargate Conspiracy,* 34.

9. Barbara Hand Clow, *The Pleiadian Agenda: A New Cosmology for the Ages of Light* (Santa Fe: Bear & Company, 1995), xix–xxi.

10. Picknett and Prince, *The Stargate Conspiracy*, xiv (author's italics).

11. Ibid., 28.

12. Ibid., 59.

12. Ibid., 105.

13. Ibid., 106–7.

14. Ibid., 255–302.

15. Picknett and Prince, *The Stargate Conspiracy*, 63.

17. Ibid., 84.

18. J. J. Hurtak, *The Book of Knowledge: The Keys of Enoch* (Los Gatos, Calif.: The Academy for Future Science, 1977).

19. Picknett and Prince, *The Stargate Conspiracy*, 87.

20. Ibid.

21. Ibid., 81–115.

22. Ibid., 100.

23. David Ovason, *The Secret Architecture of Our Nation's Capital* (New York: HarperCollins, 2000).

24. Picknett and Prince, *The Stargate Conspiracy*, 117–19.

25. Ibid., 121.

26. Ibid., 135.

27. D. S. Allan and J. B. Delair, *Cataclysm! Compelling Evidence of a Cosmic Catastrophe in 9500 B.C.* (Santa Fe: Bear & Company, 1997), 226.

28. Ibid., 227.

29. Graham Hancock, *The Mars Mystery* (New York: Crown, 1998), 48.

30. Ralph Ellis, *Thoth, Architect of the Universe* (Dorset, England: Edfu Books, 1997), 104–31.

31. John Noble Wilford, "Replying to Skeptics, NASA Defends Claims About Mars," *New York Times*, 8 August 1996, sec. D, pp.1, 20.

32. Picknett and Prince, *The Stargate Conspiracy*, 157–59; Hancock, *The Mars Mystery*, 21–22.

33. David L. Chandler, "Clinton Touts Mars Project," *Boston Globe*, 8 August 1996, sec. A, p. 1.

34. Hancock, *The Mars Mystery*, 23.

35. John Noble Wilford, "Replying to Skeptics, NASA Defends Claims About Mars," p. 20.

36. Hancock, *The Mars Mystery*, 244.

37. Ibid., 264.

38. Allan and Delair, *Cataclysm!*, 205.

39. Ibid.

40. Antony Milne, *Doomsday* (London: Praeger, 2000), 33–34; Alfred K. Mann, *Shadow of a Star: The Neutrino Story of Supernova 1987A* (New York: W. H. Freeman and Company, 1997), 56–64, 81–98.

41. Picknett and Prince, *The Stargate Conspiracy,* 163.

42. Ibid., 161–66.

43. Ibid., 167–69.

44. Ibid., 167–68.

45. Ibid., 168.

46. Ibid., 169.

47. Ibid., 171.

48. Ibid., 178.

49. Ibid., 177.

50. Ibid., 174–81.

51. Ibid., 183–87.

52. Ibid., 189–96.

53. Ibid., 205–6.

54. Ibid., 205–9, 217.

55. Ibid., 235.

56. Ibid., 239.

57. Ibid., 239–40.

58. Ibid., 240.

59. Felicitas D. Goodman, *Ecstasy, Ritual, and the Alternate Reality* (Bloomington, Ind.: Indiana University Press, 1992), 25.

60. David Ulansey, *The Origins of the Mithraic Mysteries* (Oxford: Oxford University Press, 1989), 4.

61. Ibid.

62. Ibid., 88.

63. Ibid., 68–69.

64. Ibid., 71–73.

65. Ibid., 75.

66. Ibid., 76.

67. Ibid., 78.

68. Ibid., 83.

69. Mary Settegast, *Plato Prehistorian: 10,000 to 5000 B.C.—Myth, Religion, Archaeology* (Hudson, N.Y.: Lindisfarne Press, 1990), 220.

70. Ibid., 225.

71. Ibid., 219.

72. Ibid., 240–51.

73. Andrew Collins, *From the Ashes of Angels: The Forbidden Legacy of a Fallen Race* (London: Signet, 1997), 95.

74. Ulansey, *The Origins of the Mithraic Mysteries*, 32–33, 47–49.

75. Ibid., 57.

CHAPTER NINE

1. Barbara Hand Clow, *The Pleiadian Agenda: A New Cosmology for the Age of Light* (Santa Fe: Bear & Company, 1995), 54.

2. Ibid., 73.

3. Dimitri Meeks and Christine Favard-Meeks, *Daily Life of the Egyptian Gods* (Ithaca, N.Y.: Cornell University Press, 1993), 58.

4. Ibid., 53–89.

5. Barbara Hand Clow, *The Mind Chronicles Trilogy: Eye of the Centaur* (Santa Fe: Bear & Company, 1990), 4.

6. Ibid., 8.

7. Ibid., 8–9.

8. Ibid., 9.

9. Ibid., 18–19.

10. Joscelyn Godwin, *Arktos: The Polar Myth in Science, Symbolism, and Nazi Survival* (Kempton, Ill.: Adventures Unlimited Press, 1996), 48, 76.

11. Barbara Hand Clow, *Chiron: Rainbow Bridge between the Inner and Outer Planets* (St. Paul, Minn.: Llewellyn Publications, 1989), 1–12.

12. Richard Gerber, *Vibrational Medicine: New Choices for Healing Ourselves* (Rochester, Vt.: Bear & Co., 2001).

13. Richard Gerber quoted in Barbara Hand Clow, *The Liquid Light of Sex: Kundalini Rising During Midlife Crisis* (Santa Fe: Bear & Company, 1991), xix.

14. Belinda Gore, *Ecstatic Body Postures: An Alternate Reality Workbook* (Santa Fe: Bear & Company, 1995), x.

15. Ibid., ix.

16. Ibid.

17. Ibid., 12.

18. Ibid.

19. Goodman, *Where the Spirits Ride the Wind: Trance Journeys and Other Ecstatic Experiences* (Bloomington, Ind.: Indiana University Press, 1990), 107.

20. Gore, *Ecstatic Body Postures*.

21. Ibid., 29–30.

22. Ibid., 16.

23. Ibid., xii.

24. Ibid., 17.

25. Ibid.

26. Lynn Picknett and Clive Prince, *The Stargate Conspiracy* (London: Little, Brown, 2000), 346–51.

27. Ibid., 350–51.

APPENDIX A

1.   Graham Hancock, *Fingerprints of the Gods* (New York: Crown Publishers, 1995), 381–87. The very ancient date is from Manetho, the Turin Papyrus, Diodorus Siculus, Herodotus, and the Palermo Stone.

2.   Andrew Collins, *Gods of Eden: Egypt's Lost Legacy and the Genesis of Civilization* (London: Headline, 2000).

3.   Michael Hoffman, *Egypt before the Pharaohs: The Prehistoric Foundations of Egyptian Civilization* (New York: Dorset Press, 1979); and W. B. Emery, *Archaic Egypt* (London: Penguin Books, 1961). Abydos King List. Emphasis is on pharaohs and theological periods discussed in my text.

4.   The Dynastic Chronology is the basic standard used by Egyptologists that is derived from Manetho and the King Lists, and the interpretation of events is my own.

APPENDIX B

1.   J. B. Delair, "Planet in Crisis," *Chronology and Catastrophism Review*, 2 (1977): 6–9.

Notes from J. B. Delair's article:

40. Barton, P & Wood, *Geophys.Journ.*, vol. 79, 1984, pp. 987–1022.

41. Manley, J., *Atlas of Prehistoric Britain*, Oxford, 1989.

42. Gresswell, RK, *Sandy Shores in South Lancashire*, Liverpool, 1953, see fig. 6.

43. Manley, op cit.

44. Kuenen, PH, *Marine Geology*, New York, 1950.

45. Van Bemmelen, RW, *The Geology of Indonesia*, The Hague, 1949.

46. Geyh, MA, Kudrass, HR and Strief, *Nature*, vol. 278, 1979, pp 441–443.

47. Hantoro, WS, Faure, H. Djuwansah, R, Faure-Denard, L & Pirazzoli, PA. *Quat.Intern.*, vol. 29/30, 1995, pp. 129–34.

48. Van Andel, TH, Heath, GR, Moore, TC & McGeary, DRF, *Amer.Journ.Sci.*, vol. 265. 1961, pp. 737–758.

49. Smart, J, *Geology*, vol. 5, 1977, pp. 755–759.

50. Torguerson, T, Jones, MR, Stephens, DE & Ullman, WJ, *Nature*, vol. 313, 1985, pp. 785–787.

51. Bloom, A, *Quaterneria*, vol. xii, 1970.

52. Piazzolli, PM & Montaggioni, F, *Palaeogeogr.Palaeoclimat.Palaeoecol.*, vol. 68, 1988, pp. 153–175.

53. Piazzoli, PM, Montaggioni, F, Delibrias, G, Faure, G & Salvet, B, *Proc. 5th Intern. Coral Reef Cong.* (Tahiti), 1985, vol. 3, pp. 131–136.

54. Wadia, DN, *Geology of India*, 1953, p. 37.

55. Holmes, A, *Principles of Physical Geology*, London, 1944, pp. 417–418.

56. Lees, GM & Falcon, NL, *Geogr.Journ.*, vol. 118, 1952, pp. 24–39; see p. 28 fn.

57. Grant, DR, *Canad.Journ.Earth Sci.*, vol. 7, 1970, pp. 676–689.

58. King, PB, *The Evolution of North America*, Princeton, NJ, 1937.

59. Fillon, RH, *Quat. Res.*, vol. 1, no:4, 1971, pp. 522–531.

60. Putnam, WC, *Geology*, New York, 1964.

61. Bergvist, B, *Geologiska Forengingen I Stockholm Forhandlinger*, vol. 99, 1977, pp. 347–357.

62. Velichko, AA (ed.), *Late Quaternary Environments of the Soviet Union*, London, 1984.

63. Kyasov, DD, *Late Quaternary History of Major Lakes and Inland Seas of Eastern Europe*, Leningrad, 1975.

64. Kolp, O, *Quaestiones Geogr.*, vol. 13/14, 1990, pp. 69–86.

65. Klakegg, O and Rye, N, *Norsk.Geolog.Tidskrift.*, vol. 70, 1990, pp. 47–59.

66. Svensson, N-O, *Terra Nova*, vol. 3, 1991, pp. 359–378.

67. Gams, H and Nordhagen, R, *Mitteilungen der Geographischen Gessell*, Munchen, vol. xvi, 1923, heft.2, pp. 13–348.

68. Moon, H, (trans.), *Linn.Soc.Lond.*, ser. 3, vol. 1, pt. 1, 1939.

69. Wirrmann, D & de Oliveira Almeida, LF, *Palaeogeogr.Palaeoclimat.Palaeoecol.*, vol. 58, 1987, pp. 315–323.

70. Holmes, A, op. cit.

71. Wright, HE Jr., *Bull.Res.Council Israel*, no. 7g, 1958, pp. 53–59.

72. Flint, RF, *Glacial Geology and the Pleistocene Epoch*, New York, 1947, p. 382.

73. Sayce, AH, *Hibbert Lectures*, London, 1887, p. 21.

74. Oppenheim, L, *Ancient Mesopotamia*, Chicago, 1963, p. 161.

75. Gams & Nordhagen, op. cit.

76. Gregory, JW, 1911. *Rep.Brit. Assoc. Adv. Sci.*, Portsmouth, pp. 445–446.

77. Brelsford, V, *Geogr.Journ.*, vol. 83, 1934, pp. 48–50.

78. Fowler, G, *Geogr.Journ.*, vol. 79, 1932, pp. 210–212.

79. Fowler, G, *Proc.Cambs.Antiq.Soc.*, vol. xxxiii, 1933, pp. 109–128.

80. St Joseph, JK, *Antiquity*, vol. xiviii, 1974, pp. 295–298.

81. Kendall, HGO, *Proc.Prehis.Soc.E. Anglia*, vol. 1, pt. 2, pp. 135–139.

82. Harris, M, *Cannibals and Kings*, New York, 1976.

83. Holmes, A, op. cit.

84. Mulcahy, MJ, in Jennings, JN and Marbutt, JA (eds.), *Landform Studies from Australia and New Guinea*, Cambridge, 1967, pp. 211–230.

85. Dury, GH & Logan, MI, *Studies in Australian Geography*, London, 1968, pp. 14–15.

86. Selby, MJ, Hendry, CH & Seeley, MK, *Palaeogeogr.Palaeoclimat.Palaeoecol.*, vol. 26, 1978, pp. 37–41.

87. Boocock, C & Van Straten, OJ, (trans.,) *Proc.Geol.Soc.S.Afr.*, vol 65, 1962, pp. 125–171.

88. Wright, op. cit.

89. Holm, DA, *Science*, vol. 132, 1960, pp. 1369–1379.

90. McClure, *Nature*, vol. 263. 1976, pp. 755–756.

91. Al Sayari & Zotl, JG (eds.), *Quaternary Period in Saudi Arabia*, New York, 1978.

92. Kropelin, S & Soulie-Marsche, I, *Quat.Res.*, vol. 36, 1991, pp. 210–223.

93. Pachur, J-J & Kropelin, S, *Science*, vol. 237, 1987, pp. 298–300.

94. NcCauley, JF, Schaber, GG, Breed, CS, Grolier, MG, Haynes, CV, Issawi, B, Elachi C & Blom, A, *Science*, vol. 218, 1982, pp. 1004–1020.

95. Geyh, MA & Jakel, D. *Palaeogeogr.Palaeoclimat.Paleoecol.*, vol. 15, 1974, pp. 205–208.

96. Gautier, EF, *Geograph. Rev.*, vol. 16, 1926, pp. 378–394.

97. Harvey, CPD & Grove, AT, *Geogr.Journ.*, vol. 148, pp.327–336.

98. Bowen, R, & Jux, U, *Afro-Arabian Geology: A kinematic view*, London & New York, 1987.

99. Gardner, EW, *Geol.Mag.*, vol. 64, 1927.

100. Ritchie, JC & Haynes, CV, *Nature*, vol. 330, 1987, pp. 645–647.

101. Murray, GW, *Geogr.Journ.*, vol. 117, 1951, pt. 4, pp. 422–434.

102. Ibid.

103. Ibid.

104. Murray, GW, *Journ.Egypt.Archaeol.*, vol. 17, 1931.

105. Twitchell, KS, *Saudi Arabia*, 3rd edn., New Jersey, 1958.

106. Thesiger, W, *Arabian Sands*, London, 1959.

107. Kutzbach, JE, *Science*, vol. 214, 1981, pp. 59–61.

108. Kutabach, JE & Otto Bliesner, BL, *Journ.Atmosph.Sci.*, vol. 39, no.6, 1982, pp. 1177–1188.

109. Eden, MJ, *Journ.Biogeogr.*, vol. 1, 1974, pp. 95–109.

110. Prance, GT, *Acta Amazonica*, vol. 3, no. 3, 1973, pp. 5–28.

111. Haffer, J, *Science*, vol. 165., 1969, pp. 131–137.

112. Vanzolini, PE & Williams, EE, *Archos.Zool.Est.Sao Paulo*, vol. 19, 1970, pp. 1–124.

113. Meggers, BJ, pp. 493–496 in Prance, GT (ed.), *Biological Diversification in the Tropics*, New York, 1982.

114. Mousinho de Meis, MR, *Bull.Geol.Soc.Amer.*, vol. 82, 1971, pp. 1073–1078.

115. Flemley, JR, *The Equatorial Rain Forest: A Geological History*, 1979.

116. Campbell, KE Jr. & Frailey, D. *Quat.Res.*, vol. 21, 1984, pp. 369–375.

Appendix D

1. J. B. Delair, "Planet in Crisis," *Chronology and Catastrophism Review* (1997): 4–11. Sections of the article are excerpted only.

2. Alexander Marshack, *The Roots of Civilization* (New York: Mc Graw-Hill, 1967), 9–16.

3. Ibid.

4. Richard Rudgley, *The Lost Civilizations of the Stone Age* (New York: The Free Press, 1999), 102.

5. Ibid., 102–4.

6. Ibid., 104.

7. Martin Brennan, *The Stars and the Stones: Ancient Art and Astronomy in Ireland* (London: Thames and Hudson, 1985).

8. Robert Temple, *The Crystal Sun* (London: Century Books, 2000).

9. Ralph Ellis, *Thoth Architect of the Universe* (Dorset, England: Edfu Books, 1977) 104–31.

10. Christopher Knight and Robert Lomas, *Uriel's Machine: The Prehistoric Technology that Survived the Flood* (Boston: Element, 1999), 152–82.

11. Ibid., 213–32.

12. Norman Lockyer, *The Dawn of Astronomy*, (London: Macmillan), 108.

13. Robert Temple, *The Crystal Sun*, 412–14.

Notes from J. B. Delair's article:

28. Lambeck, K, *The Earth's Variable Rotation: Geophysical Causes and Consequences* (Cambridge, 1980).

29. Rochester, MG, *Phil.Trans.Roy.Soc.Lond.*, vol. A306, 1984, pp.95–105.

30. Ray, RD, Eames, RJ & Chao, BF, *Nature*, vol. 391, 1996, n. 65831, pp. 595–597.

31. Dahlen, FA, *Geophys.Journ.Roy.Astron.Soc.*, vol. 52, 1979.

32. Guinot, B, *Astron.Astrophys.*, vol. 19, 1972, pp. 207–214.

33. Ibid. [20]

34. Harris, J, *Celestial Spheres and Doctrine of the Earth's Perpendicular Axis*, Montreal, 1976.

35. Warren, RF, *Paradise Found; The Cradle of the Human Race at the North Pole. A Study of the Prehistoric World*, Boston, 1885, p. 181.

36. Allan, D. S., and Delair, J. B., *When the Earth Nearly Died*, Bath, 1995. [This is the English edition of *Cataclysm!*, Santa Fe, (1997)].

119. Keaney, P., (ed.), *The Encyclopedia of the Solid Earth Sciences*, Oxford, 1993, p. 134.

120. Whaler, K & Holme, R, *Nature*, vol. 382, no. 6588, 1996, pp. 205–206.

121. Ramalli, G, *Rheology of the Earth*, 2nd edn., London, 1995.

122. Pellegrino, O, *Return to Sodom and Gomorrah*, New York, 1995.

123. Mansinha, L & Smylie, *DL, Journ.Geophys.Res.*, vol. 72, 1967, pp. 4731–4743.

124. Dahlen, FA, *Geophys.Journ.Roy.Astron.Soc.*, vol. 32, 1973, pp. 203–217.

125. Yatskiv, YS & Sasao, T, *Nature*, vol 255, no. 5510, 1975, p. 655.

126. Whiston, W, *A New Theory of the Earth*, London, 1696.

127. Catcott, A, *A Treatise on the Deluge*, London, 2nd edn., 1761.

128. Donnelly, I, *Ragnarok: The Age of Fire and Gravel*, 13th edn., New York, 1895.

129. Beaumont, C, *The Mysterious Comet*, London, 1932.

130. Bellamy, HS, *Moons, Myths, and Men*, London, 1936.

131. Velikovsky, I, *Worlds in Collision*, London, 1950.

132. Patten, DW, *The Biblical Flood and the Ice Epoch*, Seattle, 1966.

133. Muck, O, *The Secret of Atlantis*, London, 1978.

134. Englehardt, WV, *Sber.Heidel.Akad.Wiss.Math.Nat.KL.*, 2 abh, 1979.

135. Clube, V, and Napier, WR, *The Cosmic Serpent*, London, 1982.

Suggested Reading

Allan, D. S., and J. B. Delair. *Cataclysm! Compelling Evidence of a Cosmic Catastrophe in 9500 B.C.* Santa Fe: Bear & Company, 1987.

Bauval, Robert, and Adrian Gilbert. *The Orion Mystery: Unlocking the Secrets of the Pyramids.* New York: Crown Publishers, 1994.

Clow, Barbara Hand. *The Pleiadian Agenda: A New Cosmology for the Age of Light.* Santa Fe: Bear & Company, 1995.

Collins, Andrew. *From the Ashes of Angels: The Forbidden Legacy of a Forgotten Race.* London: Signet, 1997.

Dunn, Christopher. *The Giza Power Plant: Technologies of Ancient Egypt.* Santa Fe: Bear & Company, 1998.

Flem-Ath, Rand, and Rose Flem-Ath. *When the Sky Fell: In Search of Atlantis.* New York: St. Martin's Press, 1995.

Goodman, Felicitas D. *Where the Spirits Ride the Wind: Trance Journeys and Other Ecstatic Experiences.* Bloomington, Ind.: Indiana University Press, 1990.

Gore, Belinda. *Ecstatic Body Postures: An Alternate Reality Workbook.* Santa Fe: Bear & Company, 1995.

Hapgood, Charles. *Maps of the Ancient Sea Kings: Evidence of Advanced Civilization in the Ice Age.* London: Turnstone Books, 1966.

Jaynes, Julian. *The Origin of Consciousness in the Breakdown of the Bicameral Mind.* Boston: Houghton Mifflin, 1976.

Picknett, Lynn, and Clive Prince. *The Stargate Conspiracy.* London: Little, Brown, 2000.

Ryan, William, and Walter Pitman. *Noah's Flood: The New Scientific Discoveries about the Event that Changed History*. New York: Touchstone, 1998.

Settegast, Mary. *Plato Prehistorian: 10,000 to 5000 B.C.—Myth, Religion, Archaeology*. Hudson, N.Y.: Lindisfarne Press, 1990.

Ulansey, David. *The Origins of the Mithraic Mysteries*. Oxford: Oxford University Press, 1989.

Von Dechend, Hertha, and Giorgio de Santillana. *Hamlet's Mill: An Essay on Myth and the Frame of Time*. Boston: David R. Godine, 1977.

Bibliography

Alford, Alan F. *The Phoenix Solution: Secrets of a Lost Civilisation*. London: Hodder and Stoughton, 1998.

Allan, D. S., and J. B. Delair. *Cataclysm! Compelling Evidence of a Cosmic Catastrophe in 9500 B.C.* Santa Fe: Bear & Company, 1997.

Bauval, Robert, and Adrian Gilbert. *The Orion Mystery: Unlocking the Secrets of the Pyramids*. New York: Crown Publishers, 1994.

Bauval, Robert, and Graham Hancock. *Keeper of Genesis: A Quest for the Hidden Legacy of Mankind*. London: Heinemann, 1996.

Bellamy, H. S. *Built Before the Flood: The Problem of the Tiahuanaco Ruins*. London: Faber and Faber, 1947.

Benford, Gregory. *Deep Time: How Humanity Communicates Across Millennia*. New York: HarperCollins, 2000.

Brennan, Martin. *The Stars and the Stones: Ancient Art and Astronomy in Ireland*. London: Thames and Hudson, 1983.

Butzer, Karl W. *Early Hydraulic Civilization in Egypt: A Study in Cultural Ecology*. Chicago: University of Chicago Press, 1976.

Cabrera, Javier Darquea. *The Message of the Engraved Stones of Ica*. Lima: privately published, 1989.

Clow, Barbara Hand. *Chiron: Rainbow Bridge between the Inner and Outer Planets*. St. Paul, Minn.: Llewellyn Publications, 1989.

———. *Liquid Light of Sex: Kundalini, Astrology and the Key Life Transitions*. Santa Fe: Bear & Company, 1991.

———. *The Mind Chronicles Trilogy: Eye of the Centaur*. Santa Fe: Bear & Company, 1990.

————. *The Mind Chronicles Trilogy: Heart of the Christos*. Santa Fe: Bear & Company, 1989.

————. *The Mind Chronicles Trilogy: Signet of Atlantis*. Santa Fe: Bear & Company, 1992.

————. *Nine Initiations on the Nile*. Infinite Eye Productions, 1996. Video.

————. *The Pleiadian Agenda: A New Cosmology for the Age of Light*. Santa Fe: Bear & Company, 1995.

Clube, Victor, and Bill Napier. *The Cosmic Winter*. Oxford: Basil Blackwell, 1990.

Collins, Andrew. *From the Ashes of Angels: The Forbidden Legacy of a Fallen Race*. London: Signet, 1997.

————. *Gateway to Atlantis: The Search for the Source of a Lost Civilization*. London: Headline, 2000.

————. *Gods of Eden: Egypt's Lost Legacy and the Genesis of Civilization*. London: Headline, 1998.

Cook, Albert, and Edwin Dolin. *Greek Tragedy*. Dallas, Tex.: Spring Publications, 1972.

Cooper, Glenda. "Why We Must Now Rethink Civilization." *London Daily Mail*, 28 December 2000.

Cooper, Milton William. *Behold a Pale Horse*. Sedona, Ariz.: Light Technology Publishing, 1991.

Cornford, Francis M. *Plato's Cosmology: The Timaeus of Plato*. Indianapolis, Ind.: Hackett Publishing, 1997.

Cowan, David, and Anne Silk. *Ancient Energies of the Earth*. London: Thorsons, 1999.

Cumont, Franz. *The Mysteries of Mithra*. New York: Dover, 1956.

Dames, Michael. *The Silbury Treasure: The Great Goddess Rediscovered*. London: Thames and Hudson, 1976.

Davies, P. C. W., and J. Brown. *Superstrings*. Cambridge: Cambridge University Press, 1988.

de Lubicz, R. A. Schwaller. *The Temple of Man*. Rochester, Vt.: Inner Traditions, 1998.

Dick, Steven J. *The Biological Universe: The Twentieth Century Extraterrestial Life Debate and the Limits of Science*. Cambridge: Cambridge University Press, 1996.

Dillehay, Thomas D. *The Settlement of the Americas: A New Prehistory*. New York: Basic Books, 2000.

Dunn, Christopher. *The Giza Power Plant: Technologies of Ancient Egypt*. Santa Fe: Bear & Company, 1998.

Ellis, Ralph. *Thoth: Architect of the Universe*. Dorset, England: Edfu Books, 1997.

Emery, W. B. *Archaic Egypt*. London: Penguin Books, 1961.

Fagan, Brian. *From Black Land to Fifth Sun*. Reading, Mass.: Perseus Books, 1998.

Faulkner, R. O. *The Ancient Egyptian Coffin Texts*, vol. I. Warminster, England: Aris & Phillips, 1973.

———. *The Ancient Egyptian Pyramid Texts*. Oxford: Oxford University Press, 1969.

Feuerstein, Georg, Subhash Kak, and David Frawley. *In Search of the Cradle of Civilization*. Wheaton, Ill.: Quest Books, 1995.

Fiorenza, Nick Anthony. *Erection of the Holy Cross: Astronomical Earth-Grid Spacetime Mapping*. Fort Collins, Colo.: IANS, 1995.

Fischer, Steven Roger. *Glyph-Breaker*. New York: Copernicus, 1997.

Flem-Ath, Rand, and Rose Flem-Ath. *When the Sky Fell: In Search of Atlantis*. New York: St. Martin's Press, 1995.

Fox, Matthew. *Original Blessing: A Primer in Creation Spirituality*. Santa Fe: Bear & Company, 1983.

Frankfort, Henri. *Kingship and the Gods: A Study of Ancient Near Eastern Religion and the Integration of Society and Nature*. London: University of Chicago Press, 1948.

Gaddis, Vincent H. *American Indian Myths and Mysteries*. New York: Indian Head Books, 1977.

Galanopoulos, A. G., and Edward Bacon. *Atlantis: The Truth behind the Legend*. New York: Bobbs-Merrill, 1969.

Gerber, Richard. *Vibrational Medicine: New Choices for Healing Ourselves.* Rochester, Vt.: Bear & Company, 1988.

Gimbutas, Marija. *The Language of the Goddess.* San Francisco: Harper & Row, 1989.

Godwin, Joscelyn. *Arktos: The Polar Myth in Science, Symbolism, and Nazi Survival.* Kempton, Ill.: Adventures Unlimited Press, 1996.

Goodman, Felicitas D. *Ecstasy, Ritual, and Alternate Reality.* Bloomington, Ind.: Indiana University Press, 1992.

———. *Where the Spirits Ride the Wind: Trance Journeys and Other Ecstatic Experiences.* Bloomington, Ind.: Indiana University Press, 1990.

Gore, Belinda. *Ecstatic Body Postures: An Alternate Reality Workbook.* Santa Fe: Bear & Company, 1995.

Graves, Tom. *Needles of Stone.* London: Granada, 1980.

Hamblin, Jane, and the Time-Life editors. *The First Cities.* New York: Time-Life Books, 1973.

Hancock, Graham. *Fingerprints of the Gods.* New York: Crown, 1995.

———. *The Mars Mystery.* New York: Crown, 1998.

Hancock, Graham, and Santha Faiia. *Heaven's Mirror: Quest for the Lost Civilization.* New York: Crown, 1998.

Hapgood, Charles. *Maps of the Ancient Sea Kings: Evidence of Advanced Civilization in the Ice Age.* London: Turnstone Books, 1966.

———. *Mystery in Acambaro.* Kempton, Ill.: Adventures Unlimited Press, 2000.

———. *The Path of the Pole.* Kempton, Ill.: Adventures Unlimited Press, 2000.

Harris, David R., ed. *The Origins and Spread of Agriculture and Pastoralism in Eurasia.* Washington, D.C.: Smithsonian Press, 1996.

Hitching, Francis. *Earth Magic.* New York: William Morrow, 1977.

Hoffman, Michael A. *Egypt before the Pharaohs: The Prehistoric Foundations of Egyptian Civilization.* New York: Dorset Press, 1979.

Hurtak, J. J. *The Book of Knowledge: The Keys of Enoch.* Los Gatos, Calif.: The Academy for Future Science, 1977.

Icke, David. *The Biggest Secret*. Scottsdale, Ariz.: Bridge of Love Publications, 1999.

———. *I Am Me, I Am Free*. San Diego: Truth Seeker, 1997.

Jaynes, Julian. *The Origin of Consciousness in the Breakdown of the Bicameral Mind*. Boston: Houghton Mifflin, 1976.

Jenkins, John Major. *Maya Cosmogenesis 2012*. Santa Fe: Bear & Company, 1998.

King, L. W. *Enuma Elish: The Seven Tablets of Creation*. London: Luzac and Co., 1902.

Knight, Christopher, and Robert Lomas. *The Hiram Key: Pharaohs, Freemasons, and the Discovery of the Secret Scrolls of Jesus*. Boston: Element, 1999.

———. *Uriel's Machine: The Prehistoric Technology that Survived the Flood*. Boston: Element, 1999.

Krupp, E. C. *Beyond the Blue Horizon: Myths, Legends of the Sun, Moon, Stars, and Planets*. New York: HarperCollins, 1991.

———. *Echoes of the Ancient Skies: The Astronomy of Lost Civilizations*. New York: Harper & Row, 1983.

Kushi, Michio. *The Era of Humanity*. Berkeley, Calif.: East West Journal, 1974.

———. *Forgotten Worlds: Guide to Lost Civilizations and the Coming One World*. Becket, Mass.: One Peaceful World Press, 1992.

Lamy, Lucie. *Egyptian Mysteries: New Light on Ancient Knowledge*. London: Thames and Hudson, 1981.

Laviolette, Paul A. *Beyond the Big Bang: Ancient Myth and the Science of Continuous Creation*. Rochester, Vt.: Park Street Press, 1995.

———. *The Talk of the Galaxy: An ET Message For Us?* Alexandria, Va.: Starlane Publications, 2000.

Lawton, Ian, and Chris Ogilvie-Herald. *Giza: The Truth*. London: Virgin Publishing, 2000.

Lhote, Henri. *Tassili Frescoes*. New York: Dutton, 1959.

Lichtheim, Miriam. *Ancient Egyptian Literature* (3 vol.). Berkeley, Calif.: University of California Press, 1980.

Lockyer, Norman J. *The Dawn of Astronomy*. London: Macmillan, 1894.

Mann, Alfred K. *Shadow of a Star: The Neutrino Story of Supernova 1987A*. New York: W. H. Freeman and Company, 1997.

Marschak, Alexander. *The Roots of Civilization*. New York: McGraw-Hill, 1972.

Mavor, James W. *Voyage to Atlantis*. Rochester, Vt.: Park Street Press, 1990.

Meeks, Dimitri, and Christine Favard-Meeks. *Daily Life of the Egyptian Gods*. Ithaca, N.Y.: Cornell University Press, 1993.

Mellaart, James. *Çatal Hüyük: A Neolithic Town in Anatolia*. New York: McGraw-Hill, 1967.

———. *The Neolithic of the Near East*. New York: Charles Scribner's Sons, 1975.

Mendelssohn, Kurt. *Riddle of the Pyramids*. London: Thames and Hudson, 1974.

Michell, John. *The New View over Atlantis*. San Francisco: Harper & Row, 1983.

———. *Old Stones of Land's End*. Bristol, England: Pentacle Books, 1979.

Milne, Antony. *Doomsday: The Science of Catastrophic Events*. London: Praeger, 2000.

Milton, John. *Paradise Lost*. Norwalk, Conn.: Easton Press, 1976.

Milton, Richard. *Shattering the Myths of Darwinism*. Rochester, Vt.: Park Street Press, 1992.

Naydler, Jeremy. *Temple of the Cosmos: The Ancient Egyptian Science of the Sacred*. Rochester, Vt.: Inner Traditions, 1996.

North, John. *Stonehenge: A New Interpretation of Prehistoric Man and the Cosmos*. New York: The Free Press, 1996.

O'Brien, Christopher, and Barbara Joy O'Brien. *The Genius of the Few: The Story of Those Who Founded the Garden in Eden*. Northhamptonshire, England: Turnstone, 1985.

Oppenheimer, Stephen. *Eden in the East: The Drowned Continent of Southeast Asia*. London: Weidenfeld and Nicolson, 1998.

Ovason, David. *The Secret Architecture of Our Nation's Capital*. New York: HarperCollins, 2000.

Pauwels, Louis, and Jacques Bergier. *The Morning of the Magicians*. New York: Stein and Day, 1964.

Pellegrino, Charles. *Unearthing Atlantis: An Archaeological Odyssey*. New York: Vintage Books, 1993.

Pensée, Editors of. *Velikovsky Reconsidered*. New York: Doubleday, 1976.

Picknett, Lynn, and Clive Prince. *The Stargate Conspiracy*. London: Little, Brown, 2000.

Plato, *Timaeus and Critias*. Trans. by Desmond Lee. London: Penguin, 1965.

Rapp, George Jr., and Christopher L. Hill. *Geoarchaeology: The Earth-Science Approach to Archaeological Interpretation*. New Haven, Conn.: Yale University Press, 1998.

Ravenscroft, Trevor. *The Spear of Destiny*. York Beach, Me.: Weiser, 1982.

Reich, Wilhelm. *Cosmic Superimposition*. Rangeley, Me.: Wilhelm Reich Foundation, 1951.

Ridley, Matt. *Genome: The Autobiography of a Species in 23 Chapters*. New York: HarperCollins, 1999.

Robinson, James M., ed. *The Nag Hammadi Library*. San Francisco: Harper & Row, 1977.

Rudgley, Richard. *The Lost Civilizations of the Stone Age*. New York: The Free Press, 1999.

Ryan, William, and Walter Pitman. *Noah's Flood: The New Scientific Discoveries about the Event that Changed History*. New York: Touchstone, 1998.

Scott, Mary. *Kundalini in the Physical West*. London: Routledge & Kegan Paul, 1983.

Sellers, Jane B. *The Death of the Gods of Ancient Egypt*. London: Penguin Books, 1992.

Sesti, Giuseppe Maria. *The Glorious Constellations*. New York: Harry N. Abrams, 1987.

Settegast, Mary. *Plato Prehistorian: 10,000 to 5,000 B.C.—Myth, Religion, Archaeology*. Hudson, N.Y.: Lindisfarne Press, 1990.

Schoch, Robert M. *Voices of the Rocks: A Scientist Looks at Catastrophes and Ancient Civilizations*. New York: Harmony Books, 1999.

Starbird, Margaret. *The Woman with the Alabaster Jar: Mary Magdalen and the Holy Grail*. Santa Fe: Bear & Company, 1993.

Stewart, John A. *Drifting Continents and Colliding Paradigms*. Bloomington: Indiana University Press, 1990.

Sullivan, William. *The Secret of the Incas: Myth, Astronomy, and the War Against Time*. New York: Crown Publishers, 1996.

Temple, Robert K. G. *The Sirius Mystery*. New York: St. Martin's Press, 1976. (See also the revised edition, Rochester, Vt.: Destiny Books, 1998.)

———. *The Crystal Sun* (London: Century Books, 2000).

Tompkins, Peter. *Secrets of the Great Pyramid*. New York: Harper & Row, 1971.

Ulansey, David. *The Origins of the Mithraic Mysteries*. Oxford: Oxford University Press, 1989.

Velikovsky, Immanuel. *Ages in Chaos*. New York: Doubleday, 1952.

———. *Mankind in Amnesia*. New York: Doubleday, 1982.

Van Andel, Tjeerd H. *New Views on an Old Planet: A History of Global Change*. Cambridge: Cambridge University Press, 1994.

Van Flandern, Tom. *Dark Matter, Missing Planets, and New Comets: Paradoxes Resolved, Origins Illuminated*. Berkeley, Calif.: North Atlantic Books, 1993.

Von Dechend, Hertha, and Giorgio de Santillana. *Hamlet's Mill: An Essay on Myth and the Frame of Time*. Boston: David R. Godine, 1977.

West, John Anthony. *Serpent in the Sky*. New York: Harper & Row, 1979.

For the sacred postures discussed in chapter 9, write to the Cuyamungue Institute, Route #5, Box 358-A, Santa Fe, NM 87501.

The video of the author working with Abdel Hakim, *Nine Initiations on the Nile,* is available from New Leaf Distributors through your local bookstore.

Index

Adam and Eve, 164–67

Aeshylus, 131

Age of Aquarius, 9, 11, 13, 16, 28, 32, 36

agriculture, 14, 26, 31, 76, 112, 124,
125–56, 130, 161, 200, 208, 229,
237–38

Akhenaton, 242

Alexander the Great, 143, 242

Alexandria Library, 81

Alford, Alan F., 129

Allan, D.S., 4, 7, 13, 35, 37–51, 82, 92,
94, 95, 160, 176–77, 192–93, 233

Amenhotep I–III, 242

American Indian Myths and Mysteries,
175

Amun, 242

Anatolian Plateau, 162

Ancient Egyptian Literature, 120

Ancient Voices, 97

Andromeda Galaxy, 218

animals, 218, 219

Antarctica, xvi, xvii, 49–50, 86, 95, 96,
98–99, 135, 193, 194

antidepressants, 56

Aratos of Soli, 202

archaoastronomy, 14–16

Aristotle, 80, 149

Asclepius, 232

Association for Research and
Enlightenment, 190–91

astrology, xvi, 23, 24, 31, 155. *See also*
equinoxes, precession of
and Chiron, xv, 7, 231–34
and fixed signs, 17

and the Global Elite, 195–96
liquid light principle, 233–35
and Saturn, 124–26, 233
and Uranus, 233
Zodiac, 34

Athena, 99–101

Athenian culture, 94, 98–101, 132–34,
137–38, 143, 211

Athenodorus, 202

Atlantis, xvi–xvii, 49–50, 80–88
and Egypt, 69
fall of, 94–95, 98–99, 132–37
and Goddess worship, 99–101
location of, 95–98
and war, 87, 94–95, 100, 137

*Atlantis in America: Navigators of the
Ancient World*, 97

Augustine, Saint, 107, 166

Australian Aboriginies, 81

Avebury Henge, 192, 193, 258

axial tilt, 252–56, 258–59. *See also* earth
changes; Great Flood
Egyptian mythology, 112–15
and pole shifts, 95, 96
and precession of the equinoxes, 12,
15–16, 35, 47, 74

Aymara language, 82–83, 132

Badawy, Alexander, 71

Bailey, Alice, 190

Bauval, Robert, 16, 59, 69, 70–71, 73,
76, 188

Beaulieu, John, 51, 217

Benford, Gregory, 81

Berthault, Guy, 43–44, 174
Biggest Secret, The, 196
Black Sea, flooding of, 138–40, 162–63, 171
Blavatsky, Helena, 190
Book of Enoch, 164–65
brain, bicameral
   breakdown of, 53–55, 56–57, 119, 120, 141, 156, 217
   reactivation of, 54–58
   and Wernicke's area, 53, 55
Brandenburg, John, 193–94
"Brave New World of Antidepressants," 56
Bryn Celli Ddu, 258–59
Budge, Wallis, 58
Bundahishn, 89, 93, 148, 149, 164
Butzer, Karl, 64, 66, 68, 69

Cabrera, Javier Darquea, 171–82, 179
Cain and Abel, 92
calendars, sacred
   lunar, 256–58
   Mayan, 9, 10, 13, 30–31, 107, 240
cancer, 151, 220
Cappadocia, 161–62
Cataclysm! Compelling Evidence of a Cosmic Catastrophe in 9500 B.C., 4, 13, 35, 37–51, 94, 95, 160, 176–77, 233
Çatal Hüyük, 58, 80, 133, 134–35, 139, 140, 143–50, 161, 170, 208
catastrophobia, 10, 25–26, 50–51, 57, 156, 163, 218, 256. *See also* consciousness; Global Elite
   and the Great Flood, xiv, xv–xvi, 1, 6–7, 35
   and materialism, 26, 32
   and past–life regression, 224
   and politics, 3

and racial memory, 79–80, 94, 99
and sacred sites, 105
and scientists, 2–3, 194–95, 203
and the shadow side, 155–58
and Y2K, 25, 196
Cayce, Edgar, 69, 185, 189–91
Cayce, Hugh Lynn, 190–91
channelling, 197–99
chemistry, 151
Chiron, xv, 7, 231–34
Choroid Pulse, 51
Clark, Brian, 93
Cleito, 83–84, 100–101
Clinton, Bill, 193, 194
Clow, Barbara Hand, 141, 213–20, 228, 234
Collins, Andrew, 4, 97, 132, 134–35, 140, 145, 159, 161, 163, 167, 168–70, 177, 209–10
Columbine massacre, 56, 196
consciousness. *See also* brain, bicameral; catastrophobia; reincarnation; shamanism
   collective, 21–22, 23, 79–80, 94, 99, 213–14, 221–27
   as creator, 6, 151–53, 158
   dimensions of, 76–78, 108–9, 213–21, 239
   evolution of, 53–55
   and the Standard of Abydos, 127–30
Cooper, William, 185
Cosquer Cave, 91–92, 93, 94
Council of Nine, 197–99
Crantor, 80
Critias, 83
Crop Circles, 186
crustal shifting, 40–42, 43–44, 95, 141
Crystal Sun, The, 258
cyclopean monuments, 60–63, 83, 86,

103, 105. *See also* megalithic stones

cymatics, 217

Dalton, Nicholas, 205

Dames, Michael, 106

Dawn of Astronomy, The, 36, 100, 259

Death of the Gods, The, 74

Deep Impact, 25

*Deep Time: How Humanity
     Communicates Across Millenia,* 81

Delair, J. B., 4, 6, 7, 13, 15, 35, 37–51,
     82, 92, 94, 95, 143, 146, 150, 160,
     172, 176–77, 192–93, 233, 243–56

Di Pietro, Vincent, 193–94

Diana, Princess of Wales, 196

Dillehay, Thomas, 97

dinosaurs, extinction of, xiv, 2, 3, 111

     and the Ica Library, 171–74, 178, 181

Djed Pillar Ceremony, 75–76, 123

Djoser, 241

DNA, dormant, 2, 11

Dogon culture, 68, 188

dowsing, 104, 105

Draco, 155–57

Dunn, Chris, 76–78, 181, 182–83, 186, 236

*Early Hydraulic Civilization In Egypt: A
     Study in Cultural Ecology,* 66, 68

earth changes. *See also* Great Flood;
     Holocene Era

     and catastrophobia, 25, 47–48

     creation-centered theory, 4

     and crustal shifting, 40–42, 43–44,
          95, 141

     and the Geological Column, 42–44

     and the Gothenburg Flip, 160, 162

     and Turtle Medicine, 4, 10, 29–32,
          72, 229–30, 256

uniformitarian theory, 3, 25, 43, 57,
     79, 195

*Ecstatic Body Postures: An Alternate
     Reality Workbook,* 237–39

*Eden in the East: The Drowned Continent
     of Southeast Asia,* 90, 140

Edfu Building Texts, 134

Edison, Thomas, 186

Egypt. *See also* Giza Pyramids; Osireion
     of Abydos; Sphinx; individual gods
     and pharaohs

     and agriculture, 112, 124, 125–26,
          130

     Alexandria Library, 81

     and axial tilt mythology, 112–15

     and the Blank period, 60–64, 68, 129,
          171

     climatic changes in, xvii, 113

     and the Council of Nine, 198

     and cyclopean monuments, 60–63

     and the Djed Pillar Ceremony,
          75–76, 123

     and Goddess worship, 99–101, 211

     and the Great Flood, 132–38, 141–42

     Heb Sed Ceremony, 124–27, 161

     historical time line, 241–42

     as maritime civilization, 86–87

     mystery plays, 115–30

     mystery schools, 76–78, 111

     Nile, changes in, 64–68, 117–19

     and sacred science, 221–22, 230–31

     and the Shemsu Hor, 58–60, 63,
          68–69, 74, 85, 113, 123, 161, 241

     Valley Temple, 61, 68, 119, 160

*Egypt before the Pharaohs: The Prehistoric
     Foundations of Egyptian
     Civilization,* 65, 66–67

Einstein, Albert, 49, 186–87

Elders, 29–30, 78, 84, 108, 111, 113, 119, 134–35, 137, 160–62, 170–71, 206, 209, 211, 229, 241
elements, 151
Ellis, Ralph, 80, 106, 193, 258
Elohim, 164–65
equinoxes, precession of, xv, 6, 12–14, 257–58. *See also* astrology; Galactic Winter Solstice
  archetypes of, 18, 20–24, 33–36
  Age of Aquarius, 9, 11, 13, 16, 28, 32, 36
  and archaoastronomy, 14–16
  and Çatal Hüyük, 146–50
  and the Giza Plateau, 69–73
  and the inner stellar chronometer, 51, 55, 225
  and the Platonic Great Year, 13, 17–21
  tracking, 69–75, 203
Erikson, George, 97
ether, the, 107–8, 115
Evans, Arthur, 143
Extirpation of Idolatry, The, 107
extraterrestrials, 68, 187, 188–89, 197, 198–99
Eye of the Centaur, 141

faeries, 30
Fagan, Brian, 148
Faiia, Santha, 72
Fallen Angels, 159–67, 181, 187, 207, 209, 228
Fiorenza, Nick Anthony, 17
First Man mythology, 89–94, 164, 167
Flem-Ath, Rand and Rose, 42, 49, 82–83, 86, 95
Fox, Matthew, 4

Franchthi Cave, 137
Frankfort, Henri, 121, 126
Freemasons, 15, 34, 190, 191
Freud, Sigmund, 21
From the Ashes of Angels, 5, 161, 168, 210

Gaddis, Vincent H., 175
Galactic Winter Solstice, 9–10, 17, 18–20, 109, 157, 196, 239
Galanopolous, A. G., 142
Gateway to Atlantis: The Search for the Source of a Lost Civilization, 97
Gayomart, 92, 164, 167
Geller, Uri, 197, 199
Geological Column, 42–44
geomancy, 101, 103–4, 110–11
  and dowsing, 104, 105
  and the ether, 107–8, 115
  and ley lines, 105–6
  and megalithic stones, 103–5, 106, 110
  and the Roman Catholic Church, 106–7, 110, 160
  and safety zones, 109
geometry, 151
Gerber, Richard, 234
Giamario, Dan, 17
Gilbert, Adrian, 16, 59, 70–71, 73, 76
Gimbutas, Marija, 100, 103, 147
Giza Power Plant, The, 76, 181
Giza pyramids, 15–16, 59, 60, 63, 69–73, 76–78, 127, 133, 162, 171, 181–83, 236, 241
  and the Hall of Records, 187–91, 197, 214, 221, 225
Giza: The Truth, 71, 186
Global Elite, 3, 99, 158–60
  and the apocalypse, 163

and astrology, 195–96

bypassing, 217

and the Council of Nine, 197–99

and hypnosis, 198

manipulation of humanity by, 5, 24, 25, 159, 183–91, 222, 227–29

and Mars, 189, 191–96

and symbology, 199–201

Goddess cultures, 100–101, 140–43, 145, 204, 211–12, 259

Gods of Eden, The, 5, 132, 134–35, 140

Godwin, Joscelyn, 227

Goodman, Felicitas, 4, 5, 27, 90, 93–94, 109, 125, 200, 235–39

Gore, Al, 193

Gore, Belinda, 237–39

Gothenburg Flip, 160, 162

Great Depression, 28–29

Great Flood, the, xv–xvi, 1–2, 110–11. *See also* axial tilt; Holocene Era

and Draco, 155–57

and Egypt, 132–38, 141–42

and extinction of species, 26

and the Fall, 31, 155–57

and human evolution, 10–11, 14

and Mars, 192–93, 194

in mythology, 35

psychological effects of, xiv, xv–xvi, 1, 6–7, 35. *See also* brain, bicameral

supernova theory of, 37–42, 99, 174–82

Gregory I, Pope, 107

Guzman Rojas, Ivan, 82

Hakim, Abdel, 117, 162

Hamlet's Mill: An Essay on Myth and the Frame of Time, 34–36, 74, 148–49

Hancock, Graham, 49, 59, 72, 179–80, 188, 192, 193, 195

Hapgood, Charles, xvi, 42, 48, 80, 86, 92, 95–98, 141–42, 181–82, 187

Harmonic Convergence, 9–10

Hathor, 120, 141

Hatshepsut, 242

Hawass, Zahi, 191

health, rejuvenation of

and the Aquarian Age, 28

and ley lines, 106

and ritual postures, 236–37

Heart of the Christos, 141

Heaven's Mirror: Quest for the Lost Civilization, 72

Heb Sed Ceremony, 124–27, 161

Heliopolitan Mystery Schools, 76, 214

Hipparchus, 13, 203

Hitler, Adolf, 201

Hoagland, Richard, 192, 197

Hoffman, Michael, 63, 65, 66–67

Holocene Era. *See also* agriculture; Great Flood

and Atlantis, 82, 98–99

beginning of, xiv–xv, 14, 47–50

civilizations of, 131–51

geographical changes in, 243–51

Horus, 120–21, 122–24, 127

human evolution. *See also* brain, bicameral; consciousness; equinoxes, precession of; Great Flood

current shift, 11, 18, 22–23, 32

and materialism, 26–27, 32

spiral, 223

and symbology, 199–201, 220–21

theories of, 3–4

Hurtak, James J., 191, 192, 197, 198

hypnosis, 80, 198. *See also* past-life regresssion

hypothalamus gland, 158

Ica Library, 171–74, 177–81, 186
Icke, David, 185, 196
inner stellar chronometer, 51, 55, 225
Institute of Noetic Sciences, 198
Izady, Mehrdad, 170

Jaynes, Julian, 53, 54, 94, 156, 217, 227
Jenkins, John Major, 9, 17, 36, 72
Jung, C.G., 21
Jurassic Park, 111

Keeper of Genesis, 74
Keys of Enoch, The, 191, 197
Kingship and the Gods: A Study of Ancient Near Eastern Religion and the Integration of Society and Nature, 121–22, 124, 126
Kiyumars, 167
Knight, Christopher, 70, 258
kosmokraters, 200–201, 203–4
Kowal, Charles, 231
kundalini energy, 28, 233–34
Kurdistan, 170
Kushi, Michio, 17, 18, 22, 45, 155, 157–58

Lascaux Cave, 81, 86, 87–90, 92–93, 132, 164, 168
Lawton, Ian, 71
Lee, Desmond, 95
Leedskalnin, Edward, 182
ley lines, 105–6
Lichtheim, Miriam, 120
Liquid Light of Sex, The: Kundalini, Astrology, and the Key Life Transitions, 234
liquid light principle, 233–35

Lockyer, J. Norman, 36, 71, 73–74, 100, 259
Lomas, Robert, 70, 258
Lost Civilization of the Stone Age, The, 152, 175

Magdalenian culture, 87–94, 132–33, 211
   Cosquer Cave, 91–92, 93, 94
   Lascaux Cave, 81, 86, 87–90, 92–93, 132, 164, 168
Manetho, 59, 63, 68
Mankind in Amnesia, 80
Mann, Alfred K., 38
Maps of the Ancient Sea Kings: Evidence of Advanced Civilization in the Ice Age, 48, 80, 86, 95–98, 142, 187
Marduk, 146, 233
Mars, 189, 191–96
Mars Mystery, The, 192
Marschak, Alexander, 153, 252, 256–57, 259
Mavor, James, 142
Maya Cosmogenesis 2012, 36, 72
Mayan culture, 9, 10, 13, 30–31, 82–83, 87, 107, 132, 239–40. *See also* Ica Library
Medusa, 204
megalithic stones, 103–5, 106, 110, 192, 193, 257, 258–59. *See also* cyclopean monuments
Mellaart, James, 58, 144, 161
Men, Hunbatz, 31
Mendelssohn, Kurt, 60
Menes, 120–22, 124, 241
Mesopotamian culture, 135
Michell, John, 105, 107, 110, 115
Milton, John, 53

Milton, Richard, 43–44
Mind Chronicles, The, 54
Minoan culture, 58, 133–34, 137, 140–43, 170
Mithraism, 164, 201–7, 210–11
Monte Verde site, 97
Morris, Dick, 194
Mounts, Linda, 56
Mystery in Acambaro, 181
Mystery Play of the Succession, 122–24
mystery schools, 76–78, 111

Nagy, Bartholomew, 193–94
Narmer Palette, 205–6
Natufian culture, 138, 139
nature, symbiosis with, 53–55, 158
Naydler, Jeremy, 113, 129
Neith, 99–101
Nephilim, 164–67, 222, 228
Nevali Cori, 134–35
Neves, Walter, 97
New Grange, 257, 258
New World Order, 99, 101
Nile, changes in, 64–68, 117–19
Noah's Ark, 140, 162–63, 167, 168
Noah's Flood, 138–40
North, John, 36

O'Brien, Christopher, 169–70
Ogilvie-Herald, Chris, 71
Oklahoma City bombing, 196
Oppe, E.F., 172
Oppenheimer, Stephen, 90, 99, 140
Origin of Consciousness in the Breakdown of the Bicameral Mind, The, 53
Origins and Spread of Agriculture and Pastoralism in Eurasia, The, 238

Orion constellation, 70–73, 74, 76, 78, 191, 216, 218
Orion Mystery, The: Unlocking the Secrets of the Pyramids, 16, 59, 70–71, 73
Osireion of Abydos, xvii, 27, 61–62, 63, 65–66, 68, 70, 75–76, 119, 127–30, 133, 160, 230
Osiris, 90, 112, 118, 119, 120–21, 122–24, 127–30, 222, 230–31
Oxlac, Don Alejandro, 31

Pangea, 178
Papyrus of Ipuwer, 120
Parthenon, 19
past-life regression, 54–55, 221, 223–27, 236
Path of the Pole, 42, 49, 187
Paxson, Gregory, 141, 225–26, 227, 236
Penrose, F.C., 19
Perseus, 204–6, 210
Petrie, William Flanders, 182
Pezzia Assereto, Alejandro, 172
"Philadelphia Experiment," 186
Phoenix Solution, The: Secrets of a Lost Civilization, 129
Picknett, Lynn, 5, 162, 187–89, 197, 198
Pillinger, Colin, 194
Pitman, Walter, 138–40
"Planet in Crisis," 252–56
plate tectonics, 31, 41, 238
Plato, xvi, 30, 56–57, 60, 63, 80–81, 82–87, 94, 98, 132, 134, 151–53
Plato Prehistorian: 10,000 to 5000 B.C.– Myth, Religion, Archaeology, 57, 87–89, 92–94, 138, 143–44, 146
Platonic Great Year, 13, 17–21
Pleiades, 19, 100–101, 175–77, 210, 216, 218

Pleiadian Agenda, The: A New Cosmology for the Age of Light, 5, 19, 76, 77, 78, 213–20, 228, 239
pole shifts, 95, 96
Poseidon, 83–84, 87–88, 100–101, 146–47
Posidonius, 202
prediluvian global civilization, xvi, 10–11, 20, 30, 45–50, 80–83, 86–87, 99, 174–82, 229.
    See also individual cultures
    and cyclopean monuments, 60–63, 83, 86, 103, 105
    and technology, 27, 45, 104–5, 111, 181
    underwater sites of, 137–40
    and war, 87, 94–95, 100, 137
Primordial Bull mythology, 89–94
Prince, Clive, 5, 162, 187–89, 197, 198
Prometheus, 232
Prozac, 56
Puharich, Andrija, 197, 198–99
Pyramid Texts, 72, 73, 129, 133

quartz, 51

"Rainbow City," *xvi*
Ramsay, Jon Benet, 196
Ramses the Great, 242
Re, 118, 120
Reich, Wilhelm, 186–87
reincarnation, 54–55, 221, 223–27, 236
Riddle of the Pyramids, The, 60
Roman Catholic Church, 106–7, 110, 160, 164–67, 187, 201–2, 206, 207
Rowlands, Sherry, 194
Rudabeh, 168
Rudgley, Richard, 88, 152, 175, 257
Ryan, William, 138–40

Sacsayhuaman Temple, 61–62
Sages, 29–30, 59, 78, 119, 200, 211, 217–18, 228
Santillana, Giorgio de, 33, 34, 74, 148–49
Saturn, 124–26, 233–34
Schoch, Robert, 14
"Scourge of Prozac, The," 56
Secret of the Incas, The, 36
Secrets of the Great Pyramid, 60
Sekhmet, 16, 74–75, 114, 120, 122, 141
Sellers, Jane, 73, 74
Seth, 90, 112, 114, 118, 119, 120–21, 127, 129, 230
Seti I, 61, 62, 63, 66, 119, 127, 130, 242
Settegast, Mary, 57, 67–68, 83, 87–89, 92–94, 138, 143–44, 146, 208
settlement archaeology, 137
shamanism, 27, 69, 90, 94, 108–9, 125, 167, 178, 204, 229. *See also* consciousness
    ritual postures for, 103, 109, 235–40
    vulture shamanism, 167–71, 204–5
Shemsu Hor, 58–60, 63, 68–69, 74, 85, 113, 123, 161, 241
Sherratt, Andrew, 238
Shoemaker/Levy comet, 25
Silbury Treasure, The: The Great Goddess Rediscovered, 106
Simpson, Nicole, 196
Simurgh, 168
Sirians, 68–69, 188–89, 216, 218
Sirius Mystery, The, 188–89, 258
Social Darwinism, 3, 25, 43, 57, 81, 160
Solon, 59–60, 63, 69, 83
sound, study of, 217
South America, 97–98, 107. *See also* Mayan culture

Sphinx, 14–16, 58–60, 61, 63, 68, 70–71, 160
Spiritualism, 199
Stargate Conspiracy, The, 5, 162, 187–89, 197, 198
Starling, Edmund, 190
Stevens, H. C. Randall, 190
Stoicism, 202–7
Stone Age tools, 152–53
Stonehenge, 70, 71
Stonehenge, 36
Sullivan, William, 36
Sumerian culture, 140

Tarsus, 203
tauroctonies, 205–7, 210
Temple, Robert, 188–89, 258, 259
Teska, Nicola, 186–87
Thera's eruption, 141–42
Thoth: Architect of the Universe, 80
thymus gland, 158
Tiamat, 123, 204
Tompkins, Peter, 60
Turin Papyrus, 59, 63
Turtle Medicine, 4, 10, 29–32, 72, 229–30, 256
Tutankhamen, 242
Tutmosid I–IV, 242
twinship mythology, 89–93, 146

'Ubaid culture, 140
Ulansey, David, 202, 203–4, 210
Unas, 133, 241
Uranus, 233–34
Uriel's Machine: The Prehistoric Technology that Survived the Flood, 70, 258

Valley Temple, 61, 68, 119, 160
Van Andel, Tjeerd H., 96, 178
Van Flandern, Tom, 111
Velikovsky, Immanuel, 79–80, 94, 156
Venus, 259
Vibrational Medicine, 234
Vinod, D. G., 197
Von Dechend, Hertha, 33, 34, 74, 146, 148–49

Waco massacre, 196
Watchers, the, 163–69, 170, 187
West, John Anthony, 14, 61
When the Sky Fell, 42, 49, 50, 95
Where Spirits Ride the Wind: Trance Journeys and Other Ecstatic Experiences, 90, 93–94
Whitaker, Julian, 56
Wilkins, Harold T., xvi
Wilkinson, Toby, 68
Wilson, Woodrow, 190
Wolf, Eric, 172
Worlds in Collision, 79

Y2K, 25, 196
Yima, 89, 162

Zal, 167–68, 205
Zapp, Ivar, 97
Zarathustra, 21, 149, 163–64, 200, 208–9, 211
Zeno of Tarsus, 202
Zervanism, 146, 148–49, 208
Zolla, Elemire, 155